Mobility & Politics

Series Editors
Martin Geiger
Carleton University
Ottawa, Canada

Nicola Piper
School of Law
Queen Mary University of London
London, UK

Parvati Raghuram
Open University
Milton Keynes, UK

Editorial Board Members
Tendayi Bloom
University of Birmingham
Birmingham, UK

Michael Collyer
University of Sussex
Brighton, UK

Charles Heller
Graduate Institute
Geneva, Switzerland

Elaine Ho
National University of Singapore
Singapore, Singapore

Shadia Husseini de Araújo
University of Brasília
Brasília, Brazil

Alison Mountz
Wilfrid Laurier University
Waterloo, Canada

Linda Oucho
African Migration and Development Policy Centre
Nairobi, Kenya

Marta Pachocka
SGH Warsaw School of Economics
Warsaw, Poland

Antoine Pécoud
Université Sorbonne Paris Nord
Villetaneuse, France

Shahamak Rezaei
University of Roskilde
Roskilde, Denmark

Sergey Ryazantsev
Russian Academy of Sciences
Moscow, Russia

Carlos Sandoval García
University of Costa Rica
San José, Costa Rica

Everita Silina
The New School
New York, NY, USA

Rachel Simon-Kumar
University of Auckland
Auckland, New Zealand

William Walters Carleton University
Ottawa, Canada

Mobility & Politics

Series Editors,
Martin Geiger, Carleton University, Ottawa, Canada
Nicola Piper, Queen Mary University of London, UK
Parvati Raghuram, Open University, Milton Keynes, UK

Global Advisory Board:
Tendayi Bloom, University of Birmingham, UK
Michael Collyer, Sussex University, UK
Charles Heller, Geneva Graduate Institute, Switzerland
Elaine Ho, National University of Singapore
Shadia Husseini de Araújo, University of Brasília, Brazil
Alison Mountz, Wilfrid Laurier University, Waterloo, Canada
Linda Oucho, African Migration and Development Policy Centre, Nairobi, Kenya
Marta Pachocka, SGH Warsaw School of Economics, Poland
Antoine Pécoud, Sorbonne University Paris Nord, France
Shahamak Rezaei, University of Roskilde, Denmark
Sergey Ryazantsev, Russian Academy of Sciences, Moscow, Russia
Carlos Sandoval García, University of Costa Rica
Everita Silina, The New School, New York, USA
Rachel Simon-Kumar, University of Auckland, New Zealand
William Walters, Carleton University, Ottawa, Canada

Human mobility, whatever its scale, is often controversial. Hence it carries with it the potential for politics. A core feature of mobility politics is the tension between the desire to maximise the social and economic benefits of migration and pressures to restrict movement. Transnational communities, global instability, advances in transportation and communication, and concepts of 'smart borders' and 'migration management' are just a few of the phenomena transforming the landscape of migration today. The tension between openness and restriction raises important questions about how different types of policy and politics come to life and influence mobility.

Mobility & Politics invites original, theoretically and empirically informed studies for academic and policy-oriented debates. Authors examine issues such as refugees and displacement, migration and citizenship, security and cross-border movements, (post-)colonialism and mobility, and transnational movements and cosmopolitics.

This series is indexed in Scopus.

Jungwon Yeo
Editor

Return Migration and Crises in Non-Western Countries

palgrave
macmillan

Editor
Jungwon Yeo
School of Public Administration
University of Central Florida
Orlando, FL, USA

ISSN 2731-3867 ISSN 2731-3875 (electronic)
Mobility & Politics
ISBN 978-3-031-53561-1 ISBN 978-3-031-53562-8 (eBook)
https://doi.org/10.1007/978-3-031-53562-8

© The Editor(s) (if applicable) and The Author(s), under exclusive license to Springer Nature Switzerland AG 2024
This work is subject to copyright. All rights are solely and exclusively licensed by the Publisher, whether the whole or part of the material is concerned, specifically the rights of translation, reprinting, reuse of illustrations, recitation, broadcasting, reproduction on microfilms or in any other physical way, and transmission or information storage and retrieval, electronic adaptation, computer software, or by similar or dissimilar methodology now known or hereafter developed.
The use of general descriptive names, registered names, trademarks, service marks, etc. in this publication does not imply, even in the absence of a specific statement, that such names are exempt from the relevant protective laws and regulations and therefore free for general use.
The publisher, the authors and the editors are safe to assume that the advice and information in this book are believed to be true and accurate at the date of publication. Neither the publisher nor the authors or the editors give a warranty, expressed or implied, with respect to the material contained herein or for any errors or omissions that may have been made. The publisher remains neutral with regard to jurisdictional claims in published maps and institutional affiliations.

This Palgrave Macmillan imprint is published by the registered company Springer Nature Switzerland AG.
The registered company address is: Gewerbestrasse 11, 6330 Cham, Switzerland

Paper in this product is recyclable.

Contents

Part I Introduction ... 1

1 Return Migration and Crises in Non-Western Countries: Introduction ... 3
Jungwon Yeo

Part II Cases of Return Migration and Crises in Non-Western Countries ... 13

2 A Generation of Crisis-Responsive Reintegration in Migration Management: Reflections from the Philippines ... 15
Cherry Amor D. Yap and Jeremaiah M. Opiniano

3 Does Environmental Uncertainty Affect the Remigration Intention of Chinese Migrant Workers in the Pandemic? ... 45
Ai-xiang Zheng and Haibo Zhang

4 Soft Power Amidst a Crisis: Return Migration and India's Soft Power in the Persian Gulf ... 69
Sabith Khan

5 Reasons for Leaving and Coming Back: Migration Experiences of High-Skilled Professionals from Lithuania 83
Eglė Vaidelytė, Eglė Butkevičienė, and Jolanta Vaičiūnienė

6 Lives on Hold Between the European Union and Ukraine: Ukrainian Migrants' Return Before and After the War 103
Jungwon Yeo and Olga Pysmenna

7 Family Return Migration from Europe to Turkey in the Time of Crises 121
Filiz Kunuroglu and Demet Vural Yüzbaşı

8 Crisis, Circular Systems, and Return: A Case Study of Morocco 141
Frances D. Loustau-Williams and Abderrahim Zouggaghi

9 Building a New Home: Modes of Incorporation for 1.5-Generation Return Migrants in Mexico 157
Mónica Liliana Jacobo-Suárez

10 Venezuelan Migration in Peru: Exploring the Causes for Venezuelans' Return Migration 177
Maritza Concha and Rasha Mannaa

11 Return Migration and Return Intention in Times of Crisis: Dominican Return During the COVID-19 Pandemic 193
Carlos Manuel Abaunza

Part III Conclusion 215

12 Return Migration and Crises in Non-Western Countries: Contributions and Lessons Learned 217
Jungwon Yeo

Index 227

Notes on Contributors

Carlos Manuel Abaunza holds a PhD in Sociology and Anthropology and a postdoctoral specialization in Migration and Refugee Studies. His research spans Europe, the Caribbean, and the MENA region, reflecting his global perspective. As an international instructor, Abaunza has excelled in the areas of applied sociology, migration studies, research methods and methodologies, and academic writing. He has contributed insights as a consultant to various international organizations, helping shape policies worldwide. Over the last 20 years, Abaunza has also assisted governmental and non-governmental organizations and academic institutions. He currently works at Nazarbayev University in Kazakhstan.

Eglė Butkevičienė, PhD serves as full Professor of Sociology and head of Committee for Political Science, Sociology and Public Governance Study Programs at the Faculty of Social Sciences, Arts and Humanities, Kaunas University of Technology. She holds a visiting professor appointment at University of Central Florida. Her research and teaching focus on civil society issues, public governance, social innovations, citizen science, social entrepreneurship, migration, environmental activism, and social impact of technologies. She has over 50 articles in peer-reviewed journals and book chapters to her credit. She is responsible for co-editing the book series "Democratic Dilemmas and Policy Responsiveness," published by Lexington Books.

Maritza Concha holds a PhD in Public Affairs from the University of Central Florida (UCF). She has extensive experience in community-engaged research, focusing on vulnerable populations, including immigrants. Another area of interest includes acculturation processes of recently migrated immigrants from the Latin American and Caribbean region. Concha currently serves as the Director for the Center of Public and Nonprofit Management and as a Lecturer at the UCF School of Public Administration.

Mónica Liliana Jacobo-Suárez is a CONAHCYT Fellow Researcher currently working at El Colegio de México. Her research areas include US-Mx return migration, immigrant policies, and linguistic, educational, and labor reintegration for migrant populations. She currently coordinates the project Mexican Return Migrants: Educational Trajectories and Labor Incorporation (Funded by CONAHCYT). Her articles have appeared in the *Journal of Global Ethics*, *Latino Studies*, and the *Journal of Language and Policy*, among others. Also, she has collaborated as a chapter author in *The Routledge History of Modern Latin American Migration*, *Theorizing Transnational Youth Identities Crossing the US-Mexican Border* (Routledge), and *Accountability across borders* (UTexas).

Sabith Khan is an Associate Professor and Program Director in the MPPA program at Cal Lutheran University, California, USA. He has written on the philanthropy, migration, and remittances.

Filiz Kunuroglu works as an Associate Professor at Izmir Katip Celebi University, Turkey. She also works as an associate editor of *International Journal of Intercultural Relations*. She mainly does research on social psychological processes in culturally diverse environments. Her studies mainly focus on acculturation and reacculturation processes, discrimination, psychological resilience, and wellbeing in migrant and refugee groups.

Frances D. Loustau-Williams is an Assistant Professor in the School of Humanities and Social Sciences at Al Akhawayn University in Ifrane Morocco. Her research includes borders, migration, knowledge production systems, and social marginalization in Africa. She has a PhD in Public and International Affairs, concentrating on International Development and a Master's degree in International Development, both from the University of Pittsburgh.

Rasha Mannaa holds a bachelor's degree in international relations from Universidad del Norte in Colombia. She is currently pursuing two master's degrees at the University of Central Florida (UCF) in Public Administration and in Nonprofit Management. Mannaa works as a Graduate Assistant at the Center for Public and Nonprofit Management (CPNM), where she manages and oversees various public and nonprofit initiatives. Additionally, Mannaa works part-time as a junior consultant at socialBaq, a small consultancy firm that develops methods and programs for talent development, strategic planning, and for maximizing the impact of different companies and nonprofits worldwide.

Jeremaiah M. Opiniano holds a PhD from The University of Adelaide and teaches journalism and research methods at the University of Santo Tomas (UST) in Manila, Philippines. He is also director of UST's Research Center for Social Sciences and Education (RCSSED). Opiniano also runs a nonprofit think-tank, the Institute for Migration and Development Issues (IMDI).

Olga Pysmenna obtained a PhD in Public Affairs from the University of Central Florida. Her dissertation investigated the network collaborated capacity for service delivery for people impacted by humanitarian crisis caused by war. Her research interests include network governance, humanitarian crises, nonprofit management, international conflicts, and corruption prevention.

Jolanta Vaičiūnienė is an expert in public administration, mainly focusing on local democracy, communities, migration, local governance, sustainable public procurement, and social policy. She serves as head of the Municipal Training Centre at Kaunas University of Technology and is a member of the research group "Civil Society and Sustainability" at the Faculty of Social Sciences, Arts and Humanities. She has managed a variety of projects that have strengthened the capacity of municipal governments throughout Lithuania and has provided knowledge sharing for public officials in other European communities. She is co-editor of Palgrave Macmillan's book series "Rethinking University and Community Policy Connections".

Eglė Vaidelytė holds a PhD in Sociology and is professor, vice-dean for studies, and a member of the research group "Civil Society and Sustainability" at Kaunas University of Technology. Vaidelyte has been an external expert at the European Commission for a number of research programs including Asylum, Migration, and Integration Fund (AMIF), DG for Migration and Home Affairs. Vaidelyte often speaks at various national and international conferences, gives training to civil servants and communities, and is an author or co-author of over 40 research articles, chapters, and books on civil society, public governance, corruption prevention, and migration issues.

Cherry Amor D. Yap holds a PhD from Kyoto University. She teaches at the Global Linkage Initiative Program of the Tokyo University of Foreign Studies, and the General Studies Department of Asia University in Tokyo, Japan. She was previously a lecturer at the University of the Philippines Manila and De La Salle - College of Saint Benilde in Manila, Philippines

Jungwon Yeo is an Associate Professor in the School of Public Administration at the University of Central Florida. Her primary research focuses on enhancing attitudes, behaviors, and cognitions of diverse individuals and organizations and their collective decision-making process in critical policy contexts, such as disaster and crisis management, migration, and human security. Additionally, her research explores key topics shaping contemporary discourse in public administration, including accountability, ethics, leadership, and social justice, and their impact on public service provision. Her research experience is demonstrated through refereed publications, national and international conference presentations, and multiyear interdisciplinary research grant awards.

Demet Vural Yüzbaşı works as an Assistant Professor at Izmir Katip Çelebi University, Department of Psychology. She obtained her MA degree in Developmental Psychology and PhD in Psychological Counseling and Guidance at Ege University. Her work includes studies of intervention programs for children and youth, children with special needs and their families, immigrants, emerging adulthood, and late adulthood.

Haibo Zhang is professor and director of the Center for Risk, Disaster and Crisis Management in the School of Government at Nanjing University, China. His research interests include emergency management networks, social media and crisis communication, organizational and policy learning, and social risk governance in China. His work has been published in journals such as *Safety Science, Disasters, Risk Analysis*, the *Journal of Public Affairs Education*, and the *Journal of Comparative Policy Analysis*.

Ai-xiang Zheng is a professor at Wuxi Institute of Technology, where he is a deputy dean of school of management. His primary research interests include migration risk and unemployment risk. His work has appeared in journals including *Asian and Pacific Migration Journal*, and *PLOS ONE*.

Abderrahim Zouggaghi is an alumnus of Al Akhawayn University in Ifrane with advanced degrees in International Studies & Diplomacy. He is currently researching the intricacies of the informal economies and power structures that emerge out of border fluidity at the Melilla-Nador border. His master's thesis is a thorough investigation on how money sent home by migrants affects Moroccan migration patterns.

List of Figures

Fig. 2.1	Evolution of the Philippines' migration management bureaucracy, from the 1980s until 2022	19
Fig. 2.2	The Philippine migration management bureaucracy, starting 2023	23
Fig. 2.3	Timeline of state-run migrant reintegration policies and programs. Packaged by the Institute for Migration and Development Issues (IMDI)	26
Fig. 2.4	Organizational transitions for migrant reintegration in the Philippine government. *Sources*: Borja in Böhning (1999), Manzala (2007), and OWWA (2017). National Reintegration Center for OFWs (n.d., 2017a, 2017b). Packaged by the Institute for Migration and Development issues (IMDI)	29
Fig. 3.1	Theoretical model	53
Fig. 5.1	Paths of migrants	95

List of Tables

Table 2.1	Returning overseas Filipinos during the COVID-19 pandemic's first two years	34
Table 2.2	Forms of economic reintegration assistance provided by Philippine government agencies to pandemic affected OFWs	36
Table 3.1	Sample characteristics ($N = 317$)	56
Table 3.2	Means, standard deviations, and correlation matrix	57
Table 3.3	Regression analysis results	59
Table 5.1	Summary of the cases	90
Table 5.2	The prevailing reasons to emigrate and re-emigrate as pull and push factors	94
Table 6.1	Ukrainian refugees' urgent needs and intention	112
Table 7.1	Demographic characteristics of the participants	126
Table 8.1	News articles used to build a timeline of events and perspectives	145
Table 8.2	Surveys conducted by the Moroccan "Haut Commissariat au Plan"	146
Table 8.3	Interviews conducted	146
Table 8.4	Return migrants by year of indicated return	147
Table 9.1	Profile of participants	167
Table 10.1	Attitudes and stereotypes against Venezuelans	185
Table 11.1	Dominican population resident in Spain	196
Table 11.2	Policies and regulations in response to the pandemic during the first year of the pandemic	203
Table 11.3	Number of international entries of Dominican residents to the national territory	205

PART I

Introduction

CHAPTER 1

Return Migration and Crises in Non-Western Countries: Introduction

Jungwon Yeo

INTRODUCTION

Crises have become prominent factors in global migration. The increasing frequencies and scales of both expected and unprecedented crises shed light on diverse issues related to human displacement (Kahanec et al., 2016; Yeo, 2020; Comfort, 2023). Crises can shape multifaceted conditions for the departure or return of people and bring about cascading changes or challenges in the societies involved, all without necessarily suggesting foreseeable outcomes or resolutions (Hall & Massey, 2010; Barrett et al., 2016; Mencutek, 2022). For instance, the Russian Invasion of Ukraine in 2022 led to the displacement of over eight million Ukrainians, resulting in new economic, cultural, political, and societal challenges and opportunities for many European countries (see Yeo & Pysmenna, 2024, Chap. 6, in this volume). Similarly, the world's common responses to combat the initial spread of the COVID-19 pandemic, such as border

---

J. Yeo (✉)
School of Public Administration, University of Central Florida,
Orlando, FL, USA
e-mail: Jungwon.Yeo@ucf.edu

© The Author(s), under exclusive license to Springer Nature
Switzerland AG 2024
J. Yeo (ed.), *Return Migration and Crises in Non-Western Countries*, Mobility & Politics,
https://doi.org/10.1007/978-3-031-53562-8_1

closures and lockdowns, gave rise to unusual migration flows between countries, resulting in unprecedented socio-economic issues and challenges worldwide (see Loustau-Williams & Zouggaghi, 2024, Chap. 8 in this volume).

It requires a comprehensive understanding of the complex interplay between various types and scales of crises and the diverse backgrounds of migrants, encompassing their social, political, economic, cultural, and psychological status to address and resolve emerging issues at the intersection of migration and crises (Hall & Massey, 2010; Hazans, 2016). Despite the significance, the intersection of crises and migration remains relatively underexplored and poorly understood within migration and crisis research (Bastia, 2011; Mencutek, 2022). This limited research knowledge has hindered its potential to offer meaningful insights to policymakers and practitioners in these fields.

Additionally, there has been a growing demand for information and knowledge concerning return migration and crisis in non-Western countries. A major portion of migration studies focuses predominantly on the dichotomy between immigration—the influx of foreigners—into Western countries, and emigration—outflows of citizens—from non-Western countries (Olivier-Mensah & Scholl-Schneider, 2016; Yeo & Huang, 2020). Return migration is often viewed as the final stage of this dichotomy and is not explored extensively as an independent subject within migration studies (Olivier-Mensah & Scholl-Schneider, 2016). Moreover, significant volume of migration studies was conducted in the context of Western countries, as migrants' destinations (Yeo & Huang, 2020). When non-Western countries become the locus of migration research, it tends to revolve around the emigration of their citizens. This emphasis on emigration stems from economic factors as non-Western countries are rarely highlighted as departures for migrants seeking for new opportunities. Consequently, migration studies have rarely centered on non-Western countries as destination for migrants.

Return migration in non-Western countries has been an evolving phenomenon, particularly amid crises (Bastia, 2011; Zaiceva & Zimmermann, 2016). Moreover, the contextual conditions in non-Western countries differ significantly from those in developed Western countries. Many returnees may find that their formal status aligns with their countries of origin. When they return to their home countries, they may no longer face the same set of challenges they encountered in their host countries, especially those related to maintaining their formal status (as Jacobo-Suárez, 2024 discussed in Chap. 9 in this volume). However, returnees' experiences in other countries, primarily affluent Western ones, and their encounters with crises could introduce unique contexts that either facilitate or hinder the processes and outcomes of their return to their home countries (Comfort, 2023). Furthermore, the impacts, challenges, and issues associated with return migration are more prominent in non-Western countries (Zaiceva & Zimmermann, 2016), many of which may lack sufficient awareness and mitigation measures to address the emerging needs and demands of returnees (as discussed in Chaps. 2 and 9 in this volume).

Therefore, I have proposed this edited volume to explore diverse issues related to return migration amid various types of crises facing non-Western countries. Through a rich collection of cases and theoretical discussions featured in chapters, this book aims to expand significantly current knowledge of crisis migration and discuss the implications for a wide range of practices and policies in migration and crisis management.

Foci, Loci, and Conceptualization

As the title of this edited volume indicates explicitly, 'crisis,' 'return migration,' and 'non-Western countries' are the key terms that define the focus and locus of this book. In this section, I will briefly discuss how these terms are defined and used throughout the chapters of this book.

Firstly, this book explores various causes, types, scales, and roles of crises in the realm of human migration research and practice. In this book, 'crisis' refers to 'a difficult or a dangerous situation requiring serious policy attention.' The contributing authors investigate different forms of crises including war (see Chap. 6), public health crises (see Chaps. 2, 3, 4, 5, 7, and 11), and institutional, economic, or policy failures (see Chaps. 7, 8, 9, and 10). Some chapters focus on specific crisis as a standalone event, such as the COVID-19 pandemic in Chaps. 2 and 3, and the war in Chap. 5. Other chapters examine cascading crises that involve a series of interconnected events (see Chaps. 9, 10, and 11). Additionally, certain chapters explore how a crisis or cascading crises can create new contexts influencing various aspects of human migratory processes (see Chaps. 5, 6, 7, 8, 9, and 10), and relevant policies (see Chap. 2). Some chapters address crises as both causes and consequences of human movement across borders (Chaps. 3 and 9).

Secondly, while many studies on migration amid crises exist, this edited volume places a particular emphasis on 'return migration.' Return migration refers to 'the movement of a person going from a host country back to a country of origin, country of nationality, or habitual residence' (International Organization of Migration [IOM], 2011). Traditionally, in migration studies, return migration was often seen as the final stage of the migratory process, primarily discussed in relation to the extended period of residence in foreign countries (Pérez-López, 2001; IOM, 2011; Stark, 2019). However, both chapter authors and I acknowledge that there has not been a universally concrete definition or understanding of return migration within the field, given the varied causes, processes, and outcomes associated with return migration. In addition, existing studies on return migration tend to highlight the experiences of low-skilled international male labor migrants. Other types of returnees, such as refugees, asylum seekers, families, high-skilled migrants, female domestic workers, and 1.5 generations, received relatively less scholarly attention (Mencutek, 2022).

Therefore, this book presents a wide array of definitions of return migration, returnees, or return migrants that consider factors such as the duration of migration, types of return (permanent, medium, and temporary), causes, and locations. Several chapters delve into the issues of return migration's volatility or circularity of return migration. In examining the forces and factors driving return (or return intention), the chapter authors are allowed to adopt and explain diverse terms, including push and pull factors, as well as individual, structural, and institutional factors. The book addresses divergent types of return, distinguishing between forced returns due to external circumstances or forces and voluntary returns driven by individual choices within different contexts.

Moreover, recognizing the volatility and circulatory nature of return migration, this book broadens the concept by including 'remigration' which refers to the act or process of migrants moving from their initial location to another that may not necessarily be their home (see Zheng & Zhang, 2024, Chap. 3 in this volume). This expansion is especially pertinent for short-term or seasonal migrant laborers, for whom remigration to other cities or locations could be an integral part of the return process. As such, we anticipate that research findings on remigration will offer valuable insight into our understanding of return migration.

Finally, this book delves into the intersection of return migration and crises within 'non-Western countries.' The term 'non-Western countries' refers to nations in the Eastern part of the world, encompassing Asian, Middle Eastern, and African countries. Western countries typically denote economically developed nations primarily located in North America and Western Europe. However, it is worth noting that the distinction between Western and non-Western countries extends beyond geography; it often signifies the level of economic development. For instance, countries in Central or South America as well as Eastern Europe are not typically considered Western despite their geographical locations. Conversely, Australia and New Zealand are regarded as Western countries due to their historical and cultural ties to North America and Western Europe, even though they are situated in the Oceania region. As a result, the term 'non-Western countries' encompasses a broad range of regions, including Asia, the Middle East, Africa, Eastern Europe, Latin America, and the Caribbean, based on the aforementioned criteria. This distinction forms the framework for selecting chapter authors in this edited volume.

Book Organization and Chapter Introduction

This book is divided into three sections. **Section I**, which includes this introductory chapter (Chap. 1), serves as a foundational component of the edited volume. It introduces the volume's overarching goals and contributions by emphasizing the significance of understanding return migration and crises in contemporary society. This chapter also provides clear definitions of the main concepts—return migration, crisis, and non-Western countries. Additionally, it offers an overview of the edited volume and briefly introduces the chapters that are included in Section II.

In **Section II**, which encompasses Chaps. 2–11, the book delves into specific case studies of non-Western countries. These chapters explore a wide range of theoretical and methodological perspectives while offering practical insights to address the intricate issues surrounding return migration and crises. The topics covered within this chapters include return migration trends, the pivotal roles, and contributions of return migrants, the social, psychological, and policy challenges faced by returnees, emerging issues stemming from return migration in their home countries, and the public and formal responses to return migration and the reintegration of returned citizens. Section II is further divided into four parts, each focusing on a distinct geographical region: Asia (Chaps. 2–4), Europe (Chaps. 5–7), North Africa (Chap. 8), and Latin America and the Caribbean (Chaps. 9–11).

The Asian chapter by Yap and Opiniano (2024) (Chap. 2). In the chapter, Yap and Opiniano delve into the systematic policy efforts of Philippine government to reintegrate overseas returnees, particularly during the COVID-19 pandemic. They provide a comprehensive review of the 40-year history of migrant management policies, with a special focus on reintegration policies developed in response to various crises. The chapter analyzes how the substantial return migration resulting from the COVID-19 pandemic has led to innovative approaches to migration reintegration in the Philippines. The authors underscore the significance of return migration for the nation's development and emphasize the need for more comprehensive and inclusive reintegration policies. They advocate for a whole-of-government and a whole-of-society approach to support systemically the return of oversees migrants in the post pandemic era.

In Chap. 3, Zheng and Zhang (2024) explain empirically how environmental uncertainty, particularly uncertainty related to the global pandemic, influences the remigration intentions of Chinese migrant workers within different regions and cities of China. Through statistical analysis of survey data from 317 migrant workers, Zheng and Zhang explore the intricate relationships among environmental uncertainty, pandemic-related uncertainty, migrant workers' perception of unemployment risk, and their intentions to remigrate. While the authors did not find a significant direct association between environmental uncertainties and remigration intentions, their findings highlight the exacerbating impact of pandemic-related uncertainty on overall environmental uncertainty. Furthermore, they demonstrate that heightened perceptions regarding unemployment significantly influence migrant workers' intention to emigrate from their current locations.

In Chap. 4, Khan (2024) delves into the profound effects of return migration on the diplomatic ties between nation-states. Emphasizing the pivotal role of remittances in cementing the connection between countries of origin and destination, the author contends that the mass return of Indian expatriates from the Persian Gulf amid the COVID-19 pandemic and shifting labor market dynamics in the region have resulted in a substantial reduction in remittances. Consequently, this reduction has led to fractures in the bilateral relationship between the nations.

Chapters 5, 6, and 7 explore return migration and crises within the context of non-Western Europe. In Chap. 5, Vaidelytė et al. (2024) investigate whether various crises have reshaped migration patterns, specifically the movement between emigration and return, among high-skilled professionals in Lithuania. The authors explained that while the pandemic itself may not have significantly influenced the decisions of high-skilled labor migrants to return, the conditions in both the origin and host countries since the pandemic—such as socio-economic cultural conditions, as well as individual's perceptions of the life—may serve as push or pull factors in the return and remigration decision of high-skilled migrants in Lithuania.

Chapter 6, by Yeo and Pysmenna (2024), examines the migratory processes of Ukrainians before and after the war resulting from the Russian invasion in February 2022. The authors explore whether the factors and antecedents driving Ukrainians' emigration, return, remigration, or resettlement differ before and after the war. Findings indicate that in the pre-war period, structural factors, especially economic and institutional disparities between Ukraine and the destination countries, were the primary drivers of Ukrainians' migratory process. However, after the war, individual factors, such as family connections and patriotism, became the major forces influencing the return intentions and decisions of Ukrainian refugees.

In Chap. 7, Künüroğlu and Yüzbaşı (2024) focus on the return migration of Turkish families from Western European countries and the impact of cascading crises on their returns and reintegration in Turkey. The authors investigate the push and pull factors affecting Turkish migrant families' decisions to return, their reintegration and readaptation processes amid public health and economic crises, and the role of family dynamics in the returnees' reintegration and re-acculturation processes. Through qualitative analysis of in-depth interviews, authors find that emotional reasons, such as preserving ethnic ties, feeling at home, and avoiding discrimination in Europe, played a significant role in convincing returnees to stay in Turkey, despite the challenges of hyperinflation and unemployment challenge they faced in Turkey.

In Chap. 8 Loustau-Williams and Zouggaghi (2024) contend that the pandemic-induced border closures caused an immobility crisis in Morocco, **North Africa**. They, then, delve into how the immobility crisis reshaped the circulatory movement of migrants within Morocco. Throughout the chapter, the authors explore three forms of circulatory return migration: longer term return, seasonal return, and daily border-crossing. By analyzing government reports, statistics, and in-depth interviews, the authors discover that the mobility restrictions disrupted the migration circularity system. In particular, immobility had a significant impact on seasonal or daily circular returns, leading to a shift from short-term circularity to more permanent or illegal migration.

Chapter 9, 10, and 11 offer insights into Latin American and Caribbean countries. In Chap. 9, Jacobo-Suárez (2024) examines the reintegration process of young Mexican returnees whose forced return was a result of the U.S. government immigration enforcement policies. The chapter highlights the lack of governmental support in reintegration of the forced returnees as a crisis that has long-lasting effect on these young individuals' lives. Against the backdrop of the ongoing reintegration crisis in Mexico, the author investigates the education and labor incorporation experiences of young returnees and explores their readaptation strategies and agency manifestations to help themselves adjust to their new environment in Mexico.

In Chap. 10, Concha and Mannaa (2024) explore potential antecedents for the return of Venezuelan immigrants in Peru. The authors focus on how conflictive migratory policies led by different Peruvian administrations, xenophobic attitudes of Peruvians toward Venezuelan migrants, and return support by the Venezuelan government shape the intentions of Venezuelan immigrants to return or remigrate.

In Chap. 11, Abaunza (2024) examines the factors influencing the return migration and return intention of Dominican migrants from Spain during the COVID-19 pandemic. The chapter begins with a review of the history of Dominican return amid crises and provides a parallel investigation of Dominican return during the pandemic. The author identifies that government intervention during the pandemic had little to no influence on Dominican migrants' return intentions. Instead, the main drivers for Dominicans' return amid the crisis were concerns and fears related to the lack of access to social welfare, such as healthcare or social assistance, increasing social discrimination in Spain, and longer term family considerations.

Lastly, in **Section III**, Chap. 12 synthesizes findings from the 11 cases and offers lessons for both researchers and practitioners.

Conclusion

This book aims to broaden our understanding of the intersection between return migration and crisis by offering an in-depth exploration of various cases in diverse context. It serves as a valuable resource that brings together the perspectives of academic researchers, practitioners, and policymakers on the topic of return migration. Each chapter provides a unique opportunity to examine critically the current discourse on return migration and its relationship with crises, offering insights from different policy and operational perspectives.

REFERENCES

Abaunza, C. M. (2024). Return migration and return intention in times of crisis: Dominican return during the COVID-19 pandemic. In J. Yeo (Ed.), *Return migration and crises in non-Western countries (Chapter 11)*. Palgrave Macmillan.

Barrett, A., Bergin, A., Kelly, E., & McGuinness, S. (2016). Ireland's recession and the immigrant-native earnings gap. In M. Kahanec & K. F. Zimmermann (Eds.), *Labor migration, EU enlargement, and the great recession* (pp. 103–122). Springer.

Bastia, T. (2011). Should I stay or should I go? Return migration in times of crises. *Journal of International Development, 23*(4), 583–595.

Comfort, L. K. (2023). Dislocation after disaster: What does 'returning home' mean? *International Migration, 61*(4), 337–340.

Concha, M., & Mannaa, R. (2024). Venezuelan migration in Peru: Exploring the causes for Venezuelans' return migration. In J. Yeo (Ed.), *Return migration and crises in non-Western countries (Chapter 10)*. Palgrave Macmillan.

Hall, S., & Massey, D. (2010). Interpreting the crisis. *Soundings, 44*(44), 57–71.

Hazans, M. (2016). Migration experience of the Baltic countries in the context of economic crisis. In M. Kahanec & K. F. Zimmermann (Eds.), *Labor migration, EU enlargement, and the great recession* (pp. 297–344). Springer.

International Organization of Migration. (2011). 'Return', IOM glossary on migration (2nd ed.). Accessed September 10, 2023 from https://www.corteidh.or.cr/sitios/Observaciones/11/Anexo5.pdf

Jacobo-Suárez, M. L. (2024). Building a new home: Modes of incorporation for 1.5-generation return migrants in Mexico. In J. Yeo (Ed.), *Return migration and crises in non-Western countries (Chapter 9)*. Palgrave Macmillan.

Kahanec, M., Pytlikova, M., & Zimmermann, K. F. (2016). The free movement of workers in an enlarged European Union: Institutional underpinnings of economic adjustment. In M. Kahanec & K. F. Zimmermann (Eds.), *Labor migration, EU enlargement, and the great recession*. Springer.

Khan, S. (2024). Soft power amidst a crisis: Return migration and India's soft power in the Persian Gulf. In J. Yeo (Ed.), *Return migration and crises in non-Western countries (Chapter 4)*. Palgrave Macmillan.

Künüroğlu, F., & Yüzbaşı, D. V. (2024). Family return migration from Europe to Turkey in the time of crises. In J. Yeo (Ed.), *Return migration and crises in non-Western countries (Chapter 7)*. Palgrave Macmillan.

Loustau-Williams, F. D., & Zouggaghi, A. (2024). Crisis, circular systems, and return: A case study of Morocco. In J. Yeo (Ed.), *Return migration and crises in non-Western countries (Chapter 8)*. Palgrave Macmillan.

Mencutek, Z. S. (2022). Voluntary and forced return migration under a pandemic crisis. In *Migration and pandemics: Spaces of solidarity and spaces of exception* (pp. 185–206). Springer.

Olivier-Mensah, C., & Scholl-Schneider, S. (2016). Transnational return? On the interrelation of family, remigration, and transnationality – An introduction. *Transnational Social Review, 6*(1–2), 2–9.

Pérez-López, J. F. (2001). Pazos' economic problems of Cuba during the transition: Return migration of skilled persons and professionals. In *Annual proceedings* (Vol. 11). The Association for the Study of the Cuban Economy.

Stark, O. (2019). Behavior in reverse: Reasons for return migration. *Behavioural Public Policy, 3*(1), 104–126. https://doi.org/10.1017/bpp.2018.27

Vaidelytė, E., Butkevičienė, E., & Vaičiūnienė, J. (2024). Reasons for leaving and coming back: Migration experiences of high skilled professionals from Lithuania. In J. Yeo (Ed.), *Return migration and crises in non-Western countries (Chapter 5)*. Palgrave Macmillan.

Yap, C. A. D., & Opiniano, J. M. (2024). A generation of crisis-responsive reintegration in migration management: Reflections from the Philippines. In J. Yeo (Ed.), *Return migration and crises in non-Western countries (Chapter 2)*. Palgrave Macmillan.

Yeo, J. (2020). Collective action and vulnerable populations: Interorganizational collaboration for undocumented immigrants' disaster safety following hurricane Irma 2017. *Natural Hazards Review, 21*(1), 05019003.

Yeo, J., & Huang, X. (2020). Migration in public administration research: A systematic review and future directions. *International Journal of Public Administration, 43*(2), 176–187.

Yeo, J., & Pysmenna, O. (2024). Lives on hold between the European Union and Ukraine: Ukrainian migrants' return before and after the war. In J. Yeo (Ed.), *Return migration and crises in non-Western countries (Chapter 6)*. Palgrave Macmillan.

Zaiceva, A., & Zimmermann, K. F. (2016). Returning home at times of trouble? Return migration of EU enlargement migrants during the crisis. In M. Kahanec & K. F. Zimmermann (Eds.), *Labor migration, EU enlargement, and the great recession* (pp. 397–418). Springer.

Zheng, A., & Zhang, H. (2024). Does environmental uncertainty affect the remigration intention of Chinese migrant workers in the pandemic. In J. Yeo (Ed.), *Return migration and crises in non-Western countries (Chapter 3)*. Palgrave Macmillan.

PART II

Cases of Return Migration and Crises in Non-Western Countries

CHAPTER 2

A Generation of Crisis-Responsive Reintegration in Migration Management: Reflections from the Philippines

Cherry Amor D. Yap and Jeremaiah M. Opiniano

INTRODUCTION

The Philippines is the reputed global model in migration management among the origin countries of international migrants (International Organization for Migration, 2005). This recognition stems from the country's institutionalization of a bureaucracy and a national policy framework that tries to ensure the safe, orderly, and regular migration of overseas workers and other international migrants (e.g., emigrants, marriage migrants). A 1974 national labor code (courtesy of Philippine Presidential Decree 447) had provided the earliest regulations surrounding the

---

C. A. D. Yap
Asia University, Tokyo, Japan

J. M. Opiniano (✉)
Institute for Migration and Development Issues and the University of Santos Tomas, Manila, Philippines
e-mail: jmopiniano@ust.edu.ph

© The Author(s), under exclusive license to Springer Nature Switzerland AG 2024
J. Yeo (ed.), *Return Migration and Crises in Non-Western Countries*, Mobility & Politics,
https://doi.org/10.1007/978-3-031-53562-8_2

recruitment of workers for overseas jobs. Provisions in the said Code then led to the setting up of national government agencies that, for decades, have been managing the Philippine overseas employment program.

In essence, migration management by the Philippines covers the three phases of the migration process: pre-departure, on-site integration in the new destination, and *return* to the origin country or community. Over the decades, the Philippines is remarked to have excelled in ensuring orderly pre-departure; in leading overseas workers to government-regulated channels, contracts and processes; in regulating the overseas recruitment and manning industry (for land- and sea-based overseas workers); in negotiating for better terms and conditions for workers in host countries; in providing on-site social protection services to citizens working in foreign job sites (especially to distressed migrant workers); and in facilitating the repatriation and return of aggrieved migrant workers due to work-related abuses and natural and man-made disasters. All these elements of migration management emerged prior to and during the COVID-19 pandemic, a mega-crisis that has spurred lots of return migrations and stirred demands for economic and psycho-social reintegration services.

Migration management was then a response to the Philippines' fledgling fiscal position (e.g., balance of payments, foreign exchange) and feeble domestic labor market. Philippine migration officials even called overseas migration as a "temporary, stop-gap measure" (International Organization for Migration, 2005) to arrest economic and employment issues affecting Filipino workers. Come the new millennium, when the world got attracted to the development potential of foreign remittances, overseas Filipinos swelled in numbers and dollar remittances to the Philippines annually reached historic highs. International (labor) migration suddenly emerged as a culture (Asis, 2006), and the previous decade saw the Philippine economy consistently grow to an average of over-6%. Overseas Filipinos' remittances contributed visibly to that decade of economic growth (Opiniano, 2020b).

The desire to return home for good, however, did not automatically come for overseas Filipinos (including migrant workers). That was until the pandemic came (March 2020) and over-two million migrant workers came home the past 2.5 years (Patinio, 2022). If not for the established agencies, laws, procedures and frontline services of the Philippines' migration management system, the return of over-two million overseas workers could have been more troublesome. The services accorded to returnee overseas Filipino workers (OFWs) during this pandemic will cap off the reaching of a generation of migrant worker reintegration efforts (which started in 1983) by government.

This Chapter narrates the story of the Philippines in handling crisis-induced return migrations by OFWs through repatriation and socio-economic reintegration. From a public administration perspective, this Chapter intends to analyze (a) The place of migrant reintegration in decades-old migration management; (b) the external crises that have induced repatriations, deportations and return migrations; (c) the nearly 40-year response of the Philippine migration management bureaucracy on reintegration; and (d) how a COVID-19 pandemic may lead to new approaches in migration reintegration. Authors here will argue that the world's "global model" in migration management has long cocooned migrant reintegration into a reactionary approach that is done by a handful of migration and non-migration agencies. Crisis or no crisis, Philippine migrant reintegration in the post-pandemic era is a visible development need that may require broader, strategic approaches and a whole-of-government, whole-of-society approach. Lessons from the Philippines, even if many of these may not be applicable to other migrant-origin countries, can spur policy and scholarly discussions on institutionalizing migrant reintegration (International Organization for Migration, 2019; Haase & Honerath, 2016) while the world remains in a pandemic (Le Coz & Newland, 2021).

The Philippine Bureaucratic Configuration for Migration Management

The Philippines' migration management bureaucracy has evolved within nearly 50 years since the Labor Code's enactment. This section summarizes two evolutions, past and current, of the country's migration management bureaucracy. Such a summary will allow us to see the place of migrant reintegration.

Early Agencies

Articles 17 and 18 of that Code created two agencies, the former Overseas Employment Development Board (OEDB) and the National Seamen's Board, respectively in 1975. Given the growth of the overseas labor recruitment industry, a Bureau of Employment Services (BES) was created. When issues of migrant workers' protection emerged in the late 1970s, Presidential Decree no. 1694 (1980) created a Welfare and Training Fund for Overseas Workers or the WelFund (IOM & Scalabrini Migration Center, 2013).

The year 1982 saw a major organizational change: the OEDB, NSB and BES were merged into the Philippine Overseas Employment Administration (POEA). The POEA not only regulates overseas labor recruiters (both land-based and sea-based workers), but curbs illegal recruitment practices and their perpetrators; processes the deployment of would-be and repeat migrant workers through government-sanctioned channels; and does labor market intelligence efforts (i.e., labor marketing) for future overseas job prospects by Filipinos. The WelFund was then a unit of the former OEDB, but the POEA's creation saw the WelFund spin off into a separate agency. Both POEA and the WelFund (later renamed the Overseas Workers Welfare Administration or OWWA in 1987 (Overseas Workers Welfare Administration, 2017). OWWA is reputedly the world's largest welfare fund for migrant workers. Departing migrant workers pay a US$25 membership fee per contract for the agency to accord economic and social services for OFWs and their families, and OWWA manages the membership fees into a trust fund.

Meanwhile, Filipinos also leave the country as emigrants and spouses of foreigners. Their concerns as well as those of Filipinos who became permanent settlers and naturalized citizens abroad became the mandate of the Commission on Filipinos Overseas (CFO), created in 1980 and was then under the Department of Foreign Affairs (IOM and Scalabrini Migration Center, 2013). Under the auspices of their respective departments, POEA, OWWA and CFO serve as the long-time leading focused agencies in Philippine migration management (see Fig. 2.1).

POEA and OWWA are major attached agencies under the Department of Labor and Employment (DOLE), which works in tandem with DFA to become the major agencies handling overseas Filipino workers' (OFWs) concerns in all stages of the migration process. Also under the DOLE is the National Labor Relations Commission (NLRC), a quasi-judicial body tasked to "adjudicate labor and management disputes involving both local and overseas workers through compulsory arbitration and alternative modes of dispute resolution" (NLRC, n.d.). RA 8042 carried provisions related to illegal recruitment and to the eventual money claims for migrant workers to get from their recruitment agencies and manning agencies.

2 A GENERATION OF CRISIS-RESPONSIVE REINTEGRATION IN MIGRATION... 19

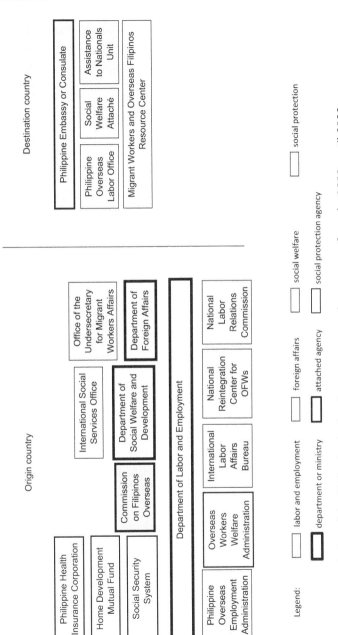

Fig. 2.1 Evolution of the Philippines' migration management bureaucracy, from the 1980s until 2022

Turning Point in Migration Management

The Philippines encountered a major setback in 1995 in terms of migration management. A domestic worker, Flor Contemplacion, was executed for allegedly killing a compatriot domestic worker and a Singaporean baby under their care. After triggering a major diplomatic issue, the Philippine legislature enacted the country's first landmark migration policy: Republic Act 8042 (the Migrant Workers and Overseas Filipinos Act of 1995). The protection of what were then called "overseas contract workers" (OCWs) formed the basis of the numerous provisions in RA 8042, including *migrant reintegration* (to be explained in succeeding sections). RA 8042 also mandated the establishment of a Re-Placement and Monitoring Center (RPMC) for returning migrant workers (IOM & Scalabrini Migration Center, 2013).

The same law helped create an office under the Department of Foreign Affairs: a legal assistant for migrant workers' affairs, which eventually became the Office of the Undersecretary for Migrant Workers Affairs (OUMWA). This Office handles mostly migrant workers' needs in host countries, especially when they are in distressed situations (including legal, welfare and workplace cases). OUMWA then coordinates with the Philippine embassies and consulates abroad when workers need to be repatriated to the Philippines (IOM and Scalabrini Migration Center, 2013).

The Office for Migrant Reintegration

DOLE also has other offices under its wings: the RA 8042-mandated National Reintegration Center for OFWs (NRCO, created by virtue of DOLE Order 79-07 in 2007), and the International Labor Affairs Bureau (ILAB, created given a rationalization plan of DOLE implemented in 2009). NRCO is the mandated RPMC by RA 8042, while ILAB (n.d.) handles all the labor attaches posted in host countries. Labor attaches and some migrant welfare officers of OWWA in some embassies and consulates from what is called the Philippine Overseas Labor Office (POLO), which directly reports to ILAB. Also in host countries, the counterpart of the RPMC in the Philippines is the Migrant Workers and Overseas Filipinos Resource Center, also created by virtue of RA 8042. If the RPMC-cum-NRCO handles the needs of returnees, the MWOFRC serves as a diplomatically sanctioned shelter catering to the needs of distressed migrant workers (including those who escaped or ran away from abusive employers).

Social Welfare Agency Helping Migrant Workers

Another relevant department or ministry came into the picture. The Department of Social Welfare and Development (DSWD) became involved in the migrant sector given the rise of returnee irregular/undocumented workers and international trafficking victims. Since 1986, DSWD, through a regional office in southern Philippines, even handles the needs of deported Filipinos coming from Malaysia given regular irregular migration crackdowns there by the Malaysian government (Abdulkarim, 2016; United Nations High Commissioner for Refugees, 2015). DSWD created the International Social Welfare Services for Filipino Nationals (ISWSFN) program at the turn of the new millennium. ISWSFN caters to the social welfare needs of distressed returning migrant workers, trafficking victims, and deportees. In the mid-2010s, the DSWD deployed social welfare attaches, and formed an International Social Services Office (ISSO), to act as backstop Philippine government personnel in overseas countries.

Social Protection Agencies

Given the growth of migrant worker deployment, social protection needs became paramount. Three agencies not technically under the ambit of migration management have become involved in migrant protection. The Social Security System (SSS) offered a pension program for OFWs through membership. The Philippine Health Insurance Corporation (PhilHealth) then offered health insurance coverage for OFWs after the Corporation acquired a previous health insurance program by OWWA for OFWs. The Home Development Mutual Fund then offered an "overseas program" so that OFWs and their families become members and avail of housing loans and other relevant credit. These agencies' programs then became requirements for departing overseas workers when they process their overseas employment documents through the POEA.

Observations and Other Sectors Involved in Overseas Migration

Thus saying, the DOLE (including POEA, OWWA, ILAB, NRCO, POLO and the NLRC), the DFA (including OUMWA and the embassies and consulates), the DSWD, the CFO, and the social protection agencies all make up the inter-agency migration management bureaucracy of the Philippines. This configuration (refer to Fig. 2.1) saw much inter-agency cooperation in both the Philippines and in host countries. Not surprisingly, there are overlaps in the provision of services, as well as reported delays in availing services, benefits and assistance in both origin and host countries.

It is also to note that the Philippines has an active civil society sector for migrant workers and overseas Filipinos in the origin country. These CSOs, formed as early as the 1980s, implement social assistance, economic interventions (savings, business development assistance) and policy advocacy measures to help improve the governance of overseas migration. Recruitment agencies, for their part, have to abide by RA 8042 and the POEA's rules and regulations for migrant worker deployment. These regulations include joint and solidary liability when a migrant worker faces distress abroad and needs to be repatriated to the Philippines.

New Chapter in Philippine Migration Management

These established migration management agencies represented the overall approach to international migration of the Philippines *until 2022*. That is because starting 2023, the Department of Migrant Workers will become fully operational. On 30 December 2021, former Philippine President Rodrigo Duterte signed Republic Act 11649 creating the Department of Migrant Workers. And when this new Department became operational on 1 January 2023, a new bureaucratic configuration will now make up the Philippines' approach to migration management (see Fig. 2.2).

Seven agencies and attached —DOLE's POEA, ILAB, NRCO, POLO and the National Maritime Polytechnic (NMP), DFA's OUMWA, and DSWD's ISSO—merged to form the DMW. OWWA becomes the sole attached agency of DMW while remaining as a social protection agency dedicated to OFWs. Even with OUMWA's transfer to DMW, the Department of Foreign Affairs (DFA) continues its diplomatic roles while continuing to implement its Assistance to Nationals (ATN) program that directly benefits Filipinos working and residing in host countries. DOLE (the previous major department for migration management) becomes solely focused on domestic employment concerns. Yet the NLRC remains the quasi-judicial body that handles the work contract-related cases of distressed migrant workers. CFO continues to handle permanent settlers, emigrants and naturalized Filipinos renewing their ties (economic, cultural) to the Philippine homeland.

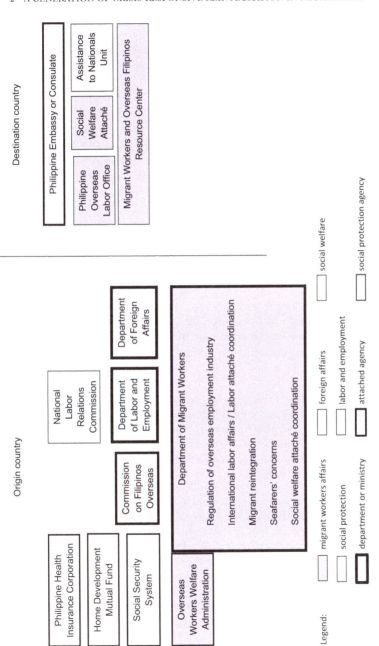

Fig. 2.2 The Philippine migration management bureaucracy, starting 2023

It is to note that in host countries, the embassy or consulate implements the one-country team approach (OCTA) in attending the needs of Filipinos abroad. OCTA means the head of an embassy or consulate handles all the affairs for the Filipino population (including migration and immigration) in the host country. The OCTA approach prevailed in the pre-DMW and now DMW era. Beginning 2023, the DMW now handles the POLO, the social welfare attaché, and the Migrant Workers and Overseas Filipinos Resource Center. Beginning 2023 also, the DMW will implement a "new" approach to migrant reintegration but let us have a historical retrace on Philippine efforts surrounding migrant reintegration.

Government-Run Migrant Reintegration

Migrant reintegration as a program of the state bureaucracy only began in 1983, nine years after the Philippine Labor Code's enactment. Prior to 1983, there have been cases of reported abuses facing overseas contract workers as well as some repatriations due to domestic conflicts in host countries (e.g., Iran [in Diampuan, 2017]). The reflection below, written by some of the leading government officials in migration management, saw the Philippines reflecting on migrant reintegration or "reabsorption" as a necessity for the country:

> *The subject of reintegrating returning migrants involves voluntary and involuntary return of contract workers. Cases of voluntary return are usually spread over a period of time while involuntary return usually involves a sizable number of workers who are forced to return as a group, for instance where natural or man-made disasters occur at their worksites. Voluntary return, especially of people unable to find employment, may be assisted by encouraging and providing advice for them to engage in livelihood and business projects. If they had sizable savings, i.e. capital, they could be advised on business opportunities available in the country and informed of the feasibility of projects suiting their own skills ... Involuntary return necessitates a contingency plan that can cope with the problems of transporting the workers back to the country, providing refuge and protection while waiting to be transported, as well as reabsorbing them into the economy when the return is affected. To ensure the protection of returning workers, including assistance for transport, labor agreements should be negotiated with the governments of immigration countries. Such agreements could request these countries to extend official assistance and protection to Filipino workers when unfavorable conditions occur, such as natural or*

man-made disasters. Reabsorption into the economy is a difficult problem when large numbers of workers are involved at the same time. However, such an eventuality makes obvious the need to generate more domestic employment opportunities. (Lazo et al., 1982: p. 32)

The first documented migrant reintegration program was a program by the former Welfare Fund on organizing migrant worker family circles. These circles were then seen as a support system to help alleviate family-level social costs of labor migration "and later towards ... reintegration" (Manzala, 2007: slide 7). Then the WelFund, in 1984, initiated a livelihood and enterprise counseling service for returning migrant workers and their families as well as provided technical information on small businesses that they can embark on (Manzala, 2007). These first two migrant reintegration programs run by the government paved the way to nearly a generation of state-led efforts on migrant reintegration (see Fig. 2.3)—be it done by migration management agencies, by agencies outside of the migrant sector, and between and among government agencies within and outside of the migrant sector.

The first entrepreneurial credit program for returnees was launched in 1986 through a program called SEED. And when the WelFund was renamed OWWA, psychosocial reintegration got bolstered by the creation of a Center for Family Assistance and Services. Meanwhile, crackdowns on irregular migrants in Malaysia (particularly Indonesians and Filipinos) were reported. That was when the DSWD's regional office in Mindanao island (southwestern Philippines) started receiving and providing social welfare assistance to deported Filipinos from Sabah. These psychosocial and economic reintegration programs were later on expanded and became more developed as the years progressed. The succeeding three decades saw the migrant reintegration effort of the state conduct the following:

1. Launch livelihood/entrepreneurial credit and family-oriented psychosocial assistance programs under OWWA.
2. Begin implementing inter-agency cooperation for specific purposes, like entrepreneurial credit that is handled by both a migrant-related and non-migration government agency.
3. Conduct repatriation and economic reintegration assistance to migrant workers during major man-made (e.g., civil strife, economic slowdown, war) and natural crises.

International labor migration and cash remittances					Reintegration-related programs, policies & institutions			
US$ - P rate	Cash remittances	Deployed		Migration-related agency		Non migration agency	
(end-year)	(US$ million)	OFWs				or inter-agency effort	
				Economic	Psychosocial	Economic	Psychosocial
14.00	944.45	434,207	1983		•		
19.76	658.89	350,982	1984	•			
20.53	680.44	378.214	1986	•	•		•
20.80	791.91	449,271	1987			•	
21.34	856.81	471.030	1988	•			
22.44	973.02	458,626	1989	•	•		
28.00	1,181.07	446,095	1990	•	•		
26.65	1,500.29	615,019	1991	•			
25.10	2,202.38	686,461	1992	•			
24.82	2,630.11	718,407	1994	•			
26.29	4,306.64	660,122	1996	•		•	
39.98	5,741.84	747,696	1997	•			
39.06	7,367.99	831,643	1998	•	•		
50.00	6,050.45	841,628	2000	•	•		
53.10	6,886.16	891,908	2002			•	•
55.57	7,578.46	867,969	2003	•		•	
56.27	8,550.37	933,588	2004			•	
53.07	10,689.00	981,677	2005				•
41.40	12,761.30	1,062,567	2007	•	•		
46.36	17,348.05	1,077,623	2009	•		•	
43.89	19,762.98	1,470,826	2010	•			
43.93	20,116.99	1,687,831	2011	•			
41.19	21,391.33	1,802,031	2012				•
44.41	22,984.03	1,836,345	2013				•
44.62	24,628.05	1,832,668	2014	•	•		•
47.17	25,606.83	1,844,406	2015	•			•
49.81	26,899.84	2,112,331	2016	•	•		•
49.92	28,059.78	2,044,877	2017	•			
48.04	29,903.25	549,841	2020	•	•	•	•
50.77	31,417.61	675,567	2021	•	•		

Fig. 2.3 Timeline of state-run migrant reintegration policies and programs. Packaged by the Institute for Migration and Development Issues (IMDI)

4. Enact national policies that include migrant reintegration and form a specific government agency for such purpose.
5. Initiate broader strategies on migrant reintegration in cooperation with migrant civil society groups and with agencies under the United Nations

These efforts spanning the past 39 years (1983–2022) all but helped establish the Philippines' migrant reintegration effort. These efforts did have their fits of inefficiencies. For example, numerous evaluations of entrepreneurial credit interventions revealed observations that reintegration by returnees-cum-loan availees "rarely happened" (Orbeta & Sanchez-Robielos, 1996: p. 29); that "sustainable incomes were not achieved" (Subbarao et al., 1996: p. 41); that marginalized migrant returnees may have not benefited from these loan programs given the financing guidelines of partner government banks (e.g., credit standing, ownership of collateral such as real property) (Borja in Böhning, 1999: p. 10); and delays in handing out checks representing returnees' entrepreneurial loans (Böhning, 1999) and even grants (Development Action for Women Network, 2021).

A Dedicated Government Agency for Returnee Migrant Workers

OWWA's mandate (dating back to the WelFund) to ensure the socioeconomic welfare of migrant workers and their families made the agency the de facto in-charge for migrant reintegration. That was what happened when the former WelFund had migrant family organizing as its first reintegration program, and a Reintegration Program Department was created in 1988. The search was then on for a national policy mandate for migrant reintegration.

As mentioned in the previous section. RA 8042 mandated the creation of the Re-Placement and Monitoring Center. However, after a few years of delays, the RPMC was established but was not funded. That was when the International Organization for Migration (IOM) helped the Philippine government (in 2007) form the National Reintegration Center for OFWs (NRCO) through technical assistance. The NRCO—the mandated RPMC in RA 8042—may represent the most institutionalized effort by a migrant origin country to specifically handle returnees' economic and social reintegration.

The NRCO then gained ground and launched multiple migrant reintegration programs in the 2010s, whether as stand-alone NRCO programs or in cooperation with the reintegration-oriented programs of DOLE and especially OWWA (Manzala, 2007). The problem, however, was the numerous disruptions to the NRCO as an organization. The Center only got its first staffing plantilla in 2013, seeing the first six years of migrant reintegration programs and services affected by limited personnel and, eventually, beneficiary outreach. And since 2007, three national laws and two department orders from the Department of Labor and Employment had seen the agency crisscross organizationally—from being under OWWA then to the DOLE and then back to OWWA, until finally a more recent law saw NRCO being merged with other relevant agencies to form the new Department of Migrant Workers (*see* Fig. 2.4). Starting 2023, NRCO becomes a unit integral to the DMW as OWWA becomes an attached agency that also implements economic and social welfare programs (including reintegration) to OFWs and their families. Admittedly, these organizational changes affected plans to expand dedicated reintegration services, and even budgets by the NRCO.

The External Crises That Have Triggered Reintegration Responses and Approaches

Since the state-facilitated overseas labor migration of Filipinos became in place in 1974, return migration by OFWs had been occurring as stereotypically crisis-induced. The observation can be gleaned from the fact that Filipino workers departing for work abroad are mostly in the low-skilled occupations, thus rendering them vulnerable from workplace abuses and exploitation. Couple that employment-related vulnerability with the natural and man-made crises that have affected Filipino workers in host countries. In the 39 years that the Philippine government had managed migrant reintegration, numerous crises and the corresponding return migrations and repatriations had occurred (including today's COVID-19 pandemic).

Twentieth-Century Crises

The 1990–91 Gulf War led what was perhaps the first major massive repatriation effort by the Philippines. Cooperating with the International Organization for Migration (IOM), the Philippine government repatriated about 29,728 Filipino migrants from Kuwait and Iraq (Battistella, 2004). The Gulf War was a learning experience for government officials and personnel tasked to handle the return of Filipinos in times of emergencies. Identified needs during those situations were properly outlined exit routes, clear logistics, close diplomatic relations with the receiving countries, and the need to work hand-in-hand with humanitarian actors and other migrant communities (IOM & Scalabrini Migration Center,

2 A GENERATION OF CRISIS-RESPONSIVE REINTEGRATION IN MIGRATION... 29

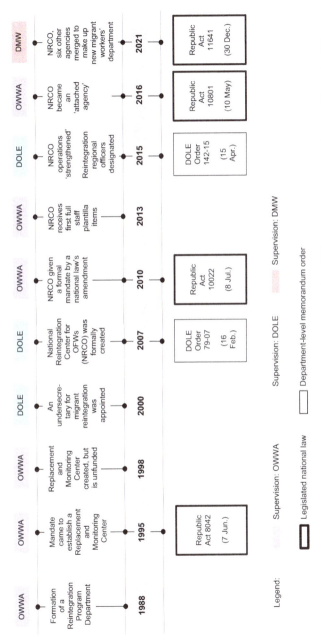

Fig. 2.4 Organizational transitions for migrant reintegration in the Philippine government. *Sources*: Borja in Böhning (1999), Manzala (2007), and OWWA (2017). National Reintegration Center for OFWs (n.d., 2017a, 2017b). Packaged by the Institute for Migration and Development Issues (IMDI)

2013; Asis, 2021). At that time also, early gaps in the government response were uncovered: the lack of inter-agency coordination, insufficient personnel at foreign service posts, and inaccurate data on the total number of Filipinos working and living in the host country. Were uncovered. The Gulf War propelled the writing of repatriation concerns in Philippine migration policies (Liao, 2020), such as a framework for preparedness and emergency responses, requiring foreign companies with Filipino workers to submit evacuation plans and the leadership of the Philippine ambassador or consul-general in facilitating repatriations (Asis, 2021: p. 228).

Perhaps the first major international economic crisis that led to some return migrations by affected Filipino workers abroad was the 1997 Asian financial crisis. That economic crisis mostly affected the large economies of Southeast and East Asia. However, not much return migrations were observed because Filipino workers were in countries not affected by the Asian financial crisis even if there were reductions in foreign work opportunities for Filipinos (Battistella, 2004). Except perhaps for some affected workers in Korea and Malaysia (the latter with a large presence of irregular migrants), no massive reduction in the number of OFWs in affected countries occurred. By that time, the RPMC still was not set up but the programs of OWWA and SSS were in place plus some entrepreneurship/livelihood interventions from other government agencies.

Health Epidemics and Continued Civil Unrest

Come the new millennium, the government is already refining its repatriation, return migration and reintegration measures. That was when a major health outbreak struck Asian countries where most overseas Filipino workers are employed.

The 2003 Severe Acute Respiratory Syndrome (SARS) epidemic was first determined in Hong Kong SAR and mainland China. Readily, the Philippine government imposed a deployment ban to send Filipino workers to Hong Kong (APEC, 2003) It is also to note that the index case of SARS in the Philippines came from a nurse working in Canada (World Health Organization, 2003; Lasco, 2020); some have died in Hong Kong (Jaymalin, 2003a) and some host countries (e.g., Libya, Hong Kong) did not allow Filipinos from entering their countries and thus losing their jobs in the process (eBalita, 2003; Jaymalin, 2003c). Not surprisingly, some OFW returnees felt ostracized by townmates in their birthplace communities (Jaymalin, 2003b).

In the advent of the war on terror, the United States invaded Iraq. Some Filipino workers had to be repatriated, as a truck driver—Angelo dela Cruz—was held hostage and freed when the Philippines withdrew its troops in Iraq. Similarly, Israel invaded Lebanon in July–August 2006 that led to another major evacuation and repatriation effort. Most of the over-7000 repatriated OFWs from Lebanon, plus some who fled to Syria, were female domestic workers and irregular migrants (the latter found to be working in the country). The Lebanon episode also highlighted the years of domestic worker abuses in that country and in other countries (e.g., non-payment of wages, excessive working hours, limits to freedom of movement, etc.). Lessons from the Lebanon evacuation and repatriation effort pushed the Philippines to institute new regulations for the hiring of Filipino domestic workers worldwide, including a US$400 minimum wage and the mandatory training of departing domestic workers by the Technical Education and Skills Development Authority (Jureidini, 2019).

If the 1997 Asian financial crisis did not affect many Filipino workers in affected Asian countries, the 2007–2008 global economic and financial crisis sent shockwaves to countries and their foreign workers. During those years, up until 2010, the Philippines provided repatriation and reintegration services to affected workers from East Asia, the Middle East, and from ocean-plying vessels. However, similar to the 1997 Asian crisis, there were not many return migrations by OFWs given the global economic crisis (Yap et al., 2009). However, with the said crisis, some migrant households reported cases that their breadwinners abroad lost work, earned reduced wages, and sent lesser amounts of remittances (Reyes et al., 2009). Note also that some migrant workers stayed put in host countries, waiting for business and income conditions in host countries to improve instead of risking to return to the Philippines. Yet during this global economic crisis, the social protection services for displaced and affected OFWs were rolled out by relevant migration and non-migration agencies (Balisacan et al., 2010). There were also observations that some displaced OFWs defaulted on the loans provided to them by OWWA (Opiniano, 2010).

The 2011 Arab Spring came, this time affecting multiple countries in the Middle East and North Africa (MENA) region. Series of protests by citizens, starting with those in Tunisia, led to a violent change of leadership in Egypt, Tunisia, Libya, and Yemen (Furagganan, n.d.). Libya became a country of concern for the Philippines given the over-30,000 OFWs present there. Syria was also affected by the Arab Spring, and so are the Filipinos (mostly domestic workers) in that country. The Arab Spring resulted in the emergency repatriation of some 10,000 OFWs with the assistance of IOM, private companies, employers, and recruitment agencies (IOM & Scalabrini Migration Center, 2013). As the Syrian civil war unfolded, the plight of Filipinos there (especially irregular migrants) remained uncertain. The Syrian situation also exposed the fact that there were around 17,000 Filipinos in Syria, a majority of whom carrying fake passports. The number contradicted a figure, 800 Filipinos, who registered in the Philippine embassy in Damascus (Sevilla, 2013). Libya's civil unrest continued to 2014–2015, and Filipino nurses were caught in the crossfire. Some of these nurses had to be repatriated (Castañaga, 2016).

Other man-made and natural crises ensued (Asis, 2021), including earthquakes and weather disturbances in host countries. With the Arab Spring, the DFA, OWWA, and DOLE repatriated a total of 6806 OFWs from conflict ridden countries in the Middle East. A global oil crisis in 2016 displaced some 15,000 OFWs in the Kingdom of Saudi Arabia, and some 4000 Filipinos returned home under "Operation Bring Them Home" (Liao, 2020). The same program provided for relief assistance, financial and legal assistance. Another health epidemic, caused by the Middle East Respiratory Syndrome coronavirus (MERS-CoV), led to some few return migrations—same with the 2003 SARS epidemic. Even the index case of MERS-CoV in the Philippines also came from an overseas worker, a domestic worker from Saudi Arabia (Racelis et al., 2015). It is also to note that numerous piracy incidents on ocean-plying vessels, perpetrated by Somali pirates, had Filipino seafarers as among the hostages. Not surprisingly, trauma and post-traumatic stress disorder (PTSD) hit on seafarers even after being repatriated (Abila & Tang, 2014).

Capacity Building for Crisis-Responsive Reintegration

With these crises becoming regular and frequent, IOM and the Philippine and US governments instituted a program called Migration in Countries in Crisis (MICIC) in 2014. MICIC built the capacities of countries to respond to natural and man-made crises and respond to the needs of their migrants /migrant workers/refugees in crisis-hit countries. MICIC even produced an emergency manual for countries and their emergency responders to be guided at (including migrants' return to the origin country). IOM also became helpful to the Philippines' efforts to upscale its reintegration measures through a funded program called the Enhanced

Reintegration Program for OFWs (International Organization for Migration Development Fund, n.d.). ERPO improved the capacities of NRCO, produced handbooks for reintegration service providers (Small Enterprises Research and Development Foundation, 2018a, 2018b), and even developed a reintegration strategic plan for the Philippines.

All these pre-COVID-19 pandemic crises witnessed the Philippines' migration management bureaucracy improve its repatriation, return migration and reintegration measures. The Philippines has already instituted a well-placed migration management system. Non-migration agencies have also cooperated to help OFWs (currently abroad and who returned to the country). The Overseas Workers Welfare Administration had cemented its place as a migrant welfare fund that responds to distressed OFWs. The National Reintegration Center for OFWs, amid its organizational transitions from 2007 to 2022 (*refer to* Fig. 2.4), has done frontline services for returning migrant workers. These developments set the stage to how the Philippines responded to the largest return migration in history.

Pandemic-Induced Return Migration and Reintegration Assistance

Not surprisingly, the COVID-19 pandemic led to the massive repatriation and return migration of Filipinos, through involuntary and voluntary circumstances. The repatriations began when what was then called the novel coronavirus (nCoV) was discovered in Wuhan, China and some 30 Filipinos had to be repatriated (Philippine News Agency, 2020). Countries locked themselves down. Borders were shut. Public health regulations and mobility restrictions became common. Countries experienced recessions in 2020. And like many nationals in host countries, Filipino workers were affected with job displacements, reduced or non-payment of wages (since employers were also affected), smaller remittance transmissions, and repatriations and return migrations. Labor markets in host countries reeled from massive job displacements and closed businesses (Opiniano, 2021a).

The Philippine government declared its first lockdown ("enhanced community quarantine") on 15 March 2020. In the first full two years of the COVID-19 pandemic (15 March 2020 to 14 March 2022), around 1,835,866 overseas Filipino workers returned to the country. The number notably included some 706,088 seafarers because the shipping industry also had its share of problems of having reduced passengers on cruise ships and delays in bringing shipments across ports (Opiniano, 2020a). Those overseas Filipinos (not the OFWs) who returned home were also sizable: 570,865 (see Table 2.1). At the same time, deployment of OFWs (new hires and repeat workers) grounded to a halt. Combining the deployment figures of 2020 (549,841) and 2021 (675,567), their combined totals still dwarf the 1,835,866 OFWs who returned to the country.

Table 2.1 Returning overseas Filipinos during the COVID-19 pandemic's first two years

		Year 1 of the pandemic (as of 15 Mar. 2021)	Year 2 of the pandemic (as of 28 Feb. 2022)
Confirmed COVD-19 cases among overseas Filipinos, running totals (reported from Philippine embassies and consulates using guidelines under the WHO's International Health Regulations)	Number of cases Deaths Countries with cases	15,881 1,043 88	25,116 1,462 107
Number of returning overseas Filipinos (including OFWs) received by the Task Group on the Management of Returning Overseas Filipinos (TG-MROF)		Year 1 of the pandemic (as of 14 Mar. 2021)	Year 2 of the pandemic (as of 14 Mar. 2022)
	OFWs – Land-based – Sea-based Non-OFWs (including permanent residents and vacationing overseas Filipinos) Deceased OFWs – COVID-19 deaths – Non COVID-19 deaths	759,733 446,524 313,209 175,402 2,947 409 2,538	1,835,866 1,054,761 706,088 570,865 6,027 636 5,391
		2020	2021
Deployed overseas Filipino workers reported by the Philippine Overseas Employment Administration (POEA)	Total deployed land-based and sea-based OFWs (annual)	549,841	675,567

Data collected by the Institute for Migration and Development Issues, citing data from the Sub-Task Group on Management of Returning Overseas Filipinos (TGMROF), the Department of Foreign Affairs and the Philippine Overseas Employment Administration (POEA)

The massive return migration (to also cover repatriations and deportations) of Filipino workers because of the pandemic saw the Philippines pivot its migration policy to return migration and reintegration (Opiniano, 2021b, 2021c; Asis, 2020). The country's inter-agency task force for emerging and infectious diseases (IATF) formed a sub-task group to manage the return of these Filipinos abroad. The quarantine, testing, and transport home of returnee OFWs alone became a big undertaking, with the Department of Health (DOH) helping out. What followed were economic and psycho-social reintegration services from migration and non-migration government agencies. The reintegration services alone saw non-traditional government agencies getting involved: the Small Business Corporation, the Agricultural Credit Policy Council (ACPC), the Department of Trade and Industry (DTI), the Department of Agriculture (DA), the Department of the Interior and Local Government (DILG) and the Department of Science and Technology (DOST). Together with DOLE and DFA and their attached agencies, these government agencies offered multifold reintegration services—from cash grants, entrepreneurial credit, business training, online skills training, to scholarships (see Table 2.2). Over-720,000 returnee and current OFWs (the latter still abroad and cannot come home) benefitted from these economic reintegration programs of various government agencies (IOM, 2021).

The COVID-19 pandemic provided the stark lesson that overall reintegration efforts by the Philippines will have to improve. For decades, civil society groups have lobbied for frameworks for a comprehensive approach to reintegration (Atikha, 2012). This comprehensive approach sees reintegration to cover the three phases of migration, to involve the family, to involve multiple stakeholders, and to cover both economic and psychosocial dimensions. With Republic Act 11649 that created the DMW, the newly created agency is tasked to implement *full-cycle reintegration*. The elements of full-cycle reintegration include:

1. *Embedded in all stages of migration for work*, from pre-deployment, on-site during employment, and upon return whether voluntary or involuntary.
2. *Covers economic, social, psychosocial, gender-responsive, and cultural dimensions of support*, including skills certification and recognition of equivalency for effective employment services.
3. *Ensures contribution to national development* through investments and transfer of technology from skilled or professional OFWs.

Table 2.2 Forms of economic reintegration assistance provided by Philippine government agencies to pandemic affected OFWs

Form of assistance	Beneficiaries (N)
Entrepreneurial credit[a]	2550
Cash grants[b]	575,607
Skills training[c]	5984
Vocational-technical education[d]	98,893
Education support (basic, higher education)[e]	45,972
Total of assisted OFWs (returnees and still abroad)	728,826
Number of returnees OFWs (two years since the first Philippine lockdown)	1,835,866
% of OFWs (returnees, still abroad) who availed of the specified forms of assistance above	At least 39.7% of returnees

This table did not include meals, transport, and hotel quarantine support (coming from OWWA), as well as loans availed by returnee OFWs from the Social Security System and the Home Development Mutual Fund.

[a]Entrepreneurial credit came from Landbank of the Philippines, Small Business Corp., the Overseas Workers Welfare Administration (OWWA data were as of 31 October 2021), Agricultural Credit Policy Council, and the Department of Science and Technology

[b]Grants came from the Department of Labor and Employment, OWWA and the National Reintegration Center for OFWs (the latter two agencies through their various programs)

[c]Skills training support, including business skills training, came from OWWA, the NRCO and DOST

[d]The Technical Education and Skills Development Authority (TESDA) primarily provided online vocational-technical education courses. OWWA also provided some vocational-technical education assistance to returnees

[e]Education support came from OWWA

Data collected by the Institute for Migration and Development Issues (IMDI) from various government agencies

4. *Social protection and financial inclusion*, by promoting access to social protection instruments and financial services.
5. *Includes unsuccessful migrations*, such as the reintegration of survivors of violence against women, and trafficking in persons (Republic Act 11649).

As of the writing of this Chapter, the United Nations family in the Philippines (2021) is implementing a two-year program on sustainable, gender-responsive reintegration. One of the outcomes of this UN-funded program is an online reintegration advisor for OFWs. The portal will feature six types of "pathways" with a range of services and government agencies providing them: those seeking employment back home, those seeking skills training, those seeking to run a business or to place investments, those who survive trafficking and violence against women, those who plan to retire back home, and those who wish to re-migrate overseas (United Nations in the Philippines, 2021). Once launched online, this reintegration advisor will further sophisticate the reintegration measures of the Philippines for returnees in crisis and non-crisis situations.

Conclusion: The Ways Forward

This Chapter shared the running history of the Philippines' migrant reintegration programs and services that span nearly 40 years, responding to various external crises. This history comes as pre-pandemic Philippine migration saw rising migrant worker deployments and formal foreign remittance inflows (*refer to* Fig. 2.1), with the latter having reached over-US$450 billion from 1975 to 2021. These economic inputs from international migration visibly contributed to the Philippines' economic surge from 2009 to 2019 (Opiniano, 2021c). With the pandemic still persisting, the Philippines may continue to need overseas jobs and foreign remittances for the homeland economy to recover (Tigno, 2021).

In this 39-year history of migrant reintegration, analysts remark that reintegration is the "weakest link" in Philippine migration governance (Go, 2012). The Philippines excels in managing and regulating the exit of overseas workers, yet not even the previous decade of economic growth has enticed Filipino workers abroad to return for good. The "weakest link" observation on migrant reintegration (Go, 2012) may have persisted since the might of the dollar remittances' development potential has yet to translate into more jobs and business activities that could make international migration a choice than a necessity. The continued deployment of overseas workers before and during this COVID-19 pandemic still provides signals that international migration and remittances remain necessary for the Philippines.

The history of migrant reintegration efforts by the Philippines reflects the efforts of civil servants to try and systematize social protection interventions for returning overseas workers. Migrant reintegration is, in fact, largely perceived to be *a response to OFWs in crisis situations abroad* even if there are voluntary returns due to old age or personal/family preference. Yet the reintegration effort by the Philippines is not only shown to be a reactionary measure after a crisis. Even with the sophistication of the economic and social reintegration programs of the Philippines, migrant reintegration remains to be a development need that is cocooned to migration-focused government agencies and bolstered by one-off inter-agency collaborations between migration and non-migration agencies.

The problem is that returning migrants go back to the social and economic conditions that made them migrate overseas in the first place. The country and its multiple stakeholders address these varied socio-economic conditions through various strategies, plans and programs across presidents and national and sectoral development plans. Whether it is addressing mental health, promulgating migrants' rights, promoting financial inclusion, assuring legal redress of contract-related issues abroad, supporting micro- and small-scale entrepreneurship, or ensuring citizens' social protection, overseas Filipino workers confront these varied development concerns upon their return to the motherland. They need all these aspects of development to aid in their socio-economic reintegration.

It is laudable that the Philippines will now embrace actions covering a full-cycle reintegration framework (United Nations in the Philippines, 2021). Yet migrant reintegration is that big elephant in the room that needs to be mainstreamed to other Philippine development concerns. These other developmental concerns also matter as the world moves forward from the raging COVID-19 pandemic. Thus, in the 40th year of Philippine migrant reintegration efforts in 2023, there may have to be clearer inter-agency, inter-sectoral collaboration in migrant reintegration-related programs and services from national to local levels. The needs of overseas workers and their families may have to be mainstreamed more in sectoral development plans of the Philippine government, covering varied development needs. With the aid of a new bureaucratic configuration for Philippine migration management (refer to Fig. 2.2), the challenge for post-pandemic migrant reintegration is to become a more visible contributor to Philippine development that ensures the improved well-being of returning migrant workers.

References

Abdulkarim, B. A. (2016). Changes in the dimensions of life of Filipino deportees from Malaysia. *Asian Social Work Journal, 1*(1), 17–29. https://doi.org/10.47405/aswj.v1i1.6

Abila, S., & Tang, L. (2014). Trauma, post-trauma, and support in the shipping industry: The experience of Filipino seafarers after pirate attacks. *Marine Policy, 46*, 132–136. https://doi.org/10.1016/j.marpol.2014.01.012

APEC Economic Committee. (2003, June 27). *Economic impact of SARS on the APEC region [meeting]*. Special senior officials' meeting on severe acute respiratory syndrome, Bangkok, Thailand. Accessed from http://mddb.apec.org/Documents/2003/SOM/SSOM/03_ssom_006rev1.pdf

Asis, M. M. (2006, January 1). The Philippines' culture of migration. *Migration Information Source* (Migration Policy Institute). https://www.migrationpolicy.org/article/philippines-culture-migration

Asis, M. M. (2020). *Repatriating Filipino migrant workers in the time of the pandemic* (Migration research series no. 63). International Organization for Migration (IOM).

Asis, M. M. (2021). Supporting overseas Filipino workers in the pandemic: An unfolding saga. In N. Shah (Ed.), *COVID-19 crisis and Asian migration* (pp. 223–246). Lahore School of Economics.

Atikha. (2012). *Return and reintegration: Women's participation and gender-responsive interventions. A participatory action research*. Accessed from https://asiapacific.unwomen.org/sites/default/files/Field%20Office%20ESEAsia/Docs/Publications/2013/Atikha.pdf

Balisacan, A., Piza, S. F., Mapa, D., Abad Santos, C., & Odra, D. M. (2010). *Social impact of the global financial crisis in the Philippines*. Asian Development Bank. Accessed from https://www.adb.org/sites/default/files/publication/27471/social-impact-crisis-ph.pdf

Battistella, G. (2004). Return migration in the Philippines: Issues and policies. In J. E. Taylor & D. Massey (Eds.), *International migration: Prospects and policies in a global market* (pp. 212–239). Oxford University Press.

Böhning, W. R. (Ed.). (1999). *Philippines: From OFWs to microentrepreneurs?* International Labor Organization.

Borja, A. L. (1999). Effects and costs of governmental support measure on the reintegration program for OFWs: The case of OWWA's assistance. In W. R. Böhning (Ed.), *Philippines: From OFWs to microentrepreneurs?* (pp. 5–10). International Labor Organization.

Castañaga, D. (2016, March). *The lived experiences of the repatriated overseas Filipino nurses from Libya [paper presentation]*. DLSU Research Congress 2016. Accessed from https://www.dlsu.edu.ph/wp-content/uploads/dlsu-research-congress-proceedings/2016/TPHS/TPHS-II-04.pdf

Development Action for Women Network. (2021). *The paths that pandemic-hit women migrant workers take for their reintegration: A policy-oriented case study*. DAWN.

Diampuan, P. (2017). A theoretical study: Iran's Islamic revolution and the Filipino people power. In S. Sevilla (Ed.), *Philippines-Iran relations: 50 years and beyond* (pp. 50–62). University of the Philippines – Asian Center.

eBalita. (2003, June 18). Filipinos continue to bear SARS stigma in Libya. *eBalita*. Accessed from http://www.ebalita.net/go/news/news.php?id=1321

Furagganan, B. B. (n.d.). *The Arab spring and the evacuation of overseas Filipino workers: A note on assistance to nationals in Riyadh PE*. Accessed from Department of Budget and Management. https://www.dbm.gov.ph/wp-content/uploads/DBM%20Publications/FPB/ZBB-2012/DFA/Annex%20A-%20Caselet%20Riyadh.pdf

Go, S. (2012). *The Philippines and return migration: Rapid appraisal of the return and reintegration policies and service delivery*. International Labor Organization. Accessed from https://www.ilo.org/wcmsp5/groups/public/%2D%2D-asia/%2D%2D-ro-bangkok/%2D%2D-ilo-manila/documents/publication/wcms_177081.pdf

Haase, M., & Honerath, P. (2016). *Return migration and reintegration policies: A primer. Deutsche Gesellschaft für Internationale Zusammenarbeit (GIZ) and German Marshall Fund of the United States*. Accessed from https://www.giz.de/static/de/images/contentimages_320x305px/Haase_Honnerath-Return_migration_primer_Dec16.pdf

International Labor Affairs Bureau (ILAB). *Official website*. Accessed from http://ilab.dole.gov.ph

International Organization for Migration. (2005). *World migration report 2005: Costs and benefits of international migration*. IOM.

International Organization for Migration. (2019). *Reintegration handbook: Practical guidance on the design, implementation and monitoring of reintegration assistance*. IOM.

International Organization for Migration. (2021). *COVID-19 impact assessment on returned overseas Filipino workers*. IOM.

International Organization for Migration (IOM), & Scalabrini Migration Center (SMC). (2013). *Country migration report 2013: The Philippines*. IOM & SMC.

International Organization for Migration Development Fund. (n.d.). *Enhancing the Reintegration Programme for Overseas Filipino Workers (ERPO) in line with the Migration and Development, and Crisis Management Frameworks in the Philippines [Brochure]*.

Jaymalin, M. (2003a, March 25). *Pinay maid in HK dies of SARS*. The Philippine Star. Accessed from https://www.philstar.com/headlines/2003/03/25/200211/pinay-maid-hk-dies-sars

Jaymalin, M. (2003b, May 3). *SARS makes ostracism the new welcome for OFWs*. The Philippine Star. Accessed from http://www.newsflash.org/2003/05/hl/hl017899.htm

Jaymalin, M. (2003c, June 30). *SARS countries unlikely to hire OFWs*. The Philippine Star. Accessed from https://www.philstar.com/headlines/2003/06/30/211934/sars-countries-unlikely-hire-ofws

Jureidini, R. (2019). Vagaries in the management of migrant domestic workers from the Philippines: A case study from Lebanon. In S. I. Rajan & P. Saxena (Eds.), *India's unskilled migration to the Middle East: Policies, politics, and challenges* (pp. 777–792). Palgrave Macmillan.

Lasco, G. (2020). The Severe Acute Respiratory Syndrome (SARS) Outbreak in the Philippines in 2003. *Philippine Studies: Historical and Ethnographic Viewpoints, 68*(3), 339–371. https://doi.org/10.1353/phs.2020.0025

Lazo, L., Teodosio, V. A., & Tomas, P. (1982). *Contract migration in the Philippines (working paper number MIG WP3)*. International Labor Organization. Accessed from https://ideas.repec.org/p/ilo/ilowps/992168343402676.html

Le Coz, C., & Newland, K. (2021). *Rewiring migrant returns and reintegration after the COVID-19 shock*. Migration Policy Institute Policy Brief. Accessed from https://reliefweb.int/sites/reliefweb.int/files/resources/mpi-covid19-return-reintegration_final.pdf

Liao, K. A. (2020). Operation "bring them home": Learning from the large-scale repatriation of overseas Filipino workers in times of crisis. *Asian Population Studies, 16*(3), 310–330. https://doi.org/10.1080/17441730.2020.1811511

Manzala, T. (2007, October 17). National Reintegration Center for OFWs (NRCO): Reintegration program for OFWs [conference session]. In *7th National PESO Congress, Iloilo City*. Accessed from https://slideplayer.com/slide/6903601/

National Labor Relations Commission. (n.d.). *Official website*. Accessed from https://nlrc.dole.gov.ph

National Reintegration Center for OFWs. (2017a). *NRCO accomplishment report 2011-2016*.

National Reintegration Center for OFWs. (2017b, January 27). *Preparing for sustainable return and reintegration of overseas Filipino Workers (OFWs)* [PowerPoint slides].

National Reintegration Center for OFWs. (n.d.). *Transition matrix report* [word document].

Opiniano, J. (2010). OFWs default on crisis-support loans. *OFW Journalism Consortium*. Accessed from http://www.philippinestoday.net/archives/2406

Opiniano, J. (2020a, July 30). Seafarers, ships sound sirens, seek solutions. *BusinessMirror*. Accessed from https://businessmirror.com.ph/2020/07/30/seafarers-ships-sound-sirens-seek-solutions/

Opiniano, J. (2020b). The "new" Philippine future beside the exodus. *Asian Education and Development Studies, 10*(1), 53–68. https://doi.org/10.1108/AEDS-02-2019-0027

Opiniano, J. (2021a, 29 April). Still on queue: Returning overseas workers, and their growing economic needs at home. *BusinessMirror*. Accessed from https://businessmirror.com.ph/2021/04/29/still-on-queue-returning-overseas-workers-and-their-growing-economic-needs-at-home/

Opiniano, J. (2021b, 7 October). Pandemic prompts PHL labor-export policy pivot. *BusinessMirror*. Accessed from https://businessmirror.com.ph/2021/10/07/pandemic-prompts-phl-labor-export-policy-pivot/

Opiniano, J. (2021c). *A reset for overseas migration? Recent developments in Filipinos' migration in the context of the COVID-19 pandemic* (Migration research series no. 69). International Organization for Migration.

Orbeta, A., & Sanchez-Robielos, M. (1996). *Micro interventions for poverty alleviation: The Philippine case (PIDS Discussion Paper DP 1996-13)*. Philippine Institute for Development Studies.

Overseas Workers Welfare Administration. (2017). *Overseas workers welfare Administration 2017 annual report*. Accessed from https://owwa-owwatest.azurewebsites.net/wp-content/uploads/2021/05/annualReport2017-min.pdf

Patinio, F. (2022, July 8). *Over 1M pandemic-hit OFWs assisted by OWWA*. Philippine News Agency. Accessed from https://www.pna.gov.ph/articles/1178547

Philippine News Agency. (2020, February 7). *OFWs in China prepare for repatriation*. Accessed from https://www.pna.gov.ph/articles/1093195

Racelis, S., De los Reyes, V. C., Sucaldito, M. N., Deveraturda, I., Roca, J. B., & Tayag, E. (2015). Contact tracing the first Middle East respiratory syndrome case in the Philippines, February 2015. *Western Pacific Surveillance and Response Journal, 6*(3), 3–7. https://doi.org/10.5365/wpsar.2015.6.2.2012

Reyes, C., Sobreviñas, A., & De Jesus, J. (2009). Impact on OFWs, remittances and local employment seen in the Philippines. *CBMS Network Updates, 7*(1), 1–8. Accessed from https://idl-bnc-idrc.dspacedirect.org/bitstream/handle/10625/42828/130005.pdf

Sevilla, Jr., H. (2013, February 13). *The emergency evacuation of overseas Filipino workers (OFWs) from Libya and Syria*. Middle East Institute. Accessed December 9, 2022, from https://www.mei.edu/publications/emergency-evacuation-overseas-filipino-workers-ofws-libya-and-syria

Small Enterprises Research and Development Foundation. (2018a). *Reintegration of overseas Filipino workers: A handbook for duty bearers and stakeholders, part I*. International Organization for Migration.

Small Enterprises Research and Development Foundation. (2018b). *Reintegration of overseas Filipino workers: A handbook for duty bearers and stakeholders, part II*. International Organization for Migration.

Subbarao, K., Ahmed, A., & Teklu, T. (1996). *Selected social safety net programs in the Philippines: Targeting, cost-effectiveness, and options for reform* (World Bank Discussion Paper no. 317). World Bank.

Tigno, J. (2021). *Beyond business as usual: Philippine labor outmigration and the COVID-19 pandemic* (UP CIDS Discussion Paper 2021-05). University of the Philippines – Center for Integrative and Development Studies.

United Nations High Commissioner for Refugees. (2015, July 9). *Thematic protection bulletin: Protection of migrants and forced returnees in Mindanao*. Accessed from http://www.protectionclusterphilippines.org/wp-content/uploads/2015/08/UNHCR-Thematic-Protection-Bulletin_Protection-of-Migrants-and-Forced-Returnees.pdf

United Nations in the Philippines. (2021). *National action plan on sustainable, gender-responsive return and reintegration global compact on migration (GCM) objective 21.*

World Health Organization. (2003). Weekly epidemiological record, 2003, vol. 78, 22 [full issue]. *Weekly Epidemiological Record = Relevé épidémiologique hebdomadaire*, 78(22), 189–196. Accessed from https://apps.who.int/iris/handle/10665/232179

Yap, J., Reyes, C., & Cuenca, J. (2009). *Impact of the global financial and economic crisis on the Philippines (discussion paper 2009-30).* Philippine Institute of Development Studies. Accessed from https://pidswebs.pids.gov.ph/CDN/PUBLICATIONS/pidsdps0930.pdf

CHAPTER 3

Does Environmental Uncertainty Affect the Remigration Intention of Chinese Migrant Workers in the Pandemic?

Ai-xiang Zheng and Haibo Zhang

Introduction

"Migrant workers" are a unique group that emerged with the economic and social development of contemporary China. They spend most of the year working in cities but return home in busy farming periods and for traditional festivals. According to the National Bureau of Statistics (2022), China currently has 292.51 million migrant workers. Compared with the local labor force in cities, migrant workers have a lower education level on average (National Bureau of Statistics, 2022) and are mainly engaged in low-technology value-added jobs, which not only exposes them to low

---

A.-x. Zheng
Wuxi Institute of Technology, Wuxi, China
e-mail: zhengax@wxit.edu.cn

H. Zhang (✉)
Nanjing University, Nanjing, China
e-mail: zhb@nju.edu.cn

© The Author(s), under exclusive license to Springer Nature Switzerland AG 2024
J. Yeo (ed.), *Return Migration and Crises in Non-Western Countries*, Mobility & Politics,
https://doi.org/10.1007/978-3-031-53562-8_3

wages and poor working conditions but also means that they are easily replaced (Wang & Lu, 2014).

Despite these disadvantages, migrant workers are willing to work in cities. Their most basic motivations are to receive an income higher than they would achieve in agricultural production, improve their living environment, enjoy urban welfare on this basis, and integrate into their host city (Chen, 2016; Zhu, 2017). However, the increasingly uncertain external environment is having a considerable impact on the work and situation of migrant workers (Deng et al., 2015). In some cases, this uncertainty is even shaking the foundations of their original intentions to migrate to their host city.

Comparing the several generations of migrant workers, we find that migrant workers who came to cities to work at the end of the twentieth century mainly faced a traditional environment at first, in which the development of markets and technology were relatively slow. At present, in contrast, migrant workers are facing an environment characterized by rapid technological developments and market competition. Some traditional industries and jobs are rapidly disappearing (Kim & Rhee, 2009; Deng et al., 2015). Coupled with the impact of COVID-19 since 2020, the intensified environmental uncertainty faced by Chinese migrant workers is increasing the fragility of their work situations and gradually increasing their risk of unemployment (Yang & Shao, 2021).

The international academic community has studied population migration from the perspective of environmental uncertainty, but this research has been mostly focused on exploring the migration decision-making process against the background of an uncertain environment. Furthermore, although there is abundant research on transnational migration, less attention has been paid to domestic immigrants, especially Chinese migrant workers. Within Chinese academia, researchers have paid most attention to the impact of the macro-environment on the objective unemployment situation of migrant workers. Although the achievements of this body of research are remarkable, there has been insufficient behavioral psychological analysis from a micro perspective. Given the above analysis, there is great value in studying the impact of environmental uncertainty on the subjective migration intention of Chinese migrant workers.

The phenomenon of migrant workers in China is a form of domestic migration and differs from international migration by having similar characteristics to those of migratory birds. Although they regularly migrate between villages and cities and continue to do so for a long period, China's migrant workers spend most of their time in their host city. For many, their behavior of migrating to the city marks a lifelong commitment. However, it is not known whether the increasing environmental uncertainty, superimposed on the impact of the current COVID-19 pandemic, will lead many of these workers to leave the city in which they are currently working and remigrate. To address this knowledge gap, this chapter examines whether environmental uncertainty affects the unemployment risk perception and remigration intention of Chinese migrant workers in the context of the current pandemic.

Literature Review

Environmental uncertainty represents the degree, speed, and unpredictability of changes in the external environment of enterprises (Keats & Hitt, 1988) and is a major factor in people's lives (Jung, 2021). One cause of uncertainty is information scarcity (Qin et al., 2022). Knight (1921) noted the impact of uncertainty early in the twentieth century. He pointed out that uncertainty refers to the unknown and unmeasurable probability of events, and that people's ability to deal with uncertainty in making judgments is unevenly distributed. Later, Alchian (1950) placed uncertainty as the starting point in introducing the evolutionary analysis paradigm. Since then, uncertainty has often been introduced through random items in the analysis of macroeconomic activities and decision-making in research fields such as industrial development, investment, and employment (Merton, 1969; Samuelson, 1969; Lucas & Prescott, 1971).

Uncertainty research is often interdisciplinary (Czaika et al., 2021), and uncertainty can take different forms in different disciplinary contexts. Some scholars have argued that uncertainty derives from the intrinsic and extrinsic levels. Han et al. (2011) labelled these two forms of uncertainty "aleatory" and "epistemic," respectively. The uncertainty that affects individual behavior often appears in its epistemic form (Han et al., 2011). Facing uncertainty in the external environment has been found to lead individuals to increase savings (Sandmo, 1970) and inhibit consumption to prevent the occurrence of uncertain risks (Wan et al., 2001; Luo et al., 2004; Qian & Li, 2013). Meanwhile, external uncertainty also threatens health and can cause economic losses and mental anguish (Quan et al., 2020; Huang, 2021).

Scholars generally believe that uncertainty is the key factor affecting migration decisions (Stirling, 2010; Williams & Baláž, 2012; Zuo & Sun,

2017). Migration decisions have been studied as the outcome of a rational decision-making process made by individuals according to their needs and desires. As information about the future and life in a potential migration destination is incomplete and uncontrollable, migration decisions face uncertain results, which entail migration risks (Stirling, 2010; Williams & Baláž, 2012; Czaika et al., 2021). For example, in the context of the current pandemic, health and economic uncertainties and the practical uncertainties associated with border closures and travel restrictions have in some cases directly affected migration decisions (Cheri, 2021). However, it should be noted that uncertainty does not always affect migration behavior independently and usually affects migration decisions together with risk perception (Czaika et al., 2021).

Environmental uncertainty is not a common consideration in the study of Chinese internal migration. Scholars have paid more attention to the migration intention of migrant workers and to their naturalization intentions after migration, for which human capital and personal competency (Chen, 2016; Chen & Ding, 2019; Li & Zhong, 2017; Zuo & Sun, 2017), social capital (Xu, 2018; Li et al., 2019), and land capital (Du et al., 2018; Liu et al., 2021) have been identified as influential variables across multiple research perspectives. Most of these factors belong to the deterministic environment, and some to the personal endowments of migrant workers.

The research field of environmental uncertainty in general is quite mature. In relation to individual behavior, migration decision-making has attracted academic attention, with an emphasis on the analysis of the individual decision-making process. Scholars believe that information uncertainty is an essential variable in migration decision-making (Stirling, 2010; Williams & Baláž, 2012; Zuo & Sun, 2017). Among domestic studies in China, most emphasis has been placed on the factors affecting migration intention. However, there is a lack of research along these lines integrating environmental uncertainty factors, especially the influence of environmental uncertainty on the remigration intention of Chinese migrant workers and its mechanisms. Strengthening this literature is especially important in the current phase of the pandemic, when the role of the uncertainties surrounding the pandemic in the remigration intention of migrant workers needs examining.

THEORETICAL FRAMEWORK AND RESEARCH HYPOTHESES

The Influence of Environmental Uncertainty on Unemployment Risk Perception

Environmental uncertainty refers here to a specifically occupational environmental characteristic driven by technological and market factors that brings potential opportunities and threats to the current and future occupations of workers and potential workers (Li et al., 2014). Migrant workers are currently embedded in a highly dynamic environment in which technological and market changes, and the resulting industrial upgrading, are having a major impact on their employment situations. In terms of the technological environment, China's industrial upgrading has significantly accelerated in recent years and has included the emergence of new formats such as "unmanned factories," "unmanned supermarkets," and "unmanned parking lots." This trend has gradually affected traditional industries that absorb large numbers of migrant workers, who thereby face the threat of unemployment (Zhang, 2016). Meanwhile, changes in the external market environment also have a major impact on the employment of migrant workers. At the macro level, China is currently at a specific stage of economic transformation in which downward pressures are prominent (Wu, 2018). With the ongoing Sino–U.S. trade war superimposed on these pressures, the overall development of the domestic market is hindered, and uncertainty intensified. In the internal market, commercial and noncommercial competition between players in various industries is widespread and encouraged by an increase in labor costs (Xu, 2016), thus further increasing the uncertainties associated with market competition. At the micro level, the speed of change in consumer preferences is accelerating, with rising demand for personalization and customization (Luo & Bian, 2020). These factors are undoubtedly exacerbating the uncertainty of the market environment.

In general, the dramatically changing external environment is and will continue to squeeze the urban living space of migrant workers and increase their risk of unemployment (Li et al., 2014), which will undoubtedly further aggravate the sense of urban crisis and the deprivation of migrant workers. In view of this, the following hypothesis is proposed:

Hypothesis 1: Environmental uncertainty has a positive effect on the unemployment risk perception of migrant workers.

The Influence of Unemployment Risk Perception on Remigration Intention

Risk perception can be defined as people's anxiety and worry about specific things or events (Parkinson, 1993) or as their beliefs, attitudes, judgment, and emotions about danger (Wildavsky & Dake, 1990). An important type of risk perception is unemployment risk perception, which refers to people's perceptions of the uncertainty of unemployment events (Zhang & Liu, 2015). In essence, unemployment risk perception is the subjective evaluation of workers of the uncertainty of unemployment.

In domestic research on the unemployment risk perception of migrant workers in China, Hu (2015) and Ni et al. (2016) both argued that the urban unemployment rate of migrant workers is closely linked to relative deprivation. Urban unemployment caused by unfair competition factors, such as competence and resource endowment, is a form of both income and opportunity deprivation. In accordance with this logic, the unemployment risk perception of migrant workers is closely related to their sense of relative deprivation in terms of urban resources. Although the possibility of migrant workers earning higher incomes in urban areas than in rural areas, compared to their rural counterparts, this constitutes the fundamental motivation for migrant workers to voluntarily migrate to cities in search of job opportunities (Chen, 2016; Zhu, 2017); however, they also face a sense of imbalance between resources and actual employment opportunities, especially when this sense of imbalance translates into unemployment risk perception and feeling of relative deprivation.

Through a study of the migrant population, Stark and Yitzhaki (1988) found that a relative deprivation of urban resources encouraged migration decisions. Given that a sense of urban deprivation increases the intention to make urban migration decisions, it is likely that the sense of income and opportunity deprivation associated with the risk of urban unemployment also affects the remigration intention of migrant workers. In view of this, the following hypothesis is proposed:

Hypothesis 2: Unemployment risk perception has a positive impact on the remigration intention of migrant workers.

The Influence of Environmental Uncertainty on Remigration Intention

According to the analytical framework of human capital investment decisions in economics (Sjaastad, 1962), workers' migration decisions are formed through an opportunity comparison between their potential migration destination and their current location. A worker's assessment of the environment in the two locations is an essential factor in this opportunity comparison. The initial migration decision is an outcome of workers' comparisons between the opportunity value of employment in their hometown and that of employment in the migration destination, given their environmental assessment; likewise, the remigration decision is an outcome of workers' comparisons between the opportunity value of employment in the current city and that of the potential target city for remigration, again given their environmental assessment of the two locations.

A highly uncertain environment for migrant workers is one that is characterized by uncertainty of employment opportunities and income. If, after making an environmental assessment, migrant workers determine that the value of the employment opportunities in local cities is lower than that in remote cities, they will choose to remigrate; if they determine that the opportunity value of migrating to urban employment is lower than that of their rural employment, they might even return to their home village.

Therefore, with regard to the decision-making basis of comparing the opportunity value of the current region with that of a potential target region, there is no difference in the decision-making framework between the initial migration of migrant workers and any subsequent remigration. Being essential to the comparison of opportunity value, the environment is the key variable in the migration decisions of migrant workers.

According to this analytical framework, the greater the environmental uncertainty, the greater its impact on the value of an urban employment opportunity for migrant workers. Given the vulnerability of migrant workers in their endowments of human capital and urban resources, the risks associated with environmental uncertainty are greater for migrant workers than for the local labor force and affect their remigration intention. In view of this, the following hypothesis is proposed:

Hypothesis 3: Environmental uncertainty has a positive effect on the remigration intention of migrant workers.

The Moderating Effect of Pandemic-Related Uncertainty

At the time of writing, the COVID-19 pandemic has not been eliminated and outbreaks are still occurring in some regions of China. As a severe public health emergency, the pandemic not only has resulted in massive loss of life and property but also had a huge impact on people's psychology (Chen et al., 2020) and on technology and markets (Yang & Shao, 2021). Compared with the local labor force, migrant workers have been more severely affected by unemployment during the pandemic and have therefore faced higher unemployment risks (Yang & Shao, 2021; Zang, 2022). The commuting difficulties caused by quarantining and other pandemic prevention policies have created challenges for certain industries and enterprises in meeting human resource needs (Qu & Chen, 2020; Zhang & Wu, 2020). To cope with the uncertainty of the pandemic, the process of "replacing labor with technology" has accelerated in relevant industries and enterprises, involving the transformation to unmanned, automated, and artificially intelligent processes. A major part of this large-scale transformation is a sharp reduction in the labor demand of enterprises, which has imposed tremendous pressure on migrant workers, who mainly work in labor-intensive enterprises. Even experienced and highly skilled workers are facing challenges to adapt to changes in their roles and maintain or secure employment.

From the perspective of enterprises, the uncertainties associated with the pandemic include disturbances to global supply chains, which have generated pressures associated with the uncertainties of delivery from suppliers, and the closure of urban and rural areas, which has made it difficult to keep up to date with consumer demand. Market shifts have had an even greater impact. For example, online and offline consumption habits are changing, new sales models are emerging, and new products and new competitors are rising in various markets. These dynamic features of the market environment have intensified the competitive pressure on migrant workers and the industries in which they are employed, thus making the management of enterprises more difficult and increasing the unemployment risk of migrant workers to varying extents.

Pandemic-related uncertainty is thus likely to affect the relationship between environmental uncertainty and the unemployment risk perception of migrant workers and aggravate their unemployment risk perception, such that greater pandemic-related uncertainty increases the effect of environmental uncertainty on the unemployment risk perception of migrant workers.

Hypothesis 4: Pandemic-related uncertainty has a positive moderating effect on the relationship between environmental uncertainty and the unemployment risk perception of migrant workers.

If pandemic-related uncertainty can strengthen the impact of the relationship between environmental uncertainty and unemployment risk perception, it is logical to posit that it can also enhance the effect of unemployment risk perception on remigration intention, given that pandemic-related uncertainty affects migrant workers' behavioral decisions by strengthening their motivation to change their status quo (Czaika et al., 2021). Scholars have argued that remigration is an employment-seeking strategy adopted by workers in the face of high unemployment risk and a sense of urban deprivation (Stark & Yitzhaki, 1988; Tian, 2019). Accordingly, pandemic-related uncertainty is likely to strengthen the relationship between the unemployment risk perception and remigration intention of migrant workers. In view of this, the following hypothesis is proposed:

Hypothesis 5: Pandemic-related uncertainty has a positive moderating effect on the relationship between the unemployment risk perception and remigration intention of migrant workers.

In summary, the theoretical model constructed in this chapter is shown in Fig. 3.1.

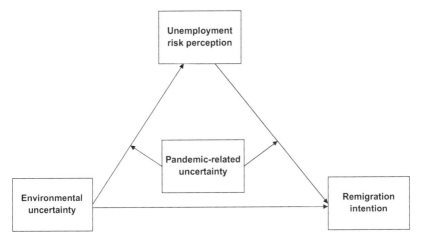

Fig. 3.1 Theoretical model

Materials and Methods

Variable Measurement

The design of the initial scale for this study was based on already-existing domestic and foreign scales. The variables were measured as follows:

1. Environmental uncertainty. With reference to the environmental uncertainty scale of Kim et al. (2016), this variable was measured through workers' perception of the technological and market environment of their industry. The items included "At present, the technical environment of my industry is highly uncertain," "At present, the technical development of my industry is difficult to predict," "The product preferences of customers in my industry change rapidly," and "The needs of customers in my industry are difficult to predict." Cronbach's alpha for this scale was 0.720.
2. Remigration intention. The withdrawal behavior selection scale of Rusbult et al. (1998) was adapted to the local situation. Representative items include "In the next year, I may leave this city to find a new job," "I often think about leaving this city," "I have recently had the intention to find a job in another city," and "I have recently had the intention to return to my hometown to find a job." Cronbach's alpha for this scale was 0.786.
3. Unemployment risk perception. The unemployment risk perception scale of Zheng and Zhang (2021) was used to measure this variable. Representative items include "I am worried that I would lose my job in the future," "If I lost my job, my quality of life would drop," and "If I lose my job, my relatives and friends will avoid me." Cronbach's alpha for this scale was 0.845.
4. Pandemic-related uncertainty. The pandemic uncertainty scale of Ma (2020) was used to measure this variable. Representative items include "Because there are asymptomatic infected people, I don't know whether there are potentially infected people among the people I have contacted," "Seeing that the number of new cases in the country is still increasing, it is unknown when the pandemic can be completely controlled," and "Since the Omicron virus may mutate, I do not know how to prevent and deal with this virus in the future." Cronbach's alpha for this scale was 0.730.

Questionnaire Distribution and Data Collection

This chapter reports on one of a series of studies of migrant workers' remigration psychology under environmental uncertainty. A stratified random sampling method was adopted. The survey was mainly conducted in the Jiangsu and Zhejiang provinces. The survey design involved fully considering the regional economy of these provinces and the spatial distribution characteristics of the population of migrant workers. As these two provinces belong to the economically developed regions of the Yangtze River Delta and are important internal migration target areas in China, they are representative of the situation of migrant workers. The survey period was from April to May 2022. To distribute the survey, the researchers selected companies that employed migrant workers in the sample areas by drawing on relationships between the companies and individual researchers and their universities.

The administration of the survey was supported by the management of each company. The survey team communicated with the human resources directors in advance. Before distributing the questionnaire, the department leaders and the research team mobilized the migrant workers to complete the questionnaire, informed them of the key points of the study, and instructed them on how to fill in the items. This effectively ensured the quality of the survey data. Zhang (2002) argued that to ensure the quality of the data collected through a questionnaire, the sample should be 5–20 times the number of items being measured. In accordance with this standard, 351 questionnaires were distributed, of which 334 were recovered. After further inspection, 22 questionnaires were found to be invalid and eliminated, leaving 317 valid questionnaires for analysis.

DATA ANALYSIS AND RESULTS

Descriptive Statistics

Table 3.1 shows the gender, age, education level, marital status, position level, and level of income of the sample. The results indicate that the sample's demographic information, such as gender, age, and marital status, closely aligns with the overall population characteristics of migrant workers in the National Bureau of Statistics' Peasant Workers Monitoring Survey Report (2022), demonstrating the high representativeness of our survey sample.

Table 3.1 Sample characteristics (N = 317)

	Classification	n	%		Classification	n	%
Gender	Male	216	68.1	Marital status	Unmarried	74	23.3
	Female	101	31.9		Married	237	74.8
Age group (years)	16–20	3	0.9		Divorced	6	1.9
	21–25	22	6.9	Position level	Basic level workers	128	40.4
	26–30	60	18.9		Junior-level management position	104	32.8
	31–35	88	27.8		Middle-level management position	64	20.2
	36–40	69	21.8		High-level management position	21	6.6
	41–45	31	9.8	Monthly income (yuan)	Below 2500	7	2.2
	46–50	26	8.2		2500–4000	71	22.4
	51–55	15	4.7		4000–6000	89	28.1
	56–60	3	0.9		6000–8000	83	26.2
Education level (highest level completed)	Primary school and below	10	3.2		8000–10,000	37	11.7
	Middle school	100	31.5		10,000–15,000	23	7.3
	High school (technical secondary school)	90	28.4		Above 15,000	7	2.2
	College	79	24.9		Total	317	100
	University	34	10.7				
	Above university	4	1.3				

Table 3.2 shows the means, standard deviations, correlations, and other descriptive data of the study variables. The correlation statistical analysis provides a solid foundation for our subsequent hypothesis testing. The results suggest that further research can be conducted.

Results

Quantitative research methods were used to explore the relationships between environmental uncertainty, unemployment risk perception,

Table 3.2 Means, standard deviations, and correlation matrix

Variable	Mean	Standard deviation	Age	Gender	Position level	Education level	Environmental uncertainty	Unemployment risk perception	Pandemic-related uncertainty	Remigration intention
Age	4.539	1.616	1							
Gender	1.319	0.467	−0.275**	1						
Position level	1.931	0.932	0.105	−0.095	1					
Education level	3.123	1.106	−0.367**	0.065	0.358**	1				
Environmental uncertainty	4.070	0.528	−0.002	0.005	0.027	−0.053	1			
Unemployment risk perception	3.222	0.488	0.121*	−0.058	−0.207**	−0.289**	0.263**	1		
Pandemic-related uncertainty	3.659	0.452	0.070	0.011	0.040	−0.024	0.363**	0.183**	1	
Remigration intention	2.067	0.613	−0.069	0.124*	−0.213**	0.041	0.025	0.312**	0.068	1

$*p < 0.05$
$**p < 0.01$

pandemic-related uncertainty, and remigration intention. SPSS 19.0 was used to test the reliability and validity of the measurement model. The relationships between the variables in the model were then calculated to test the hypotheses proposed in the study.

Table 3.3, Model 1 shows the influence of the control variables such as age, gender, position, and education level on unemployment risk perception. The results show that position and education levels had a negative effect on the unemployment risk perception of the migrant workers. Model 2 shows that environmental uncertainty had a positive effect on the unemployment risk perception of the migrant workers ($\beta = 0.256$, $p < 0.001$). These results supported Hypothesis 1.

Model 3 shows the influence of each control variable on remigration intention. Model 4 shows that the migrant workers' unemployment risk perception had a positive effect on their remigration intention ($\beta = 0.335$, $p < 0.001$). These results supported Hypothesis 2.

Model 5 shows that the influence of environmental uncertainty on the migrant workers' remigration intention was not significant. Hypothesis 3 was therefore not supported. In accordance with the mediating effect test rule proposed by Baron and Kenny (1986), the non-significant relationship between environmental uncertainty and remigration intention indicated that unemployment risk perception had no mediating effect on the relationship between environmental uncertainty and remigration intention.

In line with the suggestion of Wen et al. (2005) for testing moderation effects, the following moderation testing process was followed: (1) run the regression of the dependent variable Y on the independent variable X and the moderating variable M to obtain the coefficients; (2) run the regression of the dependent variable Y on the independent variable X, moderating variable M, and interaction term $X \times M$ to get R_2^2. The moderating effect was considered significant if $R_2^2 > R_1^2$.

Model 6 shows that adding the potential moderating variable resulted in $\beta = 0.102$, $p < 0.1$. Model 7 shows the results of adding the interaction term of the independent variable and the moderating variable. Pandemic uncertainty was found to have a positive moderating effect on environmental uncertainty and unemployment risk perception ($\beta = 0.159$, $p < 0.1$), supporting Hypothesis 4.

The moderating effect of pandemic-related uncertainty on the relationship between the unemployment risk perception and remigration intention of the migrant workers was tested in Model 8. The results show that the moderating variables were not significant in the model. Therefore, the

Table 3.3 Regression analysis results

Variable	Unemployment risk perception		Remigration intention			Unemployment risk perception		Remigration intention
	Model1	Model2	Model3	Model4	Model5	Model6	Model7	Model8
Age	0.041	0.051	0.037	0.024	0.039	0.043	0.048	0.023
Gender	−0.045	−0.046	0.101	0.116	0.101*	−0.050	−0.055	0.115
Position level	−0.135*	−0.152**	−0.258***	−0.213**	−0.261***	−0.154**	−0.159**	−0.214***
Education level	−0.223***	−0.200**	0.141*	0.216**	0.145*	−0.201**	−0.200**	0.215***
Environmental uncertainty		0.256***			0.039			
Unemployment risk perception				0.335***				0.331***
Pandemic-related uncertainty						0.102*	0.174**	0.018
Environmental uncertainty × pandemic-related uncertainty							0.159*	
Unemployment risk perception × pandemic-related uncertainty								
F	8.667	12.318	5.949	12.884	4.855	10.901	10.284	10.726
R^2	0.100	0.165	0.071	0.172	0.072	0.174	0.189	0.172

$*p < 0.1$
$**p < 0.01$
$***p < 0.001$

moderating effect of pandemic-related uncertainty on the relationship between the unemployment risk perception and remigration intention of migrant workers required no further testing, and Hypothesis 5 was not supported.

Discussion

Set against the background of the current pandemic, this chapter explores the relationship between environmental uncertainty, unemployment risk perception, and remigration intention among migrant workers with reference to human capital investment. The three main findings are discussed:

1. Environmental uncertainty had a positive and significant effect on the unemployment risk perception of the migrant workers in the study. The higher the environmental uncertainty, the stronger the unemployment risk perception of the migrant workers; when environmental uncertainty was low, the unemployment risk perception of the migrant workers decreased.

    In previous research, scholars have noted that migrant workers face objective risks as they often enter the labor market directly after primary education and can barely meet the job requirements of the occupational environment (Liu, 2009; Yang & Chen, 2012; Jin & Chen, 2017). When the external environment changes, migrant workers face a greater risk of unemployment (Li et al., 2014) than other labor groups. The conclusion of this study contributes to this literature by verifying the impact of environmental uncertainty on the unemployment risk perception of migrant workers at the subjective level.

    Furthermore, studies have focused mostly on the analysis of the migration decision-making process, pointing to information scarcity as the root of migration risks (Stirling, 2010; Williams & Baláž, 2012; Zuo & Sun, 2017). Against the backdrop of the COVID-19 pandemic, this study selected Chinese migrant workers as the research population and moved the focal point back to the stage of forming a migration intention before a decision is made. This study proposed and verified the role of environmental uncertainty on the remigration intention of migrant workers, thus improving and enriching the theory of migrant decision-making.

2. Against the pandemic background, this study further clarified the relationship between unemployment risk and the behavior of migrant workers by finding that the migrant workers' unemployment risk perception had a positive and significant effect on their remigration intention: that is, the higher the unemployment risk perception, the stronger the remigration intention of the migrant workers. One explanation for this finding can be found in the analytical framework of human capital investment decisions (Sjaastad, 1962). When migrant workers face potential net losses from urban unemployment, they will seek to maximize the opportunity value through remigration, which is effectively a human capital reinvestment scheme for migrant workers.

   The findings of this study verify the pathway to the formation of migrant workers' remigration intention from the unique perspective of their unemployment risk perception. This conclusion is consistent with the view of Stark and Yitzhaki (1988) that deprivation affects migration decision-making and improves the understanding of the mechanism behind migration psychology and the behavior of migrant workers.

3. This study was conducted more than two years after the outbreak of the COVID-19 pandemic. Scholars have claimed that the pandemic affects the psychology and behavior of migrants (Chen et al., 2020; Cheri, 2021; Zang, 2022), but no clear conclusions have been drawn on the role of the pandemic in the unemployment risk perception of migrant workers. This study found that pandemic-related uncertainty had a positive and significant moderating effect on the relationship between environmental uncertainty and unemployment risk perception. This indicates that the stronger the pandemic uncertainty, the stronger the impact of environmental uncertainty on the unemployment risk perception of migrant workers, and vice versa.

   This conclusion suggests that pandemic-related uncertainty brings negative psychological stimulation to migrant workers. When migrant workers' perception of pandemic-related uncertainty is superimposed on environmental uncertainty, it aggravates the impact of environmental uncertainty on their unemployment risk perception. This study thus provides evidence that the pandemic has intensified the unemployment risk perception of domestic migrant workers.

Nonetheless, the impact of environmental uncertainty on the remigration intention of the migrant workers in this study was not significant. This result might be related to the systemic characteristics of the risks behind the impact of environmental uncertainty. As domestic inter-city migration or returning to rural hometowns cannot eliminate the impact of macro-environmental factors such as technological innovation and market changes, environmental uncertainty is not an influential factor in the remigration intention of migrant workers.

The hypothesized moderating effect of pandemic-related uncertainty on the relationship between the unemployment risk perception and remigration intention of migrant workers was also not supported, suggesting that pandemic-related uncertainty is neither exacerbating nor mitigating the effects of migrant workers' unemployment risk perception on their remigration intention. This is again likely to be related to pandemic-related uncertainty involving uncertainties surrounding technology and the market, which are systemic risks. A remigration strategy is unlikely to improve the career situation of migrant workers who face such risks.

Conclusion and Further Directions

This research studies the remigration intention of migrant workers in the pandemic from the perspective of environmental uncertainty and further deepens the research into the migration intention, which has attracted close attention from academia in recent years. The results of this study show that environmental uncertainty positively predicts the unemployment risk perception of migrant workers, which in turn affects their remigration intention. The stronger the unemployment risk perception of migrant workers, the stronger their remigration intention. In essence, environmental uncertainty appears to intensify the employment insecurity of migrant workers, which further promotes their remigration intention. However, this chain of effects is not simply equivalent to environmental uncertainty directly affecting remigration intention, as the results indicated no direct connection between these two variables. Finally, this study also found that pandemic-related uncertainty had a positive moderating effect on the relationship between environmental uncertainty and unemployment risk perception but not on the impact of unemployment risk perception on remigration intention. It therefore appears that pandemic-related uncertainty, as a moderating variable, has different effects on the formation of migrant workers' unemployment risk perception and on that of their remigration intention. This study has certain limitations. As the research questionnaires are mainly distributed in Jiangsu Province and Zhejiang Province, future research will further expand the geographic scope of the sample and further validate existing theories. Second, the hierarchical regression method was used to analyze remigration intention among migrant workers, and their remigration decision process could be generalized by using qualitative research methods in the future, such an approach would deepen the understanding of their migration decision process of migrant workers.

REFERENCES

Alchian, A. A. (1950). Uncertainty, evolution, and economic theory. *Journal of Political Economy*, 58(3), 211–221.

Baron, R. M., & Kenny, D. A. (1986). The moderator-mediator variable distinction in social psychological research: Conceptual, strategic, and statistical considerations. *Journal of Personality and Social Psychology*, 51(6), 1173–1182.

Chen, Z. J. (2016). *Migrant workers' citizenization: Matching willingness and capability—Layer path of realistic pattern and policy design*. China Agricultural Press. (in Chinese).

Chen, L. M., & Ding, S. J. (2019). The influence factors of permanent migration intention and behavior of rural-urban migrant households. *Issues in Agricultural Economy*, 08, 117–128. (in Chinese).

Chen, Q., Liang, M., Li, Y., et al. (2020). Mental health care for medical staff in China during the COVID-19 outbreak. *The Lancet Psychiatry*, 7(4), 15–16.

Cheri, L. (2021). Perceived impact of border closure due to COVID-19 of intending Nigerian migrants. *Social Inclusion*, 9(1), 207–215.

Czaika, M., Bijak, J., & Prike, T. (2021). Migration decision-making and its key dimensions. *Annals of the American Academy of Political and Social Science*, 697(1), 15–31.

Deng, D. S., Li, Y. J., & Yan, N. (2015). On the study about risk avoidance of employment for peasant workers in new type urbanization. *Journal of Xiangtan University (Philosophy and Social Sciences)*, 39(5), 12–17. (in Chinese).

Du, W., Niu, J. K., & Che, L. (2018). The willingness of agriculture population's citizenization: The double influence of the family livelihood resilience and land policy. Journal of. *Public Management*, 15(3), 66–77+157. (in Chinese).

Han, P. K. J., Klein, W. M. P., & Arora, N. K. (2011). Varieties of uncertainty in health care: A conceptual taxonomy. *Medical Decision Making*, 31(6), 828–838.

Hu, J. H. (2015). Relative deprivation effects impact on the peasant worker's wishes to be an urban citizen. *Issues in Agricultural Economy, 36*(11), 32–41, 110–111. (in Chinese).

Huang, R. (2021). Pressure, state, and response: Configurational analysis of antecedents of hotel employees' career prospect perceptions following the COVID-19 pandemic crisis. *Tourism Tribune, 36*(9), 103–119. (in Chinese).

Jin, L. F., & Chen, X. (2017). A study on the heterogeneous knowledge diffusion of new generation of migrant workers and promotion strategy based on epidemic model. *Journal of Jiangsu University (Social Science Edition), 1,* 79–84. (in Chinese).

Jung, P. R. (2021). Hope, disillusion, and coincidence in migratory decisions by Senegalese migrants in Brazil. *Social Inclusion, 9*(1), 268–277.

Keats, B. W., & Hitt, M. A. (1988). A causal model of linkages among environmental dimensions, macro-organizational characteristics, and performance. *The Academy of Management Journal, 31*(3), 570–598.

Kim, T., & Rhee, M. (2009). Exploration and exploitation: Internal variety and environmental dynamism. *Strategic Organization, 7*(1), 11–41.

Kim, N., Shin, S., & Min, S. (2016). Strategic marketing capability: Mobilizing technological resources for new product advantage. *Journal of Business Research, 69*(12), 5644–5652.

Knight, F. H. (1921). *Risk, uncertainty, and profit.* New York: Houghton Mifflin.

Li, F., & Zhong, Z. B. (2017). Human capital, class status, identity, and migrant workers' permanent migration intention. *Population Research, 41*(6), 58–70. (in Chinese).

Li, Q., Yang, D. T., & Chen, Y. W. (2014). Unemployment and turnover of new-generation migrant workers in the context of industrial transformation and upgrading—An analytical framework based on employability. *East China Economic Management, 28*(12), 29–33. (in Chinese).

Li, D. S., Yu, H., & Zhang, L. (2019). Research on the intergenerational impact of the new generation of migrant workers' household registration migration willingness—Based on the dynamic monitoring data of floating population in Sichuan province. *The World of Survey and Research, 10,* 41–47. (in Chinese).

Liu, X. N. (2009). Citizenization of migrant workers: Path, problem, and breakthrough—An in-depth interview with peasants from a province in Central China. *Inquiry into Economic Issues, 9,* 57–61. (in Chinese).

Liu, Y. Y., Wang, H. W., & Liu, X. H. (2021). The urban housing status, farmland characteristics and the migration decision-making of the rural migrants: An analysis of the data in Chongqing's main urban districts. South China. *Population, 36*(3), 14-27+40. (in Chinese).

Lucas, R. E., Jr., & Prescott, E. C. (1971). Investment under uncertainty. *Econometrica: Journal of the Econometric Society, 39*(5), 659–681.

Luo, C. L., Zhang, Q., & Niu, J. G. (2004). Uncertainty during economic transition and household consumption behavior in urban China. *Economic Research Journal, 4*, 100–106. (in Chinese).

Luo, G. L. & Bian, W. J. (2020). Uncertainty, Risk Management, and Market Performance of New Products in High tech Enterprises. *Dongyue Tribune, 41*(8), 125–134. (in Chinese).

Ma, C. (2020). The influence of media contact on the uncertainty of infectious disease epidemic situation—The mediating role of risk perception and the regulating role of emotional response. *Shanghai Journalism Review, 10*, 57–72. (in Chinese).

Merton, R. C. (1969). Lifetime portfolio selection under uncertainty: The continuous-time case. *The Review of Economics and Statistics, 51*(3), 247–257.

National Bureau of Statistics (China). (2022). *Peasant workers monitoring survey report 2021 [cited 2022 Apr 29]*. Accessed from http://www.gov.cn/xinwen/2022-04/29/content_5688043.htm

Ni, Z. L., Jia, Z. B., & Xie, X. Y. (2016). Relative deprivation, non-agricultural employment and rural residents' happiness. *Journal of Shanxi University of Finance and Economics, 38*(12), 64–74. (in Chinese).

Parkinson, D. (1993). Risk: Analysis, perception and management. Report of a Royal Society study group. *Endeavour, 17*(2), 94–95.

Qian, W. R., & Li, B. Z. (2013). Analysis on the influencing factors of migrant workers' consumption from the perspective of uncertainty—Based on the survey data of 2679 migrant workers in China. *Chinese Rural Economy, 11*, 57–71. (in Chinese).

Qin, Q., Ke, Q., & Xie, Y. S. (2022). Public affect and cognition under global health crisis—A study from the perspective of information seeking and processing behavior. *Journal of Modern Information, 42*(4), 62–76.

Qu, X. B., & Chen, J. (2020). Impacts of COVID-19 on the labor market and policy responses. *Journal of Hebei Normal University (Philosophy and Social Sciences), 43*(4), 126–133. (in Chinese).

Quan, L., Zhen, R., Yao, B., et al. (2020). Traumatic exposure and posttraumatic stress disorder among flood victims: Testing a multiple mediating model. *Journal of Health Psychology, 25*, 283–297.

Rusbult, C. E., Dan, F., Rogers, G., et al. (1998). Impact of exchange variables on exit, voice, loyalty, and neglect: An integrative model of responses to declining job satisfaction. *The Academy of Management Journal, 31*(3), 599–627.

Samuelson, P. A. (1969). Lifetime portfolio selection by dynamic stochastic programming. *The Review of Economics and Statistics, 51*(3), 239–246.

Sandmo, A. (1970). The effect of uncertainty on saving decisions. *The Review of Economic Studies, 37*(3), 353–360.

Sjaastad, L. A. (1962). The costs and returns of human migration. *Journal of Political Economy, 70*(5), 80–93.

Stark, O., & Yitzhaki, S. (1988). Labour migration as a response to relative deprivation. *Journal of Population Economics, 1*, 57–70.
Stirling, A. (2010). Keep it complex. *Nature, 468*, 1029–1031.
Tian, Y. X. (2019). Low pay or homelessness: An empirical study on the strategy of unemployment avoidance of different generations of workers in Taiwan. *Journal of Anhui Normal University (Humanities & Social Sciences), 47*(3), 101–110. (in Chinese).
Wan, G. H., Zhang, Q., & Niu, J. G. (2001). Liquidity constraints, uncertainty and household consumption in China. *Economic Research Journal, 11*, 35–44+94. (in Chinese).
Wang, Y. J., & Lu, L. (2014). Working environment, relative deprivation and job burnout of migrant workers. *Journal of Nantong University (Social Sciences Edition), 30*(3), 107–114. (in Chinese).
Wen, Z. L., Hou, J. T., & Zhang, L. (2005). A comparison of moderator and mediator and their applications. *Acta Psychologica Sinica, 37*(2), 268–274. (in Chinese).
Wildavsky, A., & Dake, K. (1990). Theories of risk perception: Who fears what and why? *Daedalus, 119*(4), 41–60.
Williams, A. M., & Baláž, V. (2012). Migration, risk, and uncertainty: Theoretical perspectives. *Population, Space and Place, 18*(2), 167–180.
Wu, Y. W. (2018). When employment pressure meets growth slowdown: An analysis on China's urban and rural labor market. *Studies in Labor Economics, 6*(3), 54–74. (in Chinese).
Xu, D. Y. (2016). Empirical research on the regional differences and influencing factors of migrant worker's wage growth in the eastern areas. *Population Journal, 38*(2), 91–100. (in Chinese).
Xu, M. Y. (2018). Human capital, social capital and the urbanization willingness of migrant workers. *Journal of South China Agricultural University (Social Science Edition), 17*(4), 53–63. (in Chinese).
Yang, X. J., & Chen, H. (2012). The lack of employment skills of the new generation of migrant workers and the solutions. *Rural Economy, 1*, 98–102. (in Chinese).
Yang, S. L., & Shao, P. P. (2021). Study on the unemployment status of migrant workers and its influencing factors under the impact of epidemic situation. *Northwest Population Journal, 42*(5), 42–54. (in Chinese).
Zang, W. (2022). The unemployment risk of floating population in Chinese megacities during the epidemic period. *Urban Development Studies, 29*(03), 116–123+132. (in Chinese).
Zhang, W. T. (2002). *SPSS11 statistical analysis tutorial (advanced)*. Hope Electronic Press. (in Chinese).

Zhang, M. (2016). Research on the employment of migrant workers and the upgrading of industrial structure under the supply side reform. *Theoretical Investigation, 6*, 101–105. (in Chinese).

Zhang, H. C., and Liu, S. L. (2015). The impacts of unemployment risk on migrants' consumption. *Economic Review, 2*, 68–77. (in Chinese).

Zhang, G. W., & Wu, T. (2020). The impact of the COVID-19 outbreak on employment in China. Chinese journal of population. *Science, 3*, 11–20+126.

Zheng, A. X., & Zhang, H. B. (2021). The structure of unemployment risk perception among migrant workers in China: An exploratory mixed methods study. *Asian and Pacific Migration Journal, 30*(2), 169–198.

Zhu, X. K. (2017). From peasants to citizens: Logical identification and institutional induction—Reading "Citizenization of peasant workers: Matching willingness and capability." *Issues in Agricultural Economy, 38*(3), 102–104. (in Chinese).

Zuo, H., Sun, Z. L. (2017). External environment, individual capability and willingness of migrant workers urbanization. *Commercial Research, 9*, 170–177. (in Chinese).

CHAPTER 4

Soft Power Amidst a Crisis: Return Migration and India's Soft Power in the Persian Gulf

Sabith Khan

INTRODUCTION

The relations between the Persian Gulf and India date back to centuries. Consider this important fact: The oldest mosque in India (built around 629 AD) is located in Kerala, a southern state in India. The mosque, built during the time that the Prophet Muhammad lived in the Arabian Peninsula is a testament to the religious, trade, and cultural relations that existed with the region and Indian subcontinent. The story of migration and exchanges—cultural, religious, and economic—between the regions goes back to millennia.

As the birthplace of Islam, modern day Saudi Arabia enjoys unparalleled soft power in South Asia due to the presence of hundreds of millions of Muslims in the country, who live as guest-workers. As one of the largest producers of oil and natural gas, the Gulf Cooperation Council (GCC) region is also among the most strategically important, in the world. This

S. Khan (✉)
California Lutheran University, Thousand Oaks, CA, USA
e-mail: khanpgg@vt.edu

© The Author(s), under exclusive license to Springer Nature Switzerland AG 2024
J. Yeo (ed.), *Return Migration and Crises in Non-Western Countries*, Mobility & Politics,
https://doi.org/10.1007/978-3-031-53562-8_4

dual factor makes the GCC region not just important for India, but the entire South Asia region. The legend claims that the *Cheramaan Perumal Juma Mosque* was built by the King Cheraman Perumal, who witnessed the splitting of the moon, a supernatural event that is also mentioned in the holy book of Muslims, Qur'an. He summoned some of the Arab traders who were in the region, on their way to Ceylon (present day Sri Lanka) and asked them to interpret this. They shared the news of the Prophet and his mission and invited him to visit the Arabian kingdom.

With active trade, diplomatic, cultural, and religious exchanges between the GCC region and the Indian subcontinent, there is much has transpired between the regions to warrant a deep study. As Kadira Pethiyagoda from the Brookings Doha Center points out, relations between the Gulf countries (Saudi Arabia, Kuwait, Bahrain, UAE, and Oman) have taken on new dimensions since the discovery of Oil and natural gas in the region. These are "among the most important relations for both sides in the coming decades," he says (Pethiyagoda, 2015). Given the ongoing geopolitical changes and shift from a uni-polar US-led world to a multi-polar world with China and Russia staking a claim to global dominance, these relationships with its neighbors may need to be re-looked at.

This chapter takes a closer look at the diplomatic relations between the GCC countries, using UAE and Saudi Arabia as two example countries, and analyzing how the policy context in each country is determined and shaped by return migration and the changing role of remittances in the region. The argument is made here that given the changing nature of migration in the GCC, there are likely going to be some changes in the way diplomatic relations between the countries are going to be managed. While economic interests will still be the primary lens through which the countries analyzed here will view each other, there is reason to believe that religious and cultural factors will take precedence, given the rise in religious tensions in the Indian subcontinent. The lens of cultural diplomacy is becoming crucial to analyze the changes going on in the region. Migration and remittances are a big part of this narrative, and this chapter brings our focus to these factors, in analyzing the ongoing changes. This analysis follows a constructivist perspective of International Relations.

The chapter is divided as follows: Section "Remittances from Persian Gulf to India" offers a historical background to migration and remittances to the GCC region from the India and offers us some fresh perspectives on how to view this complex set of relations, from a civil society as well as state perspective. Section "India-Gulf Diplomacy: Energy,

Migration and Soft Power" offers a deeper dive into how migration and diplomacy are related. In using some past examples of diplomatic tensions between the two regions, an attempt is made to draw lessons from it, to further understand and de-construct the present. Section "Changes Amidst COVID-19 and Rise of Hindu-Majoritarianism in India" offers a critique of the existing tensions and ongoing policy changes in India, with respect to majoritarianism from the Hindu-right wing party and its affiliates (BJP) and implications on diplomacy. Finally, in Sect. "Nupur Sharma Incident: Response from UAE and Saudi Arabia", the chapter offers a deeper look at the Nupur Sharma incident, as a paradigmatic case of how one incident can shape the understanding and perception of an entire country and its politics, in the GCC region. While the ramifications of this incident are still far too numerous to offer a definitive analysis, there are indications that this incident has at least altered the public perception of India's policies with respect to Muslim minority in a big way and this will impact how migration and diplomacy is conducted, between the GCC countries and India. Finally, the conclusion offers some ways to make sense of all these changes and suggests a way forward, in terms of policy recommendations.

Soft Power and Remittances

Soft power refers to the persuasive power of a country or a group of people to get others to do what they want (Nye, 1990). In other words, it refers to the social, cultural, and other capital that a group can exert, without using actual force, to get others to comply. With the rise of the oil rich countries in the Persian Gulf, the phenomenon of guest-workers become a significant force in the relations between India and the GCC countries (Khan & Merritt, 2020; Rajan & Arokkiaraj, 2022).

Remittances (monies sent by migrant workers to their families in the country of origin) have been studied extensively as a phenomenon and a force for development. However, not much has been written about the impact of remittances as a tool for soft power. An argument can be made that they function as a soft power tool both ways—for the sending countries such as the GCC countries and also receiving countries such as India, Pakistan, Bangladesh, Sri Lanka, and others, given that they offer valuable human capital for the development of these countries.

This power has been prominent among countries that are strong and dominant, attracting the best talents and also resources, so many people want to migrate to these countries (Khan & Merritt, 2020). The soft power of superpowers lies in their ability to offer incentives, trade agreements or other modes of rewarding those countries that comply with it or benefit the country. What Nye said in 1990 holds true much more today, with a rising China, a war in Ukraine with Russia involved and a global order that is at best chaotic.

The soft power that India wields in the Persian Gulf countries goes back to its historic trade and cultural relations, spanning centuries. The Indian diaspora continues to be a strong link between India and the GCC, with a varied set of ideas, desires, opinions, attitudes, and aspirations; that often collide and conflict (Luthra, 2017).

Remittances from Persian Gulf to India

UAE is one of the largest remittance sending countries to India. With the rise of digital services and number of companies in this space, the sector is vibrant. The oil embargo of 1973–74 enriched the GCC countries in general and the UAE in particular and brought it to the fore of the global scene, in terms of an Oil and natural gas rich country (Zachariah et al., 2003). The resultant rise in migration to the country from India and other South Asian countries is a result of the favorable relations between the countries as well as the rise in opportunities to help build the country, both from a human resources perspective as well an infrastructure perspective.

As Zachariah, Prakash, and Rajan point out, there has been an ebb and flow in terms of flow of migrants from India to the UAE over the decades, due to change in immigration policy by the UAE. In early 2000, the UAE had about 1 million Indian citizens living and working in the country, and they were sending in an about 100 million USD (Zachariah et al., 2003). As they further point out and other scholars have elaborated, the nature of migration into the GCC is either in terms of "settlement or contract migration" (ILO, 1989). Settlement refers to the long-term stay of migrants in a country when they move, to live and work in a specific country, whereas contract labor referred to short-term contractual labor for specific projects in construction or service-oriented industries.

The recent Covid-19 pandemic has had a big impact on the number of Indian migrants in the UAE, with thousands having lost their jobs and returning to India (Rajan & Arokkiaraj, 2022). The stigma of migrants carrying disease was prevalent in the case of Indian migrants during the pandemic and as a result, flights were suspended between the GCC region and South Asia. There were also changes in how the oil rich nations wanted to control migration into their countries, so as not to disturb the internal balance of demographics, which was slowly skewing toward more non-citizens in these countries.

There have been restrictions on visas for workers, with them not being allowed to bring their wives and children in most cases and also the introduction of heavy visa fees (in the case of the Kingdom of Saudi Arabia) to deter migration to the country and encouraging local talent to be hired. Since the 1990s, the "Emiratization" or hiring of locals' initiative was put in place that sought to return unskilled migrants back to the countries of origin and hiring of Emirati nationals.

Zachariah et al. point out that "The policies relating to work contracts, sponsorship systems, labor disputes, restrictions on bringing dependents, worker camps, and measures to reduce unskilled labor have created very serious problems for Indian emigrant labor and their future prospects."

A recent World Bank announcement claimed that India is set to cross the $100 billion mark, when it comes to receiving remittances. This was despite the drop in remittances from the GCC countries. India receives remittances which equal to roughly 3% of its Gross Domestic Product (GDP) and are important for filling any fiscal gaps. While the weakening Rupee and strengthening dollar are factors that could have contributed to the increase in the share of remittances sent, one cannot also discount the fact that cash transfers from India climbed to more than 36% in 2020–21, up from 26% in 2016–17.

A recent media report in Arabian business, an outlet in UAE pointed out that, "The share from five Gulf countries, including Saudi Arabia and the UAE, declined to 28% from 54% in the same period, the World Bank said, citing Reserve Bank of India data (Staff writer, 2022)." The drop in remittances from the Gulf countries can be attributed to several factors: drop in employment levels, return of hundreds and thousands of migrants to India as well as higher cost of living in the Persian Gulf countries, which is eating away at the migrants' earnings.

There has been a perceptible change in migration from India and South Asian countries to the Kingdom of Saudi Arabia. This also has a gender dimension, which will be discussed shortly. Estimates point to about 12 billion dollars in remittances from Saudi Arabia to India (Staff writer, 2022).

There have been some calls for reforms in the *Kafala* system, given hi-profile events such as the World Cup (football) in Qatar, in 2022. The

Kafala system is one which allows a private citizen or company to sponsor the visa of a migrant and in some ways have total control of that person's mobility and work atmosphere. As a recent report by the Council on Foreign Relations points out "The lack of regulations and protections for migrant workers' rights often results in low wages, poor working conditions, and employee abuse. Racial discrimination and gender-based violence are endemic (Robinson, 2022)." This follows several decades of efforts by human rights activists as well as government officials both in the Kingdom of Saudi Arabia as well as in the migrant sending countries. There has been a growing awareness on labor rights etc.

Another media report points out that the remittances from Saudi Arabia to the rest of the world were at a record high, with $41 billion being sent out from Saudi Arabia. One explanation for this rise, despite the changing nature of migration in Saudi Arabia and loss of jobs is that many of the migrants may be leaving their jobs permanently and returning home, for good. Hence, they may be sending all their life savings back to their country of origin, as remittances. This is one likely explanation, though there are others, as well.

There is another angle to this story, which is that of climate change. Due to climate-change induced effects, migrants in low-lying parts of India and Bangladesh are regularly seeing their homes being flooded, and their villages and crops destroyed by unpredictable weather. This is also fueling migration to the Middle East and North Africa (MENA region), which has GCC as part of it, as several analysts and social scientists have pointed out (Gowayed, 2022).

As Gowayed writes, the MENA region is one of transit and a globally important one and also, one of the hardest hit when it comes to climate change. The MENA region is heating up twice as fast, she points out, also given that the region has countries that are "grappling with the impact of environmental calamities and political conflict." She argues that the people living in South Asia bear the brunt of the actions of the developed world and advanced countries and this change in climate is driving people to live in the Gulf countries, which are able to afford better salaries and provide some semblance of security to the millions of migrants who live there.

India-Gulf Diplomacy: Energy, Migration and Soft Power

The story of migration cannot be told without the concomitant story of diplomacy. Freedom of movement is available only between countries that have good relations with each other. Of course, there are people who leave their country, or they are forced to leave as refugees and asylum seekers. However, for mass migration, for work, such as in the case of the GCC countries and South Asia, there needs to be good healthy relations between nation-states.

Helene Thiollet writes in her chapter titled "Migration as diplomacy: Labor migrants, refugees and Arab regional politics in the Oil-Rich countries," that the flow of migrants (including refugees) is responsible for Arab integration, in the absence of effective institutions and economic integration processes (Thiollet, 2011). Helene Thiollet argues that there is something called "migration diplomacy" that can be used as an analytical framework and argues for looking at regional integration closely through a lens of migration.

Following this, and building on this argument, I suggest that there are enough historical, cultural, and religious similarities in the GCC countries with South Asia, with the presence of a large Muslim population and cross-flow of migrants of Hindu and Christian backgrounds, that make the exchange of beliefs, attitudes, and behaviors much similar, across borders.

India's ambitions to be a global leader in the world economically has given rise to a wave of thinking that prioritizes energy. This means that there is a great demand for Oil and natural gas produced by the GCC countries. As several scholars and observers have pointed out, there is a growing awareness of the shifting geo-political landscape in the GCC region, with the US backtracking from its Middle East focus and the entry of China and Russia onto the scene, with heavy investments (Pethiyagoda, 2017). Writing this a few years ago, Pethiyagoda argued that the Middle East is wracked by instability. With over 7 million Indians living in the region, it is a strategic corridor to Africa and other parts of the world, one which cannot be ignored.

The diplomatic dance that needs to be had involves not just India and the six GCC countries, but also others, such as Pakistan and China, which are vying for attention and money from these countries. With instability and poverty reigning in many countries of the region including Lebanon,

Syria, Egypt, there is growing migration from these countries to the GCC. Balancing their needs with that of the growing demand of India for jobs and opportunities for its diaspora in GCC is something we need to reckon as well.

The relationships that India enjoys with Iran may test the relationships it has with GCC, as this analyst argues. However, there is reason to believe that with the increasing realpolitik that is dominating India's foreign policy, there is likely to be less friction in this regard, as India pursues its goals of meeting GDP growth. As Pethiyagoda points out, "India also aligned with the Soviet Union over its 1980s intervention in Afghanistan, which the GCC states opposed. Many Arab countries also supported Pakistan in the dispute over Kashmir. Overall, India-GCC relations remained largely stagnant for the duration of the U.S.-Soviet Cold War." This has led to India not developing a strong foreign policy that considers the region, in any serious way. However, with the Modi government, there has been some movement on this front, despite growing religious tensions in India among religious groups, aided by the rhetoric of the ruling BJP party.

Energy diplomacy is real, as the Brookings report points out. More than 25% of the population lacks electricity and with the doubling of energy demand in India, there is likely going to be a greater need for collaborating with the GCC countries.

As argued earlier, there is a strong case to be made for studying migration as being related to diplomacy as scholars have argued (Thiollet, 2011). For the Middle East in particular, what this means is to look at the political dimensions of the movement of people. There have been changes to the movement and preferential hiring of employees in the GCC region, since the rise of Hindu-right wing government, according to some reports. Further, there has been a crackdown on Islamophobia by the ruling class in the GCC countries (PTI, 2020). An example of this is the firing of three employees in Dubai for Islamophobic posts.

War has been a factor in integrating the Middle East region. As Thiollet points out, the Palestinian diaspora's spread in the region has caused a wide-spread awareness of the Palestinian cause and support for it. Similarly, one can argue for the spread of

Together, this triumvirate of energy, people, and soft power can help us understand the dynamics of migration in the GCC region as it relates to India. The current political atmosphere in India, coupled with the growing realization of the GCC countries of their dependence on other South Asian countries for human capital is causing some frictions. Hundreds and thousands of people were laid off in the aftermath of the pandemic and we are still witnessing a gradual cut-back of visas and opportunities for expat workers in the region.

Changes Amidst COVID-19 and Rise of Hindu-Majoritarianism in India

Scholars and policy makers have written about the pandemic and how India suffered severe challenges. The migrations that occurred were massive in scale and both internal (within the contiguous states of India) and from neighboring countries (return migrants). As Bhagat, Reshmi, Harihar, and Roy point out in their chapter in article in Migration Letters, this covid-19 pandemic revealed many systemic failures within the Indian administrative system and social welfare mechanisms (Bhagat et al., 2020).

They point out that the challenges that migrants faced in India were due to a weak public distribution system (subsidized food), lack of any serious measures to provide public health facilities, and lack of support to reintegrate many of the return migrants to India. They also point out that there is lack of sufficient data on the migrants, and this can impede any meaningful efforts on the part of state and local governments (Bhagat et al., 2020).

As Irudaya Rajan and his colleagues point out, for those migrants stuck outside of India, the lockdowns and loss of jobs were a devastating situation. These migrants also faced the situation of visa cancelations, non-payment of salaries owed to them, and of also being stranded. The International Organization for Migration (IOM) estimated that at the peak of the lockdowns, there were about 1.2 million stranded migrants in the Middle East and North Africa, most of them from South and Southeast Asia, given the demographics of people who live and work there (Agarwal & Sarkar, 2022).

The total number of persons of Indian origin around the world is estimated to be 32 million (Rajan & Arokkiaraj, 2022). There has been a change in the number of migrants moving to the Gulf country, with a sharp decline over the past five years, they add. However, certain segments of the population are still in demand, with nurses from Kerala having the highest demand in Saudi Arabia, for example.

The nature of migration to the GCC countries is seen as a more temporary migration, for short term and also of people with low educational attainment. This "unskilled" labor is a main characteristic of the migration to Gulf, according to several scholars. Due to this, the migrants to the

GCC can be considered a vulnerable group, especially during a crisis such as a pandemic (Rajan, 2020; Rajan & Oommen, 2020; Rajan & Saxena, 2019).

Bhagat, Reshmi, Harihar, Roy, and Govil add that the internal migration coupled with the policy changes with regards to the lockdowns etc. caused massive loss of wages, poverty, and also anxiety among hundreds of thousands of people (Bhagat et al., 2020). A majority of the migrants who were in urban centers were daily wage earners and were left with no food or had to deplete all their earnings to get back to their homes. A similar situation played out among migrants in the GCC countries, many of whom had just started their work in these countries as construction workers, working in hotels or other service industries, which had all shut down due to the pandemic.

In March through May 2020, media outlets and social media were full of millions of migrants across India trying to get back to the villages and towns they were from. In their analysis of migration during the lockdown, Swati Agarwal and Sayantani Sarkar point out that at least in two of the major English language dailies Times of India and The Hindu, the coverage was largely neutral and focused on real issues that the migrants were facing such as food security, transportation etc.

There was also big panic about repatriating Indians stuck in the GCC countries, with several front-page articles in media outlets decrying the lack of support from the Indian government or their employers. As scholars have pointed out, migrants—both internal and those who leave India's borders—are largely economic migrants, though there are some political asylum seekers too. There is a lack of availability of programs and services for these migrants, who lack sufficient skills and at times educational level to access any services that may exist.

As Bhagat and his colleagues point out, the wave of return migrants—both within India and from outside the borders—was the largest such return migration in recent memory (Bhagat et al., 2020).

The rise of unemployment caused by the slowing economy, some of the economic policies of the current government and global economic shocks due to the ongoing war in Ukraine have created a class of unemployed youth who are anxious, worried, and desperate for solutions. This is a power keg of a challenge to Indian government and administrators and an opportunity for skilled political players to harness this distress for their political gains. This phenomenon has given rise to greater protests among the Hindu majority against the minorities and as some observers have pointed out, the numbers of hate incidents against minorities have increased many folds in the past few years. While the causality of this rise in hate cannot be singly attributed to the covid-19 pandemic, the vitriolic political rhetoric of certain political parties (including the ruling party in India) and lack of countermeasures to address real social issues such as poverty, public health, have left a vacuum for the youth, that is not being filled.

The millions of those who returned from the GCC countries have brought their life savings with them in many cases, but this situation can also be argued to have had a negative impact on the relationship between the countries, by virtue of reduced soft power of GCC in India.

Nupur Sharma Incident: Response from UAE and Saudi Arabia

In July 2022, Nupur Sharma, a politician belonging to the ruling BJP political party made some offensive remarks against the Prophet Muhammad on live TV. This sparked an outrage across the country and strong reaction from Muslims in the US as well as the Muslim world, in general. While her party dismissed her from her role as a spokesperson, the incident led to many protests as well as the deaths of several people in riots (BBC, 2022). Ms. Sharma was suspended due to complaints from several Muslim majority countries such as UAE, Saudi Arabia, and others.

The debate around her comments is taking place in a context of increased rise of Islamophobia and manufactured crises about correcting historical wrongs. The incident that sparked this particular exchange involves a sixteenth century mosque which was allegedly built on the ruins of a Hindu temple. While facts around this are slim, the BJP has consistently built its agenda on such flimsy and often misleading claims and has created rifts among communities. This observation of shift of India's secular model to one of an "ethnic democracy" is a pertinent on, as made by scholar Christophe Jaffrelot and others (Thompson & Kanjwal, 2021; Jaffrelot, 2007).

The founding ideology of the BJP is Hindutva, which is a modern right-wing and ethno-nationalist ideology, based on making all other religions (other than Hinduism) subordinate to it. This perspective contrasts with the 70 plus years of India's history since its independence in 1947 and also with centuries of co-existence with other religious groups. While this may seem like a temporary political development, Jaffrelot and other scholars argue that this could potentially be a long-term and perhaps permanent change in how India treats its minorities, with varying impacts on its domestic as well as foreign policies (Jaffrelot, 2007).

Covid-19 brought out the best and also the worst in Indian citizens. As Thomson and Kanjwal write in their report on the impact of covid-19 on Muslims in India, they argue that the treatment of Muslims in India was one of complete contempt. The ruling class blamed Muslim groups for the spread of covid-19, despite there being massive rallies among the Hindu majority led groups. This toxic spread of hate against Muslims and Christians in India has been a consistent feature of discussions among diplomats from the GCC countries and India since BJP has come to power. While the spread of covid-19 is itself attributed to the movement of people, the actual movement of people during the spread of the pandemic also caused massive global disruptions.

However, given that there has been growing awareness and also concern about the ethno-nationalist policies of the BJP government in the GCC countries, there is fear and loathing among many of the segments of Indian society. There is also increasing out-migration from India to the US and GCC countries, as a combination of lack of opportunities, high inflation and search for a safer location is rising in India. According to a news report, over 163,000 Indians relinquished their passports in 2021, up almost 50% compared to 2020 (Kumar, 2022).

Conclusion

As Ian Hall points out in his book "Modi and the reinvention of India's foreign policy," the flaws in the ways in which the BJP and other rightwing parties view international relations are many. For one, he says, these movements view international relations in gendered and racial terms, often using civilizational terminologies to argue for dominance or subjugation of people. There is no reference to modern nation-states, and this is a big weakness in conceptualization and one that can also lead to conflict where there need not be any, he points out (Hall, 2021).

The vision of India and its role in the world is rooted in a deeply ethno-nationalistic perspective, where anyone not of Aryan origin is seen as an "outsider," and a potential threat. This perspective, when translated to foreign policy, and especially, with nations that are not of Hindu origin, tends to create a conflictual basis for dealing with one another. The social Darwinism inherent in Hindutva is one of the characteristic features of the Modi government, as scholars have pointed out (Hall, 2021; Jaffrelot, 2007; Nussbaum, 2007).

The ongoing tensions between the minorities and the ruling BJP government have not just local implications, but also global impacts. This argument can be made in the context of the civilizational narratives that the BJP government continues to make and of how its worldviews have shaped Indian foreign policy (Jaffrelot, 2007; Kim 2017). Martha Nussbaum writes poignantly about "The Clash within" India, in her book of the same title. She points out that the struggles between the exclusivity policies of the Indian polity and the plural traditions of Indian culture and society are at odds and the story of it is, the resilience of Indian society will be a good one for other nations as well (Nussbaum, 2007). This internal struggle has profound ramifications for how Indian foreign policy, its migration policy, and its treatment of its diaspora are going to be shaped.

References

Agarwal, S., & Sarkar, S. (2022). Topical analysis of migration coverage during lockdown in India by mainstream print media. *PLoS One, 17*(2), e0263787. https://doi.org/10.1371/journal.pone.0263787

BBC. (2022). *Nupur Sharma: The Indian woman behind offensive Prophet Muhammad comments.* Accessed from https://www.bbc.com/news/world-asia-india-61716241

Bhagat, R., Reshmi, R., Harihar, S., Roy, A., & Govil, D. (2020). The Covid-19 migration and livelihood in India: Challenges and policy issues. *Migration Letters, 17*(2020), 705–718.

Gowayed, H. (2022). *Climate change and migration in the Middle East and North Africa.* Arab Center Washington DC. Accessed from https://arabcenterdc.org/resource/climate-change-and-migration-in-the-middle-east-and-north-africa/

Hall, I. (2021). *Hindu nationalism and foreign policy.* Bristol University Press.

ILO. (1989). *Labor Standards Guide.* Accessible at https://libguides.ilo.org/c.php?g=652469&p=4605964

Jaffrelot, C. (2007). *Hindu nationalism: A reader.* Princeton University Press.

Khan, S., & Merritt, D. (2020). *Remittances and international development: The invisible forces shaping community.* Routledge Press.

Kim, H. (2017). Understanding Modi and minorities: The BJP-led NDA government in India and religious minorities. *India Review, 16*(4), 357–376. https://doi.org/10.1080/14736489.2017.1378482

Kumar, A. (2022). *Indians leaving Indian citizenship at the fastest pace in 5 years, US top destination.* Accessed from https://www.cnbctv18.com/india/indians-leave-indian-citizenship-at-the-fastest-pace-in-5-years-us-top-destination-14183742.htm

Luthra, S. (2017). Indian diaspora policy and the "international triad": Of voices and visions beyond pragmatism. *Alternation, 24*(1), 50–75. 50, Electronic ISSN: 2519-5476. https://doi.org/10.29086/2519-5476/2017/v24n1a4

Nussbaum, M. (2007). *The clash within*. Harvard University Press.

Nye. J. (1990). Soft Power. *Foreign Policy*, No. 80, Twentieth Anniversary, (pp. 153–171).

Pethiyagoda, K. (2015). *Indian tolerance: The view from outside*. Washington D.C.

Pethiyagoda, K. (2017). *India-GCC relations: Delhi's strategic opportunity*. Doha Brookings Center.

PTI. (2020). *3 more Indians in UAE lose jobs for Islamophobic social media posts*. Accessed from https://timesofindia.indiatimes.com/nri/middle-east-news/3-more-indians-in-uae-lose-jobs-for-islamobhobic-social-media-posts/articleshow/75516328.cms

Rajan, S. I. (2020). Migrants at a crossroads: Covid-19 and challenges to migration. *Migration and Development, 9*(3), 323–330. https://doi.org/10.1080/21632324.2020.1826201

Rajan, S. I., & Arokkiaraj, H. (2022). Return migration from the Gulf region to India amidst covid-19. In A. Triandafylidou (Ed.), *migration and pandemics: Spaces of solidarity and spaces of exception*. Springer.

Rajan, S. I., & Oommen, G. Z. (2020). *Asianisation of Migrant Workers in the Gulf Countries*. Springer.

Rajan, S. I., & Saxena, P. C. (2019). *India's Low-Skilled Migration to the Middle East*. Palgrave Macmillan.

Robinson, K. (2022). *What is the Kafala system?* Council on Foreign Relations. Report. Accessed from https://www.cfr.org/backgrounder/what-kafala-system

Staff writer. (2022). *India sees record $100 bn remittances despite plunge from Saudi and UAE*. Arabian Business. Accessed from https://www.arabianbusiness.com/money/india-sees-record-100bn-remittances-despite-plunge-from-saudi-and-uae

Thiollet, H. (2011). Migration as diplomacy: Labor migrants, refugees, and Arab regional politics in the oil-rich countries. *International Labor and Working-Class History, 79*, 103–121.

Thompson, P., & Kanjwal, H. (2021). *Covid-19 and India's islamophobia*. Islamophobia Studies Center.

Zachariah, K. C., Prakash, B. A., & Rajan, I. (2003). The Impact of Immigration Policy on Indian Contract Migrants: The Case of the United Arab Emirates. *International Migration*, (pp. 161–172).

CHAPTER 5

Reasons for Leaving and Coming Back: Migration Experiences of High-Skilled Professionals from Lithuania

Eglė Vaidelytė, Eglė Butkevičienė, and Jolanta Vaičiūnienė

Introduction

The gigantic invisible broom that transforms, disfigures, erases landscapes has been at the job for millennia now, but its movements, which used to be slow, just barely perceptible, have sped up so much that I wonder: Would an Odyssey even be conceivable today? Is the epic of the return still pertinent to our time? (Milan Kundera, Ignorance)

Lithuania, as a small European country, is also the one that has demonstrated high emigration numbers over the past two decades. Following the statistics since restoration of Independence Lithuania's population has

E. Vaidelytė (✉) • E. Butkevičienė • J. Vaičiūnienė
Kaunas University of Technology, Kaunas, Lithuania
e-mail: egle.vaidelyte@ktu.lt; egle.butkeviciene@ktu.lt; jolanta.vaiciuniene@ktu.lt

© The Author(s), under exclusive license to Springer Nature Switzerland AG 2024
J. Yeo (ed.), *Return Migration and Crises in Non-Western Countries*, Mobility & Politics,
https://doi.org/10.1007/978-3-031-53562-8_5

decreased from 3.6 million (in 1990) to 2.79 million (in 2020).[1] People have been emigrating for a wide range of economic and non-economic reasons: better salary, better professional opportunities, education, personal and family reasons, etc. According to the Official Statistics of Lithuania, in 2019, the majority (67.4%) of Lithuanian emigrants declared their departure to the EU countries (in 2018 it was 72.9%). In 2019, 34.6% of all emigrants from Lithuania moved to the United Kingdom, 8.8% moved to Germany, 8.1% to Norway, and 5.5% have selected Ireland as their emigration destination.[2]

However, in recent years, with the COVID-19 pandemic, Brexit, and other global challenges the numbers of return migration to Lithuania have considerably increased. Following the Official Statistics of Lithuania, while in 2011, 10,155 persons returned to Lithuania, in 2019 there were 20,412 Lithuanians who came back to Lithuania and in 2021 the number of return migrants reached 23,712[3] and it was the first time since the restoration of the Independence in 1990 when the return migrant flow appeared to be bigger than emigration flow. It should be mentioned that in the first two decades of Independence the return migration was not significant at all. For example, in 2004 the return migrants were 5.6 thousand comparing to 37.7 thousand who left the country (in 2005 adequately 6.8 thousand to 57.9 thousand).[4]

While there are many assumptions about the reasons and causes of return migration, up to now there is no clear academic evidence whether the return migration flows were influenced by COVID-19 pandemic or any other reason. Nevertheless, the considerably high numbers of return emigration from the UK could be noticed already in 2019, thus, it might be assumed that the reasons for return migration have much wider backstage than a single pandemic. While existing literature suggests a range of emigration and return migration factors, most emigration theories (de Haas et al., 2020; Okeke, 2013, etc.) explored push and pull factors of migration decisions, which are embedded in the social context.

Lados (2014, p. 133) argues that after the EU enlargement in 2014, the pool of all emigrants was considerably supplemented by "the young

[1] datacatalog.worldbank.org **2023-05-03**
[2] https://osp.stat.gov.lt/statistiniu-rodikliu-analize?indicator=S3R0012#/ 2022-09-10
[3] https://osp.stat.gov.lt/statistiniu-rodikliu-analize?indicator=S3R0012#/ 2022-09-10
[4] Economic Commission for Europe. Conference of European Statisticians, 2014. Developments of Return Migration Statistics in Lithuania. https://unece.org/fileadmin/DAM/stats/documents/ece/ces/ge.10/2014/mtg1/WP_21_Lithuania.pdf 2023-05-03

and well-educated populations from post-socialist countries". Thus, in this chapter we analyze the emigration and return migration paths of high-skilled professionals and argue that COVID-19 pandemic was not a decisive factor of return migration to Lithuania as other reasons like family ties, national pride, quality of life changes in Lithuania were much more relevant to the high-skilled return migrants.

MIGRATION AND RETURN MIGRATION LITERATURE REVIEW

In academic and public discourse there are a wide range of definitions of migration and return migration. From an economic perspective, migration is defined through the lenses of labor aspects and is considered "as a response to better returns to human capital and lead to an improvement of occupational status of the worker" (Abraham, 2020, p. 1224). Following Lithuanian Official Statistics, an emigrant is considered as "a person who has left the country with the intention to stay in the new place for permanent residence or longer than 12 months".[5] Eventually, the return migration is "and integral part of temporary labor migration when people migrate to take up contract employment in the receiving country" (Zhao, 2002 in Abraham, 2020, p. 1224). Per the reasons for coming back to the country of origin, the return migration might be divided into voluntary and forced migration. According to the International Organization of Migration[6] (2022), the return to the country of origin, transit or another country is based on the voluntary decision of the returnee which can be based on spontaneous return which is independent return. Another encouragement for return might be assisted return related to integration programs, job offers, and other pull factors in the home of origin. The voluntary return migration can be also based on humanitarian reasons which represent a life-saving measure for migrants who are persecuted or in detention (Return and Reintegration Key Highlighted, 2019b). Meanwhile the forced return is based on diverse factors that involve force, coercion, and compulsion (IOM Glossary on migration, 2019a).

While there are many migration theories, at least two main approaches related to return migration reasons can be crystallized: neoclassical migration theory and new economics of labor migration. Neoclassical migration

---

[5] https://osp.stat.gov.lt/lietuvos-gyventojai-2021/savokos-ir-metodine-informacija 2022-11-12

[6] https://www.migrationdataportal.org/themes/return-migration 2022-11-12

theory lies on the above-mentioned economic perspective and is focused on migration motivation as individuals aim to maximize "their utility by moving to places where they can be more productive" or where they "can expect the highest returns on their human capital investments" (de Haas et al., 2015, p. 416). The New Labor Migration theory views migration as a strategy and as a temporary phenomenon which is focused on the idea of individual emigration to gain an income abroad and invest them in the home country. de Haas et al. (2015) argue that "while neoclassical migration theory links migration to the failure to integrate at the destination, the new economics of labor migration sees return migration as the logical stage after migrants have earned sufficient assets" and eventually emigrants return to "invest in their origin countries" (p. 416). Thus, in the context of the new economics of labor, the return migration appears to be a result of successful migration. Nevertheless, both theories are not directly linked to the return migration of high-skilled migrants, though they might be useful by explaining the return reasons of this migrant group as well. Lam and Rui (2023) notice that high-skilled return migrants "constitute a key mechanism for knowledge transfer" and besides traditional economic perspective enlighten contemporary migration dimension that "facilitates the flow of people and knowledge between developed and less developed countries" (pp. 311–312).

Similarly, Yang (2006, p. 1) argues, that the migrants working overseas can be divided into "target earners" and "life cycle" migrants, though "there is no consensus on the extent to which the durations of migrant's stays overseas are determined primarily by straightforward life cycle considerations, as opposed to be driven by the need to reach target earning levels". In this context "life cycle" is defined as a period that migrants choose to stay abroad "that balances marginal benefit from higher savings overseas" (Yang, 2006, p. 1). This approach falls into the investment theory, as the length of stay in emigration depends directly on economic conditions. While for "life cycle" migrants, improved economic settings in the destination country can lead to a longer emigration period, for "target earners", increased wage may result in shorter emigration period. Nevertheless, speaking about high-skilled migrants the learning dimension might be relevant as well. The gained knowledge becomes important as much as it appears applicable in their home country and has "potential to connect to local knowledge" (Schulz, 2003, p. 442).

Eventually or not, new migration theories are related to Relative Deprivation theory (Runciman, 1966), Rational Expectation theory (de

Jong & Gardner, 1981), Consumption theory (Wallace et al., 1997), and argue that besides economic factors there are non-material values as family ties, security, climate, etc. (cited by Kumpikaite & Zickute, 2012), thus their decision on return migration might be different from the ones defined by neoclassical or new labor migration theories. This social psychological aspect is very relevant in the contexts of high-skilled migrants as their decision to return is loosely related to economic factors considering the scope how their high-skilled competences were acknowledged in the host country. Relative deprivation theory firstly introduced by Runciman (1966) analyzes social determinants, socioeconomic position, and psychological need for social justice (to be fairly treated in society) (Webber, 2007). Rational expectation theory introduced by de Jong and Gardner (1981) argue about addition to value-expectations, that other factors such as personal traits, risk-taking orientation, migration norms and experiences, family and friend contacts, money constraints, individual demographic factors and household characteristics are explanatory variables for migration decision. Consumption theory introduced by Wallace et al. (1997) argues that for some groups of migrants' income it is not important, but rather value maximization and that the benefits of emigration are not economic but also noneconomic, non-material values (cited by Liebeg, 2003).

In general, all migration theories conclude that push and pull factors influence decisions on emigration and eventually influence return migration, though few of them focus on high-skilled return migrants. The recently growing flows of return migration in Lithuania raise the question, whether and how (economic and noneconomic) push and pull factors for return migration in Lithuania are affected by COVID-19 pandemics. UN International organization on migration[7] declares that during the pandemic many migrants were forced to come back to their home countries, particularly those in lower paid jobs and in irregular situations, contrary to higher skilled professionals whose return was not so much affected by the pandemic crisis and had higher resilience to cascading crises. In addition to COVID-19, social tensions within societies opened the space for xenophobia and other negative attitudes toward migrants, especially the ones who are from different region, and eventually increased their vulnerability (World migration report, 2022). Nevertheless, return migration often dwells on several dichotomic factors: success and/or failure in the host

[7] https://www.migrationdataportal.org/themes/return-migration (2022-11-15)

country or country of origin, family ties and social relations, nostalgia for the home country culture, political and economic variables, as well as safety in the origin country. Black et al. (2004) argue that there are structural, individual, and policy level factors that influence migrants' decision to return. While structural factors are related to the living conditions in the home country and host country, individual factors such as age, gender, social relations are influential too. The policy level that dwells on incentives and disincentives might also motivate individuals for a return migration. Mihi-Ramirez et al. (2016) argue that the changing quality of life in the country especially the more sophisticated aspects of quality of life such as related to innovation, integrity, knowledge protection is a decisive factor for high-skilled persons to migrate or return. Many authors (Black et al., 2004; Koser & Kuschminder, 2015) discuss that despite various theories in reality those factors rarely fall into clear economic or non-economic drivers; more often return is grounded by much wider landscape of random push and pull factors that mainly focus on conditions in the destination country and conditions in the origin country.

Methodology

The chapter is based on qualitative data. The authors of this chapter conducted six in-depth interviews with return migrants, investigating the experiences of being an international migrant and their motivations to return to their homeland. The interviews were conducted during October 2022, the duration of each interview was up to 60 min.[8]

The method that we decided to use for data analysis was a case study. The criteria for selecting four cases out of six were based on a criterion of maximum differentiation. The data allowed us to select four different cases that cover different variations regarding the reasons of emigration and re-emigration (predominance of pull or push factors). The detailed explanation is presented in Table 5.2. Case study method is also a relevant one for discussing this kind of research questions as it provides rich qualitative data. This method is good for explorative study. The interview guidelines that we used for this study included several broad topics:

---

[8] This research received no specific grant from any funding agency in the public, commercial, or not-for-profit sectors.

(1) *Tell us about yourself*: information about the interviewee (age, profession, current and/or previous work, and family situations, etc.)
(2) *Tell us about your emigration experience*: when where, and why you left. What were the reasons for leaving? (including economic and non-economic reasons)
(3) *Tell us about your life in emigration* (e.g., tell us how did you feel when you were abroad? Did you find it difficult to adapt to living abroad? How much and what kind of contact did you have with Lithuania? Did you miss Lithuania, your friends, and relatives?)
(4) *Tell us about your experience of returning to Lithuania*: when, where, and why you returned (What were the reasons for your return? (economic and non-economic reasons)), to only those who returned after 2020: Did the COVID-19 pandemic influence your decision to return to Lithuania (if so, how?)?
(5) *Attitudes toward and perceptions of migration* (e.g., how important do you think it is for people to live in their home country?)

On the other hand, the sample selection for case studies always has some limitations, and that should be considered when reading this essay as well. Authors used snow-ball sample selection method, and at the saturation has been reached when completing the 6th interview. It was noticed that these interviews are covering the different combinations of reasons for leaving the home country and returning (push and pull factors). Thus, we selected four return cases out of six interviews, as explained earlier in this chapter, to present the diversity of life-cycle situations and motivations for emigrating and returning to Lithuania before and during COVID-19 pandemic. However, the limitation of the study is that this research presents the experiences of high-skilled migrants and their stories of leaving and coming back to Lithuania. The summary of cases is presented in Table 5.1.

- **Case#1:** female, who currently works as lecturer and researcher, got back to Lithuania in 2018. She has spent 4 years abroad, living in Germany.
- **Case#2:** female, who currently works as researcher, left Lithuania in 2010. First emigration country was Georgia (Sakartvel). She stayed in Georgia for 2 years, volunteering and working as teacher assistant, and then left for MA studies to Hungary. She lived in Hungary for

Table 5.1 Summary of the cases

	Case #1	Case #2	Case #3	Case #4
Years in emigration	4 years 2014–2018	11 years 2010–2021	7 years 2013–2020	15 years 2006–2020
Country of emigration	Germany	Multiple: Georgia, Hungary, US	Scotland	UK
Pandemic as a factor for return migration	No	No	No	No
Adaption in country of emigration	Easy	Easy	Easy	Difficult
Adaptation in home country	Difficult	Easy	Easy	Easy

2 years and studied for MA, after that returning to Georgia to work for a year, but at the same time applying for Graduate School in the US. She stayed in the US for more than 6 years, finishing her PhD. She got back to Lithuania in 2021. She has spent 11 years in emigration.

- **Case #3**: male, who currently works as an IT professional. He lived in Scotland for 8 years. Left Lithuania in 2010.
- **Case#4:** female, who currently works as a high-skilled professional in academic field. She left Lithuania in 2006 and lived for 15 years in the UK. She gained her degrees in the UK. She returned to Lithuania in 2020.

The citations that are used to illustrate the findings are presented in their original form.

Findings

As it was discussed above, emigration might be fostered by many reasons. As previous research shows, the main reasons for emigrating from Lithuania are economic, however there are also non-economic reasons of leaving the homeland such as perceived low quality of working life, low confidence in the future, etc., which may be identified as push factors of emigration (Bryer et al., 2020). Thus, the four cases analyzed in this chapter present a broader picture, introducing a variety of intersections of push and pull factors of emigration as well as pull and push factors of re-emigration, highlighting a really complex picture of reasons for leaving and coming back to Lithuania.

The qualitative interviews revealed that people emigrated due to various reasons that might be classified as both push and pull factors:

Studies in another country or volunteering as a way to experience new cultures (pull factors).

Several cases revealed that one of the pull factors is the attractiveness of the opportunities for studies, work, volunteering, etc. aboard, because of various reasons, but in particular, because it is a way to experience different cultures, styles, new opportunities that could not be found in the home country. Additionally, the data indicates that having gained education abroad high-skilled migrants are more likely to return to share this knowledge in the home country.

- *"I did my PhD in Germany"; "I was just screening through possibilities where I could study that and what I could do with that. And yeah, in Lithuania I didn't find anything. So, I end up in Germany" [Case #1]*
- *"So, in 2010 I left Lithuania. I went to Georgia Sakartvelo to work as a European Voluntary service volunteer"; "It was more, you know this experience, different life, experience different culture and stuff like that and also so here where my sociological hat comes on. So, It also was about related to status stuff" [Case #2]*
- *"I went to Hungary for a couple years to do my masters" [Case #2]*

Uncertainty of living in Lithuania, including economic reasons (push factors).

Several cases indicated that uncertainty and poor economic conditions served as push factors from the home country. Emigration to higher GDP countries compared to Lithuania resulted in a more attractive situation for emigrants to stay longer than it was initially planned. These are mostly financial reasons to work abroad.

- *"It was mainly sort of career economic reasons because I didn't know what I was going to do here in Lithuania. I thought maybe I'm going to try making some money abroad" [Case #3]*
- *"My husband and I were going just for the summer to the UK as students, we just wanted to earn money. My main, my goal was just enough money to buy laptop and however when we started working there for some reason, we decided that maybe we should stay for, I can't remember*

the reasons exactly why it probably was economic reasons. Understanding the opportunities that we have, the economic value of living in a different country and earning much more. So, we decided to stay for another year and see how it goes and that year after year turned out into nearly 15 years" [Case #4]

On the other hand, the reasons for return also indicate both push and pull factors. Reasons for return migration spin around several factors:

Family reasons (pull factors).
Family is a strong pull factor of return. There are various aspects such as illnesses and bad health conditions of family members, responsibilities toward extended family members and similar, that influence on a decision of returning to the home country.

- *"As I mentioned it, it was due to family reasons"; "Personal reasons, family"* [Case #1]

Attractive changes in socio-cultural and political environment of Lithuania (pull factors).
The environment in Lithuania changed to a better one regarding the economic situation, safety, increased integrity, infrastructure developments, quality of life and became more attractive for return migration. People started to notice these changes and that influenced decisions to go back to their home country. In some cases, people just returned back for holidays, but seeing much better and favorable living condition, took decision to stay and live in Lithuania.

"I've noticed that you know, things in Lithuania have improved somewhat. It feels like it felt like that to me, so there was a lot of change. A lot of change in people's attitudes and a lot of change in how people talk to you and just economic situation has improved a lot and the jobs were starting to come up in Lithuania as well. So, I then started to think that's my future" [Case #3]

- *"I broke up with my old girlfriend and so I felt like, you know, I'm kind of free. I don't no longer have to stay there because there was nothing much left a lot of my friends have gone away and then there was this summer in 2020 I believe when I come back for a holiday and I just didn't want to go back to Scotland, I just felt it was great here in Lithuania and so that's when I just decided to just Yeah, that's it for me"* [Case #3]

The socio-cultural and political environment of the host country is not attractive (push factors).
The interviews showed that in some cases emigrants were not feeling good when living in a host country. The recent political situation in the UK (Brexit) was one of the push factors of why people decide to return to their home country. Also, some countries such as the US do not offer favorable health insurance conditions nor do they have attractive social security systems. And these ones also serve as push factors for return migration. There are also some reasons related to social-cultural differences, and social class.

- *"I know that like natural way to do it will be like apply for green card. Staying in the US, Na, na, na… but as I said… said, I don't necessarily do things for economic reasons and in US I could earn like three times more than I earn here. That's a fact. But also, I want to live a life, not to be depending on my career, I want to have more than two to two weeks off a year. I want to have… have good health insurance. I want to have state pension. I want to have all these Social Security things that US just doesn't have. <…> I don't like American working culture and I don't like the life, just centered around career and achievements, and that's not for me. [Case #2]*
- *"from my day one in grad school I was told do not list your foreign languages because that indicates you, not American, and indicates that we will… whoever wants to hire you, they'll have to go through extra paperwork to get you work Visa and people don't want to do that, and officially they cannot discriminate against it, based on your nationality, but unofficially, when you have 25 candidates, everyone with PhD's, everyone with beautiful publications, they will select the one that is American or has work permit already" [Case #2]*
- *"I suppose what we realized as well, as at different levels of society. So, you have, you know, even though it it's very clearly structured by the income of the people where you belong by the lower class or middle class or upper class, or… or you're just working class. So, working class, middle class, upper class, and there is diversity. And even though it's not, you know it's not written anywhere, but it it you feel it in the society and depending how much you earn, where you live, how you dress, where you shop for the food, you would you belong to one of the classes" [Case #4]*
- *"I asked myself that when six months into moving to Lithuania, why did you do this. And I… I don't know if it comes with an age or the period of time we spent in another country, but I think there was the political*

environment in the UK had started to change with the change of the government and Brexit with the referendum of 2016. So, naturally a lot of European migrants, expats, however you want to name them, started feeling unsafe. And that was OK. We were, you know, we were all getting our permanent settled statuses, we're applying. There was a lot of nervousness around, but you were still feeling anxious" [Case #4]

The overall summary of prevailing reasons to emigrate and re-emigrate are presented in Table 5.2.

The data of these cases show that we can draw several migration paths that are common to Lithuanians who are educated and high skilled (see Fig. 5.1):

All cases also revealed some specifics that they all have in common:

When leaving a country, emigrants didn't have a well-developed plan of what will happen next. Especially, people didn't have a clear vision of how long the emigration will last. Some emigration cases were influenced by decisions of other people, close friends or partners:

- *"I didn't have like some particular plan; I knew that I'm going for four years, and I was open for possibilities and opportunities. And yeah, and just like that, nothing was set in stone"* [Case #1].
- *"So that was I'm pretty sure that at that point I didn't think it about that much... I didn't have any mission right now. No... no"* [Case #2].

Table 5.2 The prevailing reasons to emigrate and re-emigrate as pull and push factors

Cases	Reasons for emigration	Reasons for re-emigration
Case #1	**Pull factors** (studies)	**Pull factors** (family reasons)
Case #2	**Pull factor** (volunteering as a way to experience new cultures)	**Push factor** (non-attractive socio-cultural and political conditions in destination country)
Case #3	**Push factor** (uncertainty of living in home country)	**Pull factors** (changed to a better environment in Lithuania)
Case #4	**Push factor** (uncertainty of living in home country, economic reasons)	**Push factor** (non-attractive socio-cultural and political conditions in destination country)

5 REASONS FOR LEAVING AND COMING BACK: MIGRATION EXPERIENCES... 95

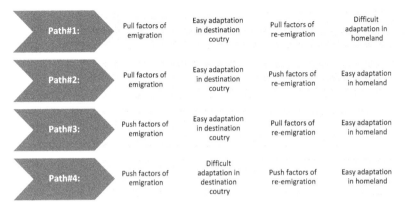

Fig. 5.1 Paths of migrants

- *"I met this girl and then she said, oh listen, I am studying abroad let's… let's move in together. So, I moved with her to Scotland"* [Case #3].
- *"so, emigration was quite spontaneous"* [Case #4].

Emigrants lived in a multicultural environment which facilitated the adaptation process, however in most cases they haven't kept relations with diaspora (other Lithuanians, living in a destination country). Emigrants preferred the networking with the same social class or interest communalities rather than based on ethnicity:

- *"So, but till that time it was a very mixed group. A lot of them came of course from university, so all the university crowd, so it was German, India, Ecuador, Mexico… uhm, what else? The Netherlands, yeah, France, Italy and so on. You know it's a was a very mixed crowd"* [Case#1].
- *"also got like new friend groups in the US. I got friend groups in in in from Hungary times, from in in Georgia as well"* [Case#2].
- *"Most of them were also immigrants to Scotland. I had a couple of… of Scottish friends but they were never really close friends, and I don't know why it was that way because I never felt like the people that I worked with were really close friends and I didn't really find any other friends in the area that were Scottish"* [Case#3].

- *"And since then, we actually probably made just one couple Lithuanian friends, all the rest of our friendship circle were either British or other expats, so French, German. Uh, you know Spanish as well. So, we were, since the beginning, we kind of understood unconsciously that we have to integrate you know. So, we have to go, if you want to fit in, we need to go to the pubs that the locals are going" [Case#4].*
- *"And it's interesting if we would hear somewhere if it was out, let's... let's say visiting castle for a day somewhere because there's lots of castles and the gardens and you would hear somebody talking Lithuanian, you would just hush, like you know there's this identity that you didn't want to be associated with Lithuanians. And... and I think so that comes from a very bad reputation since the borders opened and so you would try to kind a hide it and it... it kind of disappeared towards the end of staying when we felt more comfortable that we integrated ourselves and who we are. But at the beginning with all the bad press Lithuanians getting since 2004, you really didn't want to be associated with, be behind them" [Case#4].*

People were not missing Lithuania, and even in some cases were feeling as strangers after returning. Some cases show that people found friends in the host country, but they missed family that was still living in Lithuania:

- *"No, no, I didn't miss. How to say. I never counted the days till Christmas holidays, let's say this way" [Case#1]*
- *"Cold and struggle... a bit of lost and feeling alien" [Case#1]*
- *"Not at all. Yeah, because I found a lot of new friends there. I didn't really miss the old ones that much back home, but I obviously missed my family. So yeah, so I used to come back twice a year to... to go and visit them. But I didn't really feel like I missed the country then at the beginning of my leave, yeah, but yeah, it changed later" [Case#3]*

The feeling of being a stranger was amplified by the changes that they find after being back. The situation is changing and the friends, situations, infrastructure, etc. are not any more the same:

- *"a lot of my colleagues, friends, and so on they moved on, let's say they changed very much, and I wasn't involved in these changes. You know, they got married, they got children, and it was like massive explosion of that in my friends' circle. So, like I came back and suddenly you know the girl who was like a bar hopper. Suddenly, she's like, uh, having one child in in the hand and there other is expected and suddenly she's married and living in suburbs, you know, and having all the loan for the new house and something like this, you know" [Case#1].*

- *"But I wouldn't say that I love all my friends in Lithuania. I mean, it's it was naturally I grew up. They grew up. Our... our uh... Ideas about life changed, our lives changed. They have families and kids. Now I don't. I don't have kids" [Case#2].*

Data show that differences appear in adaptation when going to the new country and when returning to Lithuania. In most cases the adaptation in the destination country went quite smoothly, as emigrants received support either from the system or from individuals:

- *"after some time, I wished to stay there. Uhm, because I liked there" [Case#1].*
- *"It had some challenges, but in general, uhm I mean they do have a very well established... let's call it ... in a wide, broad, wide understanding... social system. So, it's, you know, uhm, you could rent a place to live, you could arrange your life there, you know, easily" [Case#1].*
- *"Additionally in university they really have a very good system, you know all the people there they were very helpful" [Case#1].*
- *"I got involved with another program, which was called 'teach and learn with Georgia' the Mikhail Saakashvili then president. He was very keen on Georgians learning English, so he was hiring all the foreigners basically who were in Georgia" [Case#2].*
- *"And I was sadly paid like twice as much as my Co teachers who actually had to do the job. So that was very unfair for them, but good for me I guess" [Case#2].*
- *"Feeling that you know you like one of the cool foreigners <...> like people want to hang out with you. You are the English-speaking ones <...> You have these cool friends we all like this gang of Westerners <...> I can go to cool parties" [Case#2].*
- *"It was some of the best years of my life because a lot of people were same my age and everyone was student, and it was great. But also, the locals were very tolerant, and I felt like the job there. The people that I worked with were very friendly and the college seemed like... like they wanted me because they had to fill in the quarter for students. So obviously Eastern European students were welcomed because they're qualified, and they're good students. So yeah, so that's why I felt pretty much at home" [Case#3].*

However, in some cases the adaptation in the destination country was not easy. People arriving to host country are situated in a different cultural context which is not easy to comprehend and adapt to:

- *"It was difficult to adapt, I think, so we were very critical of everything. We were astonished by variety things, uh by the habits like eating habits in terms of the food in terms of the culture, the support, and the love for the monarchy, which we don't didn't have in the Lithuania and we... we were surprised in terms of English language, because the English that we were taught in school is very much... It's not different, it's just spoken differently. In in, in, in the UK and you know we were not aware of different sayings, or the acronyms or the way the words are being played to explain something, but saying all of that, so we always being praised by our excellent English. Or everybody, even though we had an accent, everybody would ask – Oh, where did you learn to speak English? Your English is excellent"* [Case#4].
- *"I think we're very adaptable. And but at the same time we missed the seasons, we missed seasons, we missed the cleanliness as well of the streets and... and surroundings. We missed open spaces"* [Case#4].

The same might be said about adaptation after returning to Lithuania. In most cases the process was smooth and easy:

- *"I feel it's interesting... <...> Yeah, not bad, uh ... I forgot how long fall lasts. I was ready for it to snow already"* [Case#2].
- *"I think socialization processes is smooth like we both are still in the process of building our community again"* [Case#2].
- *"I feel like I'm at home and you know I'm walking around in the streets in Vilnius and it's it feels great and a lot of my family and friends here and... and yeah found a really nice girl. And you know it's it was great so. So very easy to go back to the old ways, yeah"* [Case#3].

However, there were cases in which the adaptation was rather difficult. People who lived abroad for a long time got used to different rules, values, and mentality. This made adaptation in home country difficult.

- *"But I didn't expect that it would be so hard <...> and suddenly you are in this cold icy shower <...> ... So, you know you're like OK, what I will do now?"* [Case#1].

Discussion

The empirical study confirmed that emigration and return migration have many reasons which at theoretical level are summarized in neoclassical, new labor, new migration theories which focus on economic and non-economic reasons for migration; and in reality, those reasons appear as push and pull factors. Data show that while having economic background the variety of push and pull factors relevant to high-skilled migrants is also highly dependent on many social and emotional factors such as education, professional achievements, career path, family relations, as well as political factors, such as security, human rights, and Brexit. Those factors are equally relevant in the country of destination and in the country of origin and are usually translated into push or pull factors.

In the last decade Lithuania has become one of the fastest growing economies in Europe. Until the end of February 2022, when Russia-Ukraine war broke out and highly influenced economic factors in all of Europe, Lithuania experienced outstanding progress in economic and social life. Following the neoclassical migration theories, it could be noticed that return migration in this period might be influenced by the life cycle of migrants when they identify that the benefits in the country of origin might be higher than the benefits in the country of emigration. According to OECD Economic Surveys 2020 and 2022, Lithuania in recent years experienced high rates of economic growth. Following the OECD[9] statistics, the latest 5-year average real economy growth in 2019 measured 3.3% (the OECD average was 2.2%) and in 2021 5-year average real economy growth was 3.5% (while the OECD average was 1.5%). According to the Index of Public Integrity 2021,[10] Lithuania in 2021 had a public integrity index 7.34 (out of 10) and human development index (HDI)- 0.882. Moreover, in the world rank Lithuania took the position of 34 (out of 114) for integrity and was ranked 11 (out of 123) for transparency, with the forecasted trend to improve those indexes in the coming years. Thus, the quality of life in Lithuania in recent years appears to be rather high and in the case of return migrants, it might be assumed that the quality of life is considerably higher than the one at the time of departure. Nevertheless, the migration paths of four selected cases studies

---

[9] https://www.oecd-ilibrary.org/docserver/0829329f-en.pdf?expires=1670409200&id=id&accname=ocid56029046&checksum=44AD180AED14C4EE61B7976C239BCBD9

[10] https://corruptionrisk.org/country/?country=LTU#integrity

discussed above in this chapter, indicate that while the economic factors appeared to be the dominating push factors for leaving Lithuania in the past, they are not that relevant for the return migration nowadays. The interview results indicate that positive changes of whole environment in Lithuania was mentioned quite often as a pull factor for return. The increased social and economic welfare in Lithuania appears as a pull factor for return migration. This pull factor was often strengthened by the negative changes in the socio-cultural environments in the country of emigration and this worked out as a strong push factor for re-emigration. Following the interviews, the COVID-19 pandemic had no influence or very minor influence for the return migration, thus the crisis had no direct influence on the return decision. On the other hand, Brexit was a much stronger factor for re-emigration. Nevertheless, it should be considered that the participants of the interviews were high-skilled professionals that in the neoclassical migration theory are identified as seeking for place where they can expect higher returns for their "human capital investment" (De Hass et al., 2015). Thus, the participants of interviews left Lithuania not only for economic reasons, but also for professional development, seeking wider horizons. In most cases they had easy adaptation in emigration and home countries and their return was based more on social life cycle model, voluntary return, and social cultural reasons than on reasons related to COVID-19.

Conclusions

The results of the interviews with the high-skilled return migrants indicated that the push factors for emigration among interview participants were uncertainty of living and economic situation in Lithuania of that time. The pull factors for emigration were studies abroad and opportunities for volunteering as a way to experience other cultures.

The pull factors for return emigration were family reasons, improved settings, and quality of life in Lithuania, meanwhile the push factors were related to non-attractive socio-cultural and political conditions in the host country.

The participants of the interviews declared that being in emigration they lived in multicultural environment and received individual or institutional social support which accelerated and smoothed their adaptation in a foreign country. The interviews also showed the different experiences of return migrants coming back to their homeland, ranging from difficult adaptation (because of climate change or social environment) to very easy and smooth adaptation, showing satisfaction with this decision as well as their satisfaction living abroad.

The limitation of the research is related to the case study sample and that should be considered when reading this essay as well. Authors used snow-ball sample selection method, and the sample is limited to the high-skilled professionals.

References

Abraham, A. (2020). International migration, return migration and occupational mobility: Evidence from Kerala, India. *Indian Journal of Labour Economics, 63*(4), 1223–1243. https://doi.org/10.1007/s41027-020-00284-9

Black, R. et al. (2004). *Understanding voluntary return.* Home Office Report 50/04.

Bryer, T., et al. (2020). Non-economic emigration factors that might be pushing citizens out of Lithuania. *Viešoji politika ir administravimas, 19*(1), 35–52. https://doi.org/10.5755/j01.ppaa.19.1.25114

de Haas, H., Fokema, T., & Fihri, M. F. (2015). Return migration as failure or success? *The International Migration and Integration, 16,* 415–429. https://doi.org/10.1007/s12134-014-0344-6

de Haas, M., Faber, R., & Hamersma, M. (2020). How COVID-19 and the Dutch 'intelligent lockdown' change activities, work and travel behaviour: Evidence from longitudinal data in the Netherlands. *Transportation Research Interdisciplinary Perspectives, 6,* 100150, ISSN 2590-1982. https://doi.org/10.1016/j.trip.2020.100150

de Jong, G. F., & Gardner, R. W. (Eds.). (1981). *Migration decision making.* Pergamon.

Index of Public Integrity 2021. Accessed from https://corruptionrisk.org/country/?country=LTU#integrity

International Organisation on Migration. (2019a). *IOM glossary on migration.* Accessed November 12, 2022, from https://publications.iom.int/system/files/pdf/iml_34_glossary.pdf%22%20%5Ct%20%22_blank

International Organisation on Migration. (2019b). *Return and reintegration key highlights.* Accessed November 20, 2022, from https://publications.iom.int/system/files/pdf/avrr_2019_keyhighlights.pdf

International Organisation on Migration. (2022). *World migration report 2022.* Accessed November 25, 2022, from https://publications.iom.int/books/world-migration-report-2022-chapter-5

Koser, K., & Kuschminder, K. (2015). *Comparative research on the assisted voluntary return and reintegration of migrants.* International Organization for Migration.

Kumpikaite, V., & Zickute, I. (2012). Synergy of migration theories: Theoretical insights. *Inžinerinė Ekonomika, 23*(4), 387–394. https://doi.org/10.5755/j01.ee.23.4.1240

Lados, G. (2014). The impact and importance of return migration in East Central Europe. *Forum Geographic, XII*(2), 132–137.

Lam, A., & Rui, H. (2023). Global human mobility and knowledge transfer: High skilled return migrants as agents of transnational learning. *Global Networks, 23*, 311–331. Accessed from https://wileyonlinelibrary.com/journal/glob

Liebeg, T. (2003). *Migration theory from a supply perspective. Discussion paper.* Accessed November 10, 2022, from https://www.researchgate.net/publication/251790229_MIGRATION_THEORY_FROM_A_SUPPLY-SIDE_PERSPECTIVE

Mihi-Ramirez, A., Gacia-Rodriguez, Y., & Cuenca-Garcia, E. (2016). *Innovation and international high skilled migration. Engineering economics.* KTU. https://doi.org/10.5755/j01.ee.27.4.14396

OECD. (2020). *Economic surveys: Lithuania.* Accessed from https://www.oecd-ilibrary.org/economics/oecd-economic-surveys-lithuania-2020_62663b1d-en

OECD. (2022). *Economic surveys: Lithuania.* Accessed from https://www.oecd-ilibrary.org/economics/oecd-economic-surveys-lithuania-2020_62663b1d-en

Okeke, E. N. (2013). Brain drains: Do economic conditions "push" doctors out of developing countries? *Social Science and Medicine, 98*, 169–178.

Runciman, W. G. (1966). Relative deprivation and social justice. A study of attitudes to social inequality in twentieth century England. *The British Journal of Sociology, 17*(4), 430–434.

Schulz, M. (2003). Pathways of relevance: Exploring inflows of knowledge into subunits of multinational corporations. *Organization Science, 14*(4), 440–459. https://doi.org/10.1287/orsc.14.4.440.17483

Wallace, S., et al. (1997). Migration as a consumption activity. *International Migration, 35*(1), 37–58.

Webber, C. (2007). Re-evaluating relative deprivation theory. *Theoretical Criminology, 11*(1), 97–120. https://doi.org/10.1177/1362480607072737

Yang, D. (2006, July). *Why do migrants return to poor countries? Evidence from Philippine migrants' responses to exchange rate shocks.* NBER Working Paper No. 12396.

Zhao, Y. (2002). Causes and consequences of return migration: Recent evidence from China. *Journal of Comparative Economics, 30*(2), 376–394.

CHAPTER 6

Lives on Hold Between the European Union and Ukraine: Ukrainian Migrants' Return Before and After the War

Jungwon Yeo and Olga Pysmenna

INTRODUCTION

The ongoing mass displacement of Ukrainians since the Russian invasion on February 24, 2022, has emerged as one of the most significant humanitarian crises in the world since the end of World War II. The war has compelled millions of Ukrainians to leave their home country. As of January 31, 2023, the United Nations High Commissioner for Refugees (UNHCR) reported that over 8 million Ukrainian refugees were scattered throughout Europe (UNHCR, 2023).

Since the onset of the war, European governments have implemented open-door policies, demonstrating a commendable commitment to solidarity and democratic principles by welcoming Ukrainian refugees. As of January 31, 2023, approximately 4.9 million Ukrainian refugees have

---

J. Yeo (✉) • O. Pysmenna
School of Public Administration, University of Central Florida, Orlando, FL, USA
e-mail: Jungwon.Yeo@ucf.edu; ol457564@ucf.edu

© The Author(s), under exclusive license to Springer Nature Switzerland AG 2024
J. Yeo (ed.), *Return Migration and Crises in Non-Western Countries*, Mobility & Politics,
https://doi.org/10.1007/978-3-031-53562-8_6

103

been granted temporary protection or an equivalent national protection status in Europe (UNHCR, 2023). Nevertheless, despite the concerted efforts of European nations, an estimated 3 million registered Ukrainian refugees in Europe still need essential humanitarian and healthcare assistance (Ukraine: Humanitarian response and regional refugee response plan, 2023). Moreover, as the war persists, it is expected that the unmet humanitarian needs of the Ukrainian population will continue to escalate, underscoring the pressing nature of the crisis. The refugee population in need may need to choose to return to Ukraine or remigrate to some other countries that they can have refuge and needed assistance.

In October 2022, the Ukrainian government issued an advisory urging its citizens to refrain from returning home. This precautionary measure was prompted by the devastating impact of Russian attacks, which destroyed 40% of the country's power stations, leading to widespread blackouts and heating problems (BBC News, 2022). Given the persisting security risks in Ukraine and the government's limited capacity to address the basic needs of its population, one might reasonably assume that Ukrainians would opt to prolong their stay abroad and postpone their return to their homeland.

However, multiple sources underscore the strong desire of Ukrainians to return back to Ukraine (German Federal Ministry of the Interior and Community, 2022; UNHCR, 2023). For instance, as of January 31, 2023, UNHCR reported that approximately 10 million Ukrainians had already chosen to return to their home country despite the ongoing war and the foreseeable threats and devastation in the country (Ukraine Situation Regional Refugee Response Plan, 2023). These return movements may not necessarily represent a sustainable or permanent return for Ukrainians (Ukraine: Humanitarian response and regional refugee response plan, 2023). Nonetheless, the sheer number of returnees indicates the unwavering determination and wants among Ukrainians to return home.

The return of displaced citizens will play a pivotal role in the post-war reconstruction of Ukraine. Once the war ends, the actual return of individuals may be compelled by mandates or enforced through legal regulations imposed by either Ukraine or the host countries where they presently reside. Yet, studies underscore many other factors that may affect migrants' return intentions (Toruńczyk-Ruiz & Brunarska, 2020). As Ukraine needs to prepare for its national rebuilding upon the war, it becomes crucial to understand the factors influencing the Ukrainian refugees' intention or decision regarding their return to homeland or remain in European countries.

This chapter explores Ukrainian return, remigration, or resettlement before and following the war caused by Russian invasion in February 2022. In particular, following Koser and Kuschminder (2015), we focus on investigating the role played by individual factors, structural determinants, and policy interventions in influencing Ukrainians' decision on resettlement in host countries or return to Ukraine. Employing a systematic content analysis method on publicly accessible data, we found that individual factors, especially the extent of familial and communal connections, have become the leading determinants of Ukrainian war refugees' return from European countries. Structural determinants and policy interventions, on the other hand, were the key factors of Ukrainian migrants' return during the pre-war period. The conclusion discusses some implications for post-war return preparation in Ukraine.

Determinants of Return

Human migration is the movement of individuals from one location to another to establish permanent or temporary residence in a new place (Anderson, 2019). Migration can occur voluntarily, motivated by personal aspirations for improved living conditions in other countries, including economic opportunities, political freedom, access to healthcare, and social prospects (Taran, 2001; Beaman et al., 2022) or self-realization in foreign contexts, such as obtaining better education opportunities and professional achievement. It can also be involuntary, forced by dire circumstances, and potential threats to people's lives, such as natural disasters, political oppression, technological catastrophes, military interventions, and wars (Hein, 1993; Jacobsen, 2006; Salehyan & Gleditsch, 2006).

Migration studies explain migration as a cycle between immigration and emigration. This cyclical approach considers return migration the final phase of the migration process (Olivier-Mensah & Scholl-Schneider, 2016). However, return migration is a continuing part of the migration process. Return migration can be permanent or volatile, existing, and repeating within the cycle of emigration and immigration. Migrants may plan their return with their emigration decision. It can develop slowly and voluntarily during the immigration process or occur abruptly or involuntarily due to emerging circumstances in the host country (Chandra, 1997; Olivier-Mensah & Scholl-Schneider, 2016). Returnees may subsequently leave their home countries again in response to different factors and circumstances upon their return. Therefore, return is not the final phase of the migration process but a continuing or revolving process within the migration cycle.

Migrants' return to their homeland is a complex and multidimensional process influenced by various interacting factors and reasons (Mohamed & Abdul-Talib, 2020; Tezcan, 2019). Studies often categorize the multidimensional causes into push/pull factors, which encourage and discourage people's migration or return decisions. However, migration is the function of multiple push/pull factors originating simultaneously and interdependently in transnational contexts. In addition, such push and pull factors exist at different levels and dimensions. In this regard, Koser and Kuschminder (2015) provide a framework that embeds transnational context (host and home countries) and categorizes multifaceted reasons and factors for return into three groups:

1. Structural factors (e.g., comparative social, economic, political, and security conditions of home and host countries).
2. Individual factors (e.g., migrants' capacity, emotions, and social connections in home and host countries).
3. Policy interventions (e.g., government policies and interventions that accommodate/segregate migrants in host and home countries).

We adopted Koser and Kuschminder's (2015) framework to explain the factors of Ukrainians' resettlement in their host country and return home before and after the war caused by the Russian invasion in February 2022. Prior to the analysis, we discuss the three-factor groups of the framework in the following subsections.

Structural Factors

Structural factors encompass social, economic, political, and security conditions in the host country compared to those in the home countries. The decision to return is made based on constant comparisons between the circumstances of the host and those of the home countries, including economic opportunities (Qehaja & Krasniqi, 2021), income differentials (Olesen, 2002), and social rights, such as employee rights (Koser & Kuschminder, 2015; Black et al., 2004). In addition, the level of access to diverse infrastructures and systems in the given circumstances becomes a cause for both emigration (accompanying resettlement in host countries) and return. For example, political restrictions and barriers in host countries, such as limited freedom of choice and expression, may affect migrants' return decisions, as those conditions in their home country became the critical factors of emigration (Klinthäll, 2007). Structural drivers of return migration also include inequitable access to public services and the labor market in host countries (Goodman & Wright, 2015). For those who were forced to emigrate due to war or terrorism, homeland security becomes a primary consideration for returning to their countries of origin (Arowolo, 2000; Fagen, 2011). The stability of systems, encompassing economic, political, institutional, and social aspects, of home and host countries influences migrants' return and resettlement decisions (Kaya & Orchard, 2020).

Individual Factors

Individual factors encompass perceptions, emotions, abilities, willingness, and knowledge of migrants and their social and cultural connections to wider communities (Koser & Kuschminder, 2015). In addition, numerous studies have emphasized the influence of individual psychological, emotional, and demographic factors on the decision to return (King & Christou, 2014; Mohamed & Abdul-Talib, 2020; Tezcan, 2018, 2019).

First, the level of emotional attachment or patriotism toward the home country needs to be examined when explaining return migration (Jeffery & Murison, 2011). The perception of the home plays a significant role, as it represents a place where they feel familiar, relaxed, and comfortable and can establish historical and personal connections and reclaim their identity (Wessendorf, 2007). Therefore, the stronger the emotional attachment to their home countries, the higher the chance for migrants to return home.

Second, studies discuss the effects of social and cultural connections to communities in their resettlement and return decisions. These connections encompass social or professional networks (Black et al., 2004), family ties, and community relations (Koser & Kuschminder, 2015) in host or home countries. In the host country, these community connections are crucial for migrants' economic, personal, emotional, and social integration. Particularly for refugees and asylum seekers, the impact of community support and affiliation is significant for both short-term adjustment and long-term settlement in foreign environment (Montgomery, 2011). Similarly, studies have observed a higher likelihood of return among migrants who lack social and professional connections in the host country but maintain active relationships and ties with family members and friends in their home country (King & Christou, 2014).

Third, individual factors also encompass individual migrants' demographic characteristics. Studies indicate that the decision to return may vary depending on migrants' age groups. Younger migrants, despite facing challenges, are more inclined to stay longer in their host countries due to the comparative advantages and benefits of remaining. Conversely, older migrants prioritize their social and familial connections and ties back home, leading them to choose to return.

Lastly, migrants' skill sets are another essential factor of resettlement that may impede return. Migrants with language skills have better access to social systems, such as healthcare, education services, and job markets, in host countries. Language proficiency also facilitates communication with the local population and enables migrants to establish or join support networks (Tezcan, 2018, 2019).

Policy Interventions

Government interventions play a crucial role in determining whether migrants resettle in host country or return home (Thielemann, 2012). Migration policies, such as integration or resettlement programs, aim to help migrants adapt to their new contexts and may discourage them from returning. Likewise, return support and benefits from the home country may facilitate migrants' return.

Migration policies and the subsequent public services of host countries ensure that migrants' immediate needs are met. The policies guide local governments, nonprofits, and faith-based organizations to provide migrants with direct services and benefits, such as legal assistance, housing, public services, healthcare, and education. These direct services and benefits are essential for the initial resettlement and integration of migrants, especially for refugees who lack the necessary resources in their new environment. The policy interventions can mediate between structural determinants and migrants' return intentions, particularly influencing migrants' perceptions of structural conditions and circumstances in their host country. As a result, migrants are more likely to return home or relocate to other countries if they do not have sufficient level of access to these essential provisions (Black & Gent, 2006).

In addition, host countries implement policies that aim to prepare newcomers to become productive and contributing members of their societies in the long term. These policies include various training opportunities and access to job markets, which can help increase refugees' economic engagement (Baez, 2011) and enable them to become catalysts for economic growth and development (Kibreab, 1985). In this sense, these policy interventions can mediate the individual factors of return by helping migrants obtain or utilize their skills, achieve their societal and economic goals, and establish professional networks. As a result, adequate and proactive policy interventions may encourage migrants to remain in host countries rather than return home.

Furthermore, policies and the accompanying programs and services can help foster intercultural understanding between the host society and migrants (Phillimore, 2011; Yeo, 2022, 2023). Intercultural learning programs and events can promote cultural awareness and sensitivity among migrants and native residents, mitigating potential conflicts and tensions arising from cultural misunderstandings. These interventions also create opportunities for migrants to develop personal relationships with native residents and establish supportive communities in host countries (Yeo, 2022, 2023). As a result, these policies are more likely to enhance migrants' chances of remaining in host countries rather than returning home.

Conversely, studies have shown that more restrictive policies are associated with lower rates of refugees and asylum seekers (Neumayer, 2004). Insufficient policy support can lead to limited access to employment, education, and housing opportunities for refugees in their host countries (Whyte & Hirslund, 2013), resulting in social and economic immobility and isolation (Tazreiter, 2019). Policy responses aimed at rapid integration may place excessive pressure on refugees, potentially causing stress and mental health issues (Phillimore, 2011). Some policy interventions can promote negative narratives or images about refugees, further limiting opportunities and fostering isolation (Shaw & Funk, 2019).

Methodology

We employed a qualitative study design to understand the determinants of Ukrainian migration and return before and after the war. Qualitative study designs offer a comprehensive understanding of social phenomena, including detailed context, processes, and outcomes (Yin, 2011, 2015). The data used in this study were obtained from various publicly available data sources, including government reports, policy briefs, legal acts, white papers, and media/press reports, especially covering the period from February 2022 to January 2023 for the post-war data. We employed qualitative content analysis techniques (Forman & Damschroder, 2007; Mayring, 2004) to examine how the individual, structural, and policy factors influenced Ukrainians' choices to stay in or leave their host countries or return to Ukraine.

Ukrainians' Emigration and Return

Pre-war

Emigration has always been a significant trend in Ukraine, but it has become even more so since its independence in 1991 (Kubal, 2015). Facing the structural instability of the country (i.e., significant economic hardship, social and political instability) following the process of national independence, a large number of Ukrainians left the country in search of new economic opportunities and lives in Western countries since the 1990s (Lapshyna, 2022).

Between 2005 and 2008, approximately 1.5 million Ukrainians left the country permanently to work abroad. Then, Ukrainian migrant workers increased by 1.2 million between 2010 and 2012 (Jaroszewicz, 2015). Then, about 3.3 million Ukrainians left the country following the Russian military aggression in 2014 (Tyshchuk, 2018). As of 2020, the size of the Ukrainian diaspora has increased to 6.6 million worldwide (United Nations Department of Economic and Social Affairs, 2021). These statistics make Ukraine the eighth most significant migrant-sending country in the world (McAuliffe & Triandafyllidou, 2021; Van Mol et al., 2018).

During the pre-war period, the interaction between structural factors and policy interventions has been the primary inhibitor of Ukrainians' return. First, Ukrainian migrant workers permanently left the country due to economic hardship, such as high unemployment and low income, caused by the lack of development in relevant infrastructures and markets (Vianello, 2014; Portnikov, 2018). Second, the policy interventions of EU countries (e.g., visa waivers and eased work permit regulations) facilitated the long-term settlement of Ukrainian workers who need and want economic and financial stability.

In addition, the returns of Ukrainian migrant workers who left the country temporarily were often delayed due to structural factors. According to Vianello (2014), Ukrainian migrant workers, particularly female domestic workers in their 40s and 50s, intended to engage in short-term labor emigration. Initially, they expected to return home within one to two years of working abroad. However, the study found that the actual duration of their stay abroad was at least four years. In many cases, Ukrainian migrant workers postponed their return plans and extended their stay in host countries to send more remittances home.

In the case of actual returns of Ukrainian migrants, the interplay between structural factors and policy interventions was still a significant factor during the pre-war period. Among the returnees, retiree migrant workers were back in Ukraine to secure their national pensions, as they were unlikely to receive retirement benefits in their host countries. In addition, Ukrainian migrant workers returned to their home country when facing a lack of policy support, such as necessary healthcare for treatment and rehabilitation abroad (Libanova, 2019). Many host countries did not grant full labor protections to these returnees, who had previously been migrant workers (Libanova, 2019). Without sufficient labor protection, Ukrainian migrant workers lacked access to unemployment benefits and were often left uncompensated for job-related accidents or disabilities. However, Ukraine provides universal healthcare to its nationals. Therefore, Ukrainian migrants who needed healthcare and other social services returned.

Post-war

Since the full-scale war in Ukraine, about 18 million citizens have left the country and about 10 million have returned amid the war (UNHCR, 2023). Before the war, about 26% of Ukrainians desired to immigrate to another country (Elinder et al., 2022). People dreamed of having better economic opportunities abroad, particularly in EU countries. Since the war, the situation drove Ukrainians out to the dream places they always wanted to be. But many people returned regardless, and many more are planning to return.

The abrupt immigration to new countries might involve some challenges, e.g., status or employment, language issues, and immediate needs for different social and financial assistance for Ukrainian refugees to resettle in their host countries. According to a study conducted by the UNHCR (as shown in Table 6.1), refugees face a list of challenges and urgent needs, i.e., cash, employment, accommodation, and material assistance. The

Table 6.1 Ukrainian refugees' urgent needs and intention

Rank	Urgent needs	Stay (63%)	Leave (9%)	Return (15%)
1	Cash (49%)	Safety (46%)	Family ties (30%)	Improved situation in Ukraine (26%)
2	Employment (36%)	Family ties (15%)	Safety (20%)	Financial reasons (13%)
3	Accommodation (33%)	Employment (7%)	Employment (17%)	Other (11%)
4	Material assistance (26%)	Asylum procedure (6%)	Community ties (9%)	Reunite with family (11%)
5	Healthcare (23%)	Community ties (5%)	Asylum procedure (9%)	Family visit (8%)
6	Food (15%)	Language (5%)	Advised (6%)	Advised by family (6%)
7	Education (14%)	Other (5%)	Other (4%)	Family evacuation (5%)
8	Family reunification (10%)	Close to Ukraine (4%)	Education (2%)	Employment (5%)
9	Legal advice (8%)	Advised (3%)	Language (2%)	Education (3%)
10	Information about services (8%)	Education (3%)		Healthcare (2%)

Source: UNHCR (2023). Regional Protection Profiling & Monitoring Factsheet: Profiles, Needs & Intentions of Refugees from Ukraine

challenges and needs, however, are common in any immigration process. In normalcy, migrants often overcome those issues with strong a desire to survive and achieve their goals in their dream countries. In addition, unlike other recent migration crises, i.e., Syrian war refugees, most European countries have provided immense policy and social support to Ukrainian refugees. Therefore, structural factors (e.g., economic hardship and financial difficulty) and policy intervention facing the refugees may not explain fully the reasons for their return.

The crisis, the Russian invasion of Ukraine, has reshaped the reasons behind the return of Ukrainian migrants. Currently, individual factors have a significant impact on Ukrainian refugees' intention and decision to return. In particular, the involuntary departure could have strengthened the impact of migrants' emotional and psychological aspects on their return decision. The process of forced emigration also caused people's involuntary and unprecedented separations from their families, communities, and country. As the war refugees' initial departure was not by their choice, and they left many things behind in Ukraine, most war refugees desire to return home and be reunited with their families and relatives rather than resettle in the host countries (Panchenko & Poutvaara, 2022). The statistics shown in Table 6.1 support that Ukrainian war refugees prioritize family ties and social connections over their economic and financial status in their lives halted between European countries and Ukraine.

In the same line, refugees may choose to return regardless of the war-torn situation in Ukraine if they face challenges in making family and social connections in their host country. Additionally, other challenges that the refugees encountered in host countries, whether personal, systemic, or structural, may amplify refugees' doubts about their value and sense of belonging in the host country. The emotions and thoughts together with physical challenges could also lead the refugees to return to their war-torn homeland (Mohamed & Abdul-Talib, 2020; Tsuda, 2010).

Lastly, the patriotism among Ukrainians became much stronger after the full-scale Russian invasion than ever before.

There is no Ukraine, no second Dnipro. (Visit Ukraine, 2023).

Ukrainian refugees are returning to the country, longing for the improved domestic (war) situation and country's independence. Especially, younger generations aged between 18 and 35 have strong willingness to return to restore and rebuild Ukraine as an independent country (Rubryka, 2023, September 28).

Conclusion

Close to 6 million Ukrainians' lives are on hold between the European Union and Ukraine since the Russian invasion of Ukraine in February 2022. Since then, many European countries have welcomed Ukrainian refugees, responding to their urgent needs. Temporary protection status accompanied by monthly social benefits, cash allowances, accommodation subsidies, and open job market and education systems have helped Ukrainian refugees sustain their lives in the host countries.

Migration studies often explain emigration and return as a function of the interplay between structural factors (i.e., domestic financial or economic situations in home countries) and host countries' policy intervention. However, this chapter finds that the determinants of return may change depending on how the emigration started. Had it not been for the war in Ukraine or forced migration, all the benefits provided by the host countries' policies might have significantly prevented or slowed Ukrainian migrants from returning home. In normalcy, such proactive policy efforts by host countries help migrants address their own needs (economic prosperity or financial security) and overcome the structural barriers they face in resettlement or integration challenges in the host countries. However, in the case of forced migration, especially when it causes involuntary family and community separation, migrants may value their family, social, and community connections more than their economic prosperity or political freedom when deciding to return to their home countries.

> *It is huge to take a train from a peaceful EU country with a child to your home where the air alarm rings every day. But we are still going to kindergarten and trying to find the best football section. We explain a new reality to kids while having Zoom calls at work and still taking kids to the best sweets. It is all about care, bravery, love, and adjusting to a new reality. (Conkling, 2022)*

As the quote above shows, some Ukrainian migrants are willing to return and reestablish their personal, family, and communal lives in Ukraine regardless of the current situation in Ukraine. The findings on Ukraine's strong willingness to return are very hopeful for Ukraine as a nation because the returnees will be essential contributors to Ukraine's restoration and rebuilding process in the near future.

In response to Ukrainian refugees' strong willingness to return, it is necessary to have some systematic preparation for accommodating those returnees. It may be impossible for the Ukrainian government to build such a system for its citizens' returns now. However, EU countries and other countries supporting Ukraine can initiate the return preparation in coordination with the Ukrainian government.

Current host countries can develop and add some programs that assist in the long-term returns and reestablishment of Ukrainian refugees. For example, capacity-building initiatives for future returnees may include technical assistance, training programs, and information exchange platforms. These capacity-building programs for individual returnees can contribute to the recovery of Ukrainian infrastructure and economy.

Other countries can contribute to the return initiative by providing more humanitarian aid to Ukraine, focusing on addressing the urgent needs of returnees, such as essential food supplies, healthcare services, accommodation assistance, and education for the younger generation in

Ukraine. They can also collaborate with the Ukrainian government to develop and implement comprehensive reintegration policies and return programs for war refugees. By supporting refugees in rebuilding their lives in their home country, these countries can facilitate Ukrainian refugees' smooth transition back to Ukraine and the nation-rebuilding and reconstruction process in Ukraine.

References

Anderson, B. (2019). New directions in migration studies: Towards methodological de-nationalism. *Comparative Migration Studies, 7*(1), 1–13.

Arowolo, O. O. (2000). Return migration and the problem of reintegration. *International Migration, 38*(5), 59–82.

Baez, J. E. (2011). Civil wars beyond their borders: The human capital and health consequences of hosting refugees. *Journal of Development Economics, 96*(2), 391–408.

BBC News. (2022, October 25). *Ukraine war refugees asked not to return this winter*. BBC News. Accessed from https://www.bbc.com/news/world-europe-63389270

Beaman, L., Onder, H., & Onder, S. (2022). When do refugees return home? Evidence from Syrian displacement in Mashreq. *Journal of Development Economics, 155*, 102802.

Black, R., & Gent, S. (2006). Sustainable return in post-conflict contexts. *International Migration, 44*(3), 15–38.

Black, R., Koser, K., Munk, K., Atfield, G., D'Onofrio, L., & Tiemoko, R. (2004). *Understanding voluntary return*. Home Office Publications.

Chandra, V. P. (1997). Remigration: Return of the prodigals—An analysis of the impact of the cycles of migration and remigration on caste mobility. *International Migration Review, 31*(1), 162–170.

Conkling, A. (2022, September 15). 'You feel trapped': Why some Ukrainian refugees are now heading home. *Euronews*. Accessed from https://www.euronews.com/my-europe/2022/09/15/you-feel-trapped-why-some-ukrainian-refugees-are-now-heading-home

Elinder, M., Erixson, O., & Hammar, O. (2022). *How large will the Ukrainian refugee flow be, and which EU countries will they seek refuge in?. Delmi Policy Brief, 3*.

Fagen, P. W. (2011). *Refugees and IDPs after conflict*. US Institute of Peace.

Forman, J., & Damschroder, L. (2007). Qualitative content analysis. In *Empirical methods for bioethics: A primer* (Vol. 11, pp. 39–62). Emerald Group Publishing.

German Federal Ministry of the Interior and Community. (2022, April 6). *Survey of Ukrainian War Refugees*. Federal Ministry of the Interior and Community.

Accessed from https://www.bmi.bund.de/SharedDocs/kurzmeldungen/EN/2022/04/survey-ukraine.html

Goodman, S. W., & Wright, M. (2015). Does mandatory integration matter? Effects of civic requirements on immigrant socio-economic and political outcomes. *Journal of Ethnic and Migration Studies, 41*(12), 1885–1908.

Hein, J. (1993). Refugees, immigrants, and the state. *Annual Review of Sociology, 19*(1), 43–59.

Jacobsen, K. (2006). Refugees and asylum seekers in urban areas: A livelihoods perspective. *Journal of Refugee Studies, 19*(3), 273–286.

Jaroszewicz, M. (2015). *The migration of Ukrainians in times of crisis. OSW COMMENTARY Number 187, 2015-10-19.*

Jeffery, L., & Murison, J. (2011). The temporal, social, spatial, and legal dimensions of return and onward migration. *Population, Space and Place, 17*(2), 131–139.

Kaya, S., & Orchard, P. (2020). Prospects of return: The case of Syrian refugees in Germany. *Journal of Immigrant & Refugee Studies, 18*(1), 95–112.

Kibreab, G. (1985). *African refugees: Reflections on the African refugee problem.* Africa World Press.

King, R., & Christou, A. (2014). Second-generation "return" to Greece: New dynamics of transnationalism and integration. *International Migration, 52*(6), 85–99.

Klinthäll, M. (2007). Refugee return migration: Return migration from Sweden to Chile, Iran, and Poland 1973–1996. *Journal of Refugee Studies, 20*(4), 579–598.

Koser, K., & Kuschminder, K. (2015). *Comparative research on the assisted voluntary return and reintegration of migrants* (Vol. 343). International Organization for Migration.

Kubal, A. (2015). Legal consciousness as a form of social remittance? Studying return migrants' everyday practices of legality in Ukraine. *Migration Studies, 3*(1), 68–88.

Lapshyna, I. (2022). Migration and Diaspora at Times of Crisis: Public Perceptions of Emigrants in Ukraine. In *Diaspora Engagement in Times of Severe Economic Crisis: Greece and Beyond* (pp. 405–431). Cham: Springer International Publishing.

Libanova, E. (2019). Labour migration from Ukraine: Key features, drivers, and impact. *Economics and Sociology, 12*(1), 313–328.

Mayring, P. (2004). Qualitative content analysis. *A Companion to Qualitative Research, 1*(2), 159–176.

McAuliffe, M., & Triandafyllidou, A. (Eds.). (2021). *World migration report 2022.* International Organization for Migration (IOM). Accessed April 26, 2022, from https://publications.iom.int/system/files/pdf/WMR-2022.pdf

Mohamed, M. A., & Abdul-Talib, A. N. (2020). Push-pull factors influencing international return migration intentions: A systematic literature review. *Journal of Enterprising Communities: People and Places in the Global Economy, 14*(2), 231–246.

Montgomery, E. (2011). Trauma, exile and mental health in young refugees. *Acta Psychiatrica Scandinavica, 124*, 1–46.

Neumayer, E. (2004). Asylum destination choice: What makes some west European countries more attractive than others? *European Union Politics, 5*(2), 155–180.

Olesen, H. (2002). Migration, Return, and Development: An Institutional Perspective. *International Migration, 40*(5), 125–150.

Olivier-Mensah, C., & Scholl-Schneider, S. (2016). Transnational return? On the interrelation of family, remigration, and transnationality – An introduction. *Transnational Social Review, 6*(1–2), 2–9.

Panchenko, T., & Poutvaara, P. (2022). Intentions to stay and employment prospects of refugees from Ukraine. *EconPol Policy Brief, 46*(6), 1–15.

Phillimore, J. (2011). Refugees, acculturation strategies, stress, and integration. *Journal of Social Policy, 40*(3), 575–593.

Portnikov, V. (2018). *Asians will come instead of Ukrainians. Libanova about labour emigration from Ukraine [Замість українців прийдуть азійці – Лібанова про трудову міграцію з України].* Accessed August 31, 2023, from https://www.radiosvoboda.org/a/29202444.html

Qehaja, D., & Krasniqi, A. (2021). Who is Most likely to Remigrate? Evidence from Kosovo's returned migrants. *International Journal of Economics & Business Administration (IJEBA), 9*(4), 98–110.

Rubryka. (2023, September 28). Poll: 89% of young people plan to build their future in Ukraine. https://rubryka.com/en/2023/09/28/opytuvannya-bilsha-chastyna-molodi-v-ukrayini-ne-hoche-pereyizhdzhaty-a-89-bachyt-svoye-majbutnye-v-ridnij-krayini/

Salehyan, I., & Gleditsch, K. S. (2006). Refugees and the spread of civil war. *International Organization, 60*(2), 335–366.

Shaw, S. A., & Funk, M. (2019). A systematic review of social service programs serving refugees. *Research on Social Work Practice, 29*(8), 847–862.

Taran, P. A. (2001). Human rights of migrants: Challenges of the new decade. *International Migration, 38*(6), 7–51.

Tazreiter, C. (2019). Temporary migrants as an uneasy presence in immigrant societies: Reflections on ambivalence in Australia. *International Journal of Comparative Sociology, 60*(1–2), 91–109.

Tezcan, T. (2018). 'I (do not) know what to do': How ties, identities and home states influence Mexican-born immigrants' return migration intentions. *Migration and Development, 7*(3), 388–411.

Tezcan, T. (2019). Return home? Determinants of return migration intention amongst Turkish immigrants in Germany. *Geoforum, 98*, 189–201.
Thielemann, E. R. (2012). How effective are national and EU policies in the area of forced migration? *Refugee Survey Quarterly, 31*(4), 21–37.
Toruńczyk-Ruiz, S., & Brunarska, Z. (2020). Through attachment to settlement: Social and psychological determinants of migrants' intentions to stay. *Journal of Ethnic and Migration Studies, 46*(15), 3191–3209.
Tsuda, T. (2010). Ethnic return migration and the nation-state: Encouraging the diaspora to return 'home'. *Nations and Nationalism, 16*(4), 616–636.
Tyshchuk, T. (2018). *The great migration: No one in Ukraine knows how many of our compatriots have moved abroad*. Accessed August 31, 2023, from https://voxukraine.org/en/the-great-migration-no-one-in-ukraine-knows-how-many-of-our-compatriots-have-moved-abroad/
Ukraine | United Nations Department of Economic and Social Affairs. (2021). Accessed from https://sdgs.un.org/statements/ukraine-15148
Ukraine Situation Regional Refugee Response Plan. (2023). Global Focus. Accessed from https://reporting.unhcr.org/ukraine-situation-regional-refugee-response-plan
Ukraine: Humanitarian response and regional refugee response plan summary. (2023). Global Focus. Accessed from https://reporting.unhcr.org/ukraine-humanitarian-response-and-regional-refugee-response-plan-summary
United Nations High Commissioner for Refugees (UNHCR). *Ukraine refugee situation*. Operational Data Portal. Accessed February 6, 2023., from https://data.unhcr.org/en/situations/ukraine
Van Mol, C., Snel, E., Hemmerechts, K., & Timmerman, C. (2018). Migration aspirations and migration cultures: A case study of Ukrainian migration towards the European Union. *Population, Space, and Place, 24*(5), e2131.
Vianello, F. A. (2014). Ukrainian migrant workers in Italy: Coping with and reacting to downward mobility. *Central and Eastern European Migration Review, 3*(1), 85–98.
Visit Ukraine. (2023, May 11). *Why Ukrainian refugees are returning home: Importance reasons*. Accessed September 1, 2023, from https://visitukraine.today/blog/1825/why-ukrainian-refugees-are-returning-home-important-reasons#:~:text=Ukrainians%20highly%20value%20family%20ties,return%20because%20of%20their%20family
Wessendorf, S. (2007). 'Roots migrants': Transnationalism and 'return' among second-generation Italians in Switzerland. *Journal of Ethnic and Migration Studies, 33*(7), 1083–1102.
Whyte, Z., & Hirslund, D. V. (2013). *International experiences with the sustainable assisted return of rejected asylum seekers (No. 2013: 13). DIIS report*.

Yeo, J. (2022). Beyond immigration and customs enforcement: Understanding interorganizational collaboration for border management. *Journal of Borderlands Studies, 37*(5), 975–997.

Yeo, J. (2023). Interorganizational coordination for immigrant integration into local society. *Journal of International Migration and Integration, 24*, 567–585.

Yin, R. K. (2011). *Applications of case study research*. Sage.

Yin, R. K. (2015). *Qualitative research from start to finish*. Guilford.

CHAPTER 7

Family Return Migration from Europe to Turkey in the Time of Crises

Filiz Kunuroglu and Demet Vural Yüzbaşı

Introduction

Over the past decade, residents of Turkey have experienced multiple crises like economic crises and recession, mass migration from Syria, political crises with several European countries, and the COVID-19 pandemic. These crises, as important but neglected aspects of the migration phenomena, have rarely been addressed in return migration literature. Further, return migration has been mostly perceived as an individual decision ignoring the familial embeddedness of the returnees and therefore studies have failed to capture the interconnectedness of the families (Konzett-Smoliner, 2016). This chapter addresses these gaps in the literature by investigating the role of crises and families in the return migration processes of Turkish migrants from Europe.

The huge diversity of migrant categories such as refugees, asylum seekers, expats, and students necessitate close analysis of the distinct types of

---

F. Kunuroglu (✉) • D. V. Yüzbaşı
Izmir Katip Celebi University, İzmir, Turkey
e-mail: filiz.kunuroglu@ikc.edu.tr; demet.vural.yuzbasi@ikcu.edu.tr

© The Author(s), under exclusive license to Springer Nature Switzerland AG 2024
J. Yeo (ed.), *Return Migration and Crises in Non-Western Countries*, Mobility & Politics,
https://doi.org/10.1007/978-3-031-53562-8_7

returns. Return migration has been defined in diverse ways by different scholars. However, in this chapter we focus on voluntary return and opt for the definition of Dustmann and Weiss (2007) who define return migration as a situation where the migrants return to their home country, by their own will, after a considerable time abroad (Dustmann & Weiss, 2007). The word 'return' is largely used within inverted commas to show the unique experiences of subsequent generations who actually return to the countries of their parents, though they have never lived (King & Christou, 2011). Subsequent generations refer to 1.5-, second-, and third-generation immigrants. The 1.5 generation refers to Turkish migrants who came to Europe as children, the second generation are born in Europe but have parents who are born in Turkey, and the third generation refers to immigrants whose grandparents are born in Turkey. Therefore, as home country might have different connotations for different generations, we refer to Turkey when we use the term home country and refer to Europe when we use the term host country to avoid ambiguity throughout the text. Similarly, 'return' for all generations refers to moving from Western Europe to Turkey.

Previous studies have revealed that major economical and geopolitical events tend to lead to a substantial increase in migration rates (Massey et al., 1999). In line with it, the Global Economic crises after 2008, the refugee crises after 2014, and Brexit were reported to have a profound effect on migration patterns within Europe (Apsite-Berina et al., 2020; King, 2018), creating more diversified and variegated migration and return migration patterns (King, 2018).

Reasons and Consequences of Return Migration

Previous studies pointed at economic and financial gaps between the home and host countries and perceived economic and professional prospects in the destination country as the main motives of migration (Todaro, 1969). Therefore, return migration was initially interpreted as a failure of immigrants and occurring as a result of the discrepancy between the expected earning and the reality (Todaro, 1969). Although economical perspectives provided valuable insight on return migration motivations and experiences upon return, recent studies on motives for return migration illustrate that return is triggered by multiple, interrelated factors. Therefore, these studies highlight the need to focus on the psychological, personal, and familial factors as well as economic factors in return migration decision (Yehuda-Sternfeld & Mirsky, 2014, p. 54).

For several groups, ethnic ties and emotional reasons were reported to act as pull factors for return migrants. Second-generation Greek migrants from Germany listed lifestyle, family reasons, and life stage (King et al., 2011) and Japanese return migrants from Brazil reported their previous social network and ethnic ties as their individual motives for return (Tsuda, 2009). Similarly, many Turkish return migrants reported to have returned as they wanted their children to keep their ethnic ties and adapt to Turkish education system (Kunuroglu et al., 2018). As well as individual and familial factors, contextual reasons such as economic and social crises and the negative climate created afterward in the host countries push migrants to their home countries. To illustrate, Bolognani (2007) reported that second-generation Pakistani migrants perceive their home countries as a way of escaping from stigmatization after 9/11. Negative social atmosphere in the immigrated country creates integration problems as well as difficulties in sense of belonging to the host country.

On the other hand, studies on post return experiences of immigrants report most migrants who live for years with a dream of return tend to realize the dream may turn into an experience of disappointment. Yehuda-Sternfeld and Mirsky (2014) reported that Israeli returnees from US tended to seek for identity and belonging in their home countries but deeply disappointed due to challenging experiences upon return. The contextual factors in the home countries such as economic or political crises might create a discriminatory atmosphere toward return migrants. Christou and King (2006) stated that return experiences trigger similar feelings of exclusion and alienation that the first generation experienced in the Western cities. In studies on Irish return migrants, the majority of respondents reported to have problems about belonging due to the negative attitudes of non-migratory Irish peers (Ní Laoire, 2008; Ralph, 2012).

Acculturation and Re-acculturation

When immigrants enter a new society, they go through an acculturation process, which is defined as "the process of cultural change that occurs when individuals from different cultural backgrounds come into prolonged, continuous, first-hand contact with each other" (Redfield et al., 1936, p. 149). According to Berry's acculturation model (1997), immigrants face two major issues in the immigrated context: maintaining their culture of origin and adopting the values of the host society with a desire to develop close relations with the members of the new group. The ability to form a multifaceted identity incorporating both identities is associated with less stress (Berry, 1997), higher levels of mental and physical health (Virta et al., 2004), and better psychological and sociocultural adaptation (Nguyen & Benet-Martinez, 2012). According to Searle and Ward (1990), psychological adaptation refers to feelings of feeling well in the new context, and sociocultural adaptation refers to the ability to fit in to the host culture.

When migrants return to their homelands, a process of re-acculturation begins (Dona & Ackermann, 2006). Re-acculturation is defined as the readjustment to one's own culture (or culture of origin) after having lived in another culture for a significant period of time. It is widely stated that continuous intercultural contact in returned context also leads to challenges, that is, re-acculturating individuals experience the acculturative stressors at the second time upon return. Return migrants need to renegotiate their behaviors and values. Their orientations toward heritage and host cultures influence both their psychological and sociocultural adaptation (Ward & Geeraert, 2016). The re-acculturation process is a rather multilayered process (Kunuroglu et al., 2015; Sussman, 2000). Migrants will have developed partly or entirely new identities during the migration period (Kim, 2001; Sussman, 2000), which makes their re-acculturation experience different from—and sometimes more complicated than—their original acculturation experience in the host country.

Turkish Return Migration from Europe

Starting from the early 1960s, hundreds of thousands of Turkish workers migrated to European countries. The flow started with the bilateral labor agreements with European countries which required the so-called Gasterbeiter (German for guest worker) to stay for a couple of years and then return to Turkey. However, the rotation principle did not work out for both sides and most Turkish migrants stayed for much longer time periods than they had expected (Abadan-Unat, 2006). Turkey is the ethnic origin of one of the largest immigrant communities with currently more than 3.5 million people with Turkish ethnic origin residing in Europe (İçduygu, 2012). The profiles of contemporary Turkish-origin immigrants, especially of the third generation, are quite different from guest worker stereotype of the past. They are more familiar and comfortable with both cultures and actively involved in dynamic business sector and social life (Kaya & Kentel, 2008). Still, they face particular challenges in European context as a result of economic and socio-political crises. They tend to face considerable social and educational exclusion that arises from government policies (e.g., the imposition of official languages and consequent devaluation of minority language) and immigration policies (e.g., assimilationism), and their image has suffered from the Islamophobic and racializing discourse in Western media particularly following 9/11 and other terrorist acts (Kılıç & Menjívar, 2013).

Return migration of Turkish citizens from Europe is not a new phenomenon. Between 1980 and 1999, approximately 1.5 million emigrants including rejected asylum seekers returned to Turkey (TUSIAD, 2006). Return migration is still ongoing to date and around 30,000 migrants of Turkish origin are reported to return to Turkey only from Germany every year (Bundesamt für Migration und Flüchtlinge (BAMF), 2016), and therefore, return migration is an important phenomenon influencing large numbers of people in contemporary Turkey, which requires close academic attention.

This study sets out to find the answer to the following questions:

1. Why have Turkish immigrants in Europe returned to Turkey and what are their migratory plans?
2. Which aspects of home/host country function as push/pull factors in return migration decision?
3. To what extent have the current multifaceted crises (financial, the public health) influenced reintegration process of Turkish returnees?

Method

Participants

Nine participants who returned from Europe to Turkey after 2016 were recruited in this study. The two-step snowball sampling method was used. First, the study was announced via social media and volunteer participants were included in the study. They were asked whether they could assist in identifying other potential participants. The circular migration where migrants spend several months in both countries was the exclusion criteria. Only migrants who return permanently were included in the study. The personal characteristics of the participants are presented in Table 7.1.

Table 7.1 Demographic characteristics of the participants

	Age	Gender	Marital status	Generation	Date of return migration	Host country	Duration of residence in Europe
P1	52	Female	Married	First	2020	Switzerland	14 years
P2	67	Male	Married	First	2020	Switzerland	44 years
P3	24	Female	Single	Third	2017	Germany	19 years
P4	27	Female	Single	Second	2018	England	16 years
P5	33	Female	Married	Third	2020	Germany	30 years
P6	28	Female	Single	Third	2020	Germany	26 years
P7	29	Female	Married	Third	2016	Germany	23 years
P8	52	Male	Married	First	2017	Germany	37 years
P9	35	Female	Married	Third	2020	Germany	33 years

Data Collection and Instrumentation

Ethics committee approval was obtained from the Social Research Ethics Committee of the university in order to conduct interviews with the participants who returned to Turkey with their families. Then, an announcement was made through an online platform and the data collection process was started. Before the interviews, the purpose of the study was explained to the participants, and they were informed that the results of the study could be used in scientific publications. The interviews were conducted face to face and via zoom at a predetermined date and time. The interviews started with an open-ended question concerning the migration history of the respondents or their families. Subsequently, a flexible interview guide—which included key topics and questions—was used for gathering information. A wide range of topics were discussed, including respondents' initial migration motives, their life in the host country, their reasons and preparation for return, their experiences upon return, the role of their families in the decision-making process, and their personal plans for their future. The interviews lasted 45 minutes in average. The interviews were conducted between October and November 2022 in Izmir and were recorded and transcribed.

Analysis

Inductive analysis method was used for qualitative data analysis, and it is aimed to base the results completely on the data and the experiences and the perspectives of the participants (Thomas, 2006). The data obtained from the interviews were analyzed with the thematic analysis (Braun & Clarke, 2006). First, the data obtained during the interviews were transcribed and organized. After reading the data set, the initial ideas were noted. Second, the initial codes were generated by collating meaningful data units in the data. Third, the codes were collated into potential themes. Then, the thematic map of the analysis was generated. After refining the themes, each theme was defined and named. Lastly, after selecting extracts, the report was produced.

Results

The themes reported by the participants in terms of their experiences of return migration amid multifaceted crises revealed four main clusters: reasons for return, the readaptation process in Turkey, cultural differences in parenting experiences, and issues related to the crisis.

Reasons for Return

The participants conveyed a wide range of factors affecting their decision to return to Turkey. When the responses are examined, these factors could be categorized under two basic dimensions as pull and push factors; the factors that push the participants to return and the factors that attract participants to return to Turkey. Both push and pull factors are discussed from individual, familial, and contextual perspectives.

From an individual point of view, one of the push factors was the strong concern about losing their own or their children's ethnic ties and ethnic identities. Not feeling at home was a major concern for most participants. They stated that they never felt like they belonged to the migrated country, while participant below expressed this concern as a mother with the following words:

> *Because we never felt like we belonged to anywhere. It comes to mind right now, as I speak. I didn't want my child to experience this. I wanted to let him know his place. Because you are neither from here, nor from there, in Germany. It's like you don't have a place(home) like this. (P5)*

Most participants reported that they or their families always had a dream of return. The return plan was reported to be an item on their agenda all the time, and their stay in Europe was perceived temporary even it lasts a lifetime. Two third-generation participants explained what they and their families went through with these words:

> *My father continued to stay there, of necessity. But it (return) was always a dream... 'We will return, we will not stay.' This is how we grew up even for that reason. You know, this is not our home, don't settle down. For example, if something breaks, nothing can be said like 'let's buy a new one.' 'We can't handle it. We'll go anyway, let's not buy stuff here.' I've always grown up like that, I've always been like this since I knew myself. (P3)*

Similarly, some participants stated that they waited for quite some time to actualize the return plan.

> *I've been wanting to return for a long time, I waited 20 years. My wife said let the children grow up, or etc. Our children grew up, so when our little son wanted it, my wife came too. (P8)*

Loneliness was another issue reported by respondents. Some of the participants reported that they felt isolated in the host county. Especially being away from their families and home country was stated to be challenging for them. A participant who immigrated to Europe due to marriage expressed these feelings as follows:

> *You are alone, there is no family there. In other words, for example, you are just giving birth, other people's mothers come and help but you also need that. You make some friends, okay, it's not an issue. However, one feels very lonely without family there. (P1)*

In addition to the abovementioned individual factors, a perceived cultural distance between the home and the host country such as more severe weather conditions in the host context and perceived difficulties in the education system compared to Turkish system and differences in the practices in private and public domains were other push factors. Most participants expressed that they perceive the life more monotonous in the migrated country. Although the rules were stated to bring ease to their lives at one side, they stated that they missed the flexibility of a rich social life in Turkey. The quotation below illustrates a similar experience:

We also go to work and come home back here, of course. You know, there is a monotony here, too. However, there's more extreme out there. In fact, I like discipline, I like order, but there is too much. I mean, it's so boring.... That's extreme. How can I say? Everything will be on time; you will sleep at this time. You will get up at this time, so I can't afford to be even a minute late, it's punished immediately. (P7)

To illustrate, one of the family-related factors that pushes the participants to leave the host country is acculturation gap experienced by the individual. As the parents were reluctant to integrate to the host culture, they seemed to feel frustrated not to get involved in the cultural practices of the country that they live in. One participant stated that the differentiation of his/her family's acculturation level challenged her as a child as follows:

So never being able to feel like them. Actually, feeling close, like wanting to be like them. But on the one hand, there is always a question mark in mind. Well; for example, the best example is Christmas time. You see the trees, you are a child, they give gifts, here are those red candles, ornaments, I don't know what. You take care and you want to see it at home. And your family explains to you: This is not right in our religion. For example, we cannot have this tree. You always envy there, but at the same time you have to accept it: No, we can't. It is obviously difficult for the child to understand. (P3)

From a familial point of view, it has been seen that the other members of the family have taken the decision to return, which also pushes other members to return. One participant stated that his wife returned, albeit reluctantly, after the decision to return and that she did her best to delay the process with the following sentences:

I didn't want to come lately either. Because I said, look, the kid has a routine here, he goes to school. If we go to Turkey now, what will this child do, what will he do? What language? That's a very, very difficult decision.... He told me to throw it now. Let's go out let's go. I said, look, think carefully, I wonder if we are doing right or wrong. I made a very difficult decision, let me say I came reluctantly, actually. (P1)

On the other hand, when some family members, especially children, were enthusiastic about return, it made it easier for parents to give the return decision as expressed by a father participant below:

My son already loved Turkey. That was one of the reasons we came. He wanted so much. (P8)

Similarly, it is seen that the perception and orientation of other members of the family toward losing their cultural identity also have an impact on their individual return decisions.

(My father said) you know Turkish, you know you are Turkish. Will your grandchildren know about you? Can you afford to lose it? I mean, I said yes at that time, too, he's actually right. Okay, this place is fine, but I don't know. (I asked myself) How long are you going to go on like this? When how long will you not have a home? When will you feel belong? They (My family) want to go, they will go, too. You will stay here alone. This time I found it more rational, and I returned. (P3)

The deteriorating economic condition in Europe was stated to be a factor changing the life standards of migrants. As the currency in Turkey is quite low, they occurred to them that they could lead a more decent life in Turkey when they have income from the host country. An example of this experience is given below:

When we exchange that money here, when we change it this way, then a very comfortable life seems to wait for us. (P1)

When evaluated from a contextual point of view, all participants reported that they and/or their family members were exposed to discrimination and this discrimination had a very important influence on their return decision. Some of the participants expressed their experiences as follows:

No matter how much multiculturalism (is salient there), we say, there is prejudice in Germany. I didn't want my daughter to grow up in that prejudice. (P5)

I have been subjected to racism so much. I mean, I always felt it in every context, at school, at work, in internships. Even though I am not as a Turkish, I act like a German, I have been exposed to (discrimination) a lot. For example, you're sitting on the bus, they say, "Get up, Turk." (P3)

It is seen that there are several factors that attract the participants to Turkey. While some of these factors are individual factors such as the critical age of the child to adopt to Turkish school system, some are educational opportunities such as comparatively easier admission to university or getting a job offer. However, the most highlighted themes could be listed as missing social support, family solidarity, tranquility, and homesickness.

> Then I remember 15–16-year-old me back in Germany now. Crying at home like this. We have no one. We are alone. Here's something that happened when I was bullied at school. Then I say "No, even if they give me the most beautiful car and the most beautiful items as much as you want. There's nothing like tranquility. … like this. Everything feels more sincere and from the heart (in Turkey)". (P3)

Readaptation in Turkey

There were various factors that make the readaptation period more difficult or easier for the participants after returning to Turkey. A majority of the participants reported that they perceived the cultural distance back at home as well. In particular, the distance was more experienced in personal relationships in family and business life, in traffic, at other public places. The quotation below indicates a perceived discrepancy in the working conditions and personal relations at workplace.

> *It doesn't matter where you work in the UK and what position you're in. You know whether you work in a store or with a very large company, everyone works 9-5. Normal shift. There is no such hierarchy between you and your supervisor as it is here. Yes, he is only responsible for asking the tasks like did you send those e-mails or not. You know, there are not such things like digging a pit for you, shouting or mobbing. In other words, everyone is actually doing their own work there. They just go home, that's it. You know, here, they mean here I am, let me be such a boss, I'm your supervisor, be careful. There is no such thing in England. I have also many friends who are in business life there, I have not heard anything like this from any of them. There are many here in Turkey. (P4)*

The respondent below also expressed the difficulties in her personal relationships with external relatives and her friends, due to the distance perceived in culture and values.

> *Here, your mother-in-law, sister-in-law, sometimes even some of the neighbors get involved (in your decisions). I say that I don't want to live according to the norms that you or your society has made, or the norms the society has accepted.*

We have our own values. We know very well what means what. We live according to it. Accept this. I mean, we come from a slightly different place. What society finds right is not always right for me. (P5)

When the reality met the expectations, the participants were surprised to see the changes in Turkey compared to the time they left. Although they lived in Turkey before and they thought that they came to a familiar context, the experience of the participants below shows the difficulty resulted from the changes experienced.

After coming here, it is as if we have never lived here before. So (we felt like) we have come to a completely different place. I said, "God, what happened?". So, I'm bored like this. My son also started to say "Mom, what are we going to do? Mom let's go". (P1)

The values of the Turkish mainstreamers were also reported to be more different from their expectations and even felt more distant from their cultural and religious identity.

The way of thinking of the people here and the fact that money is always being a priority bothers me a lot. People who settled in Germany from Turkey have always been attached to that Turkish culture. You know, so that we don't lose Turkish culture. (We say) Let's not become a German. But now I came here. I saw that unfortunately there is no trace of that Turkish culture for everyone. Not like a Muslim, Let me openly declare that (they are) not like a Muslim. (P6)

In addition to these difficulties, some of the participants stated that having language problems, missing their families due to split family situations, and the adaptation problems of their children and the perceived discrimination were found to make the readaptation process more challenging. The data revealed that discrimination was so difficult to cope particularly when migrants return to feel home. The participant below expressed that she was deeply disappointed when she felt discrimination in Turkey:

I hired a person to work at my farm and it is 250 liras per day for everybody, but I pay 275 liras as I came from Germany. They understand it from my accent, but I also earn my money here and pay taxes like everybody. (P9)

Besides difficulties experienced, there were also factors that facilitated the readaptation of the participants to Turkey. The main facilitators are having some of the family members returning beforehand, knowing the city/ previously coming, and having bought an apartment before. Not having to worry about financial issues was always expressed to be a protective factor.

I don't think I've had any difficulties. Because as I told you before, when the finance was good, I never had any difficulties. I didn't miss (the host county). (P2)

In addition, in line with the return motives, when migrants did not feel lonely, and they could get social support from family members, they stated to go through a smoother adaptation process.

Yeah, that feeling. I can find a solution when something happens. There is someone I can call. I am not alone; I am not alone. (P3)

Most participants stated that having a dual citizenship and preserving the right to go back to the host country relieve them in the readaptation period. They perceive this as a serious and guaranteed alternative in life.

I am also a dual citizen. I am both Swiss citizen and Turkish. Actually, now I have two passports and I have a Swiss passport. Also, my Turkish passport. So as soon as I feel bad, I will go back. It's that simple. (P2)

Cultural Differences Regarding Parenting Experiences

As one of the research questions was the role of familial issues in return migration process, the participants extensively reflected on the differences and similarities regarding parenting experiences in the host country and in Turkey. The main perceived difference was the child rearing practices between two groups. On the one hand, Turkish families were reported to be overly protective and therefore rather restrictive in daily lives of the children. Most interviewees reported that they were strictly controlled by the families in the migrated context which prevented them to fully integrate in host culture. This also led them to have less social network from host community.

Such an extra protectionism, I suppose. By the way, for example, my mother was very sensitive there. They were burning mosques, burning cars by identifying

Muslim neighborhoods. They were killing doner staff. Such a thing happened; it was in 2014/2015. My mother was definitely not sending us anywhere. You know, you're already a target, so she would be afraid of that too. (P3)

Despite this more authoritarian style of families, participants stated they have a deeper bond with them, and they could get more social support from the families compared to families in European countries. Although the familial system is based on making the children more independent, Turkish family members seemed to be more embedded both in daily lives and practices.

For example, when they turn 18, they separate their house to get their child be responsible. Even if you are a student, the child should work part time and shift for himself. Be responsible and live your life. I mean, they (the parents) say that my responsibilities for you are over, but we (Turks) can't have such a thing. ... For example, when I was a student, I was also working part time. When I bought clothes, my mother would still pay. They don't have anything like that either. In other words, they do not support their children even for a penny so that they can learn how to stand. We always hug our mothers and act warmly, but they don't have such a thing. They are more distant. (P7)

Issues Related to the Multifaceted Crises

As the return and reintegration periods of our participants coincided with the COVID-19 pandemic and the economic crisis, they appeared as salient themes in the interviews. The results are analyzed under two axes as difficulties related to COVID-19 and difficulties related to economic crises.

The issues regarding COVID-19 were listed as not being able to meet with family members in the host country, the uncertainty felt, job loss, and difficulties experienced by their children. One participant described her experience with the following words:

I couldn't see my family for a year or two. It was such a problem. Because Turkey was on the red list in England. Therefore, the arrivals from England were free, but the return was a problem. That's why my family couldn't come. If they had come, they would not go back. It was such a problem. I used to live here alone. (P4)

Although the themes were categorized under two main axes, economic crises started before COVID-19 pandemic in Turkey and felt more intensely afterward. Almost all participants stated that they could not find proper jobs in this period in Turkey. Even some of them were planning to return back to the host country as they lost their job during COVID-19 pandemic and could not find another one afterward. Mothers stated to have difficulty in coping with both readaptation process of their children and online teaching at the same time. One participant, who planned to stay home until her child adapts to school system, changed her mind due to the crises after COVID-19 pandemic as stated in the quotation below.

> *Yes, in our plan, I would stay at home for 2 years. It would be great if I gave my full energy to my child this year, but really, why do we say that? A single salary now only meets our basic needs. I have to work. Because, you know, my daughter has also standard. Everyone has their own standards, but if we have a certain standard, no one wants to live below that. (P5)*

The economic crisis seems to affect even the participants who get their income from the host country. However, they state that they have incomparably more easier lives compared to people who do work in and earn their income in Turkey. The interviewee below claims that it would not be possible for her to lead a life if she did not get support from the family members in Europe.

> *In 2018, I started to work with the minimum wage, I will never forget, it was 2200 liras. The rent of my house was already 2700 liras. I mean, if I were the only one here, you know, if I were to live alone without the support of my family, it would be impossible, impossible. My father paid my rent for 12 months in advance when I moved here. Namely, Turkey was not that expensive compared to today. So, I was getting 2200 liras, yes, but half of that money was in my pocket…. But as the years passed, the money had no value. In other words, 2200 liras are something like 10 thousand liras of the moment. That's why I say it again, I couldn't spend it alone. (P4)*

The economic crisis and deteriorating conditions in Turkey unexpectedly created social problems with the native peers for return migrants. Most interviewees stated that they are perceived to be weird as they chose to be in Turkey though they have to lead a life in Europe. They feel discriminated and not understood and even sometime question themselves for their decision. One participant emphasized her discomfort with the fact that people in Turkey find it strange that people are staying here:

People here are a little bit like that, so "you don't have a mind, what are you doing in Turkey? We are trying to escape, why are you here?" How logical that is debatable, but now how long can money make you happy? How much time? We lived very well, so we had everything. We had my father's Mercedes, this phone, this toy, everything, but were we happy? We were not. I mean because we've always been...We were different. We were like the other. (P4)

Discussion and Conclusion

This research described the return migration experiences of Turkish return migrants from Europe. Through a qualitative micro study with nine returnees, push and pull factors affecting return decision, their reintegration processes in the middle of economic and public health crises, and the role of family dynamics in return migration process were investigated. The study revealed that keeping their own and their children's ethnic ties, not feeling at home, perceiving discrimination, and deteriorating social and economic conditions in the host country were the main push factors for returnees. On the other hand, social support and being close to family members as well as believing in a brighter prospect in Turkey were the main pull factors. Perceived cultural distance, perceived discrimination in Turkey, discrepancy between expectations and the reality, and hyperinflation in Turkey were main challenges experienced in the readaptation period.

This chapter contributes to literature by focusing on the hardly studied untraditional group of migrants who return from Western, industrialized, and developed countries to their less developed homelands. Most studies in literature primarily explain migration as a cost-benefit optimization (Massey et al., 1993); founding theories on migration mostly focus on economic determinants of migration. However, our study, in line with several studies, highlighted the importance of non-economic factors such as family ties, ethnic roots, sense of belonging, as well as concerns about family members (Kunuroglu et al., 2018; Tezcan, 2022; Vlase, 2013). Our study provides a key finding showing that these emotional motives are so strong that the migrants return to home country in the midst of crisis.

Previous literature stated that Turkish families in Europe keep the traditional model in household despite being exposed to more egalitarian values and personal autonomy (Phalet & Güngör, 2009). All interviewees in our study reported that they had even more traditional family lives back in the host countries compared to the families in Turkey. Young generation who found it easier to integrate into the host culture and accept their values seemed to experience acculturation gap with their parents leading them to feel different from their peers and not belonged to the host country which eventually encouraged them to go to a place where they feel normal.

Despite being raised in traditional households and parental gender ideology, young female migrants were observed to look for job or education opportunities without their parents in Turkey. It is in line with the recent research which states that in recent decades, female migrants can also be active decision makers seeking new professional opportunities in other countries (He & Gerber, 2020; Hofmann & Buckley, 2013).

Parental concerns were occasionally reported as related to return migration decision. First of all, having a child was reported to motivate to return to look for assistance in caring for children from relatives in the home country (Reynolds, 2010; Vlase, 2013). Besides, as previous literature documented, the participants reported that they perceived the Turkish education system to be superior to the European system (Kunuroglu et al., 2018). Therefore, educational concerns for their children were found to be a strong motivation. Further, all parents stated that they were discriminated at school context and wanted to protect their children from the discriminating context in Europe. The last but not the least, some migrants have reported to return to provide support for their relatives, particularly if their parents are old or sick, they tend to return to help them. Therefore, multilayered parental concerns were reported as strong cause of return decision.

The study had some limitations. Due to the nature of data collection process, the research is based on self-reports and the self-reported data can contain several potential sources of bias such as selective memory. In this study, interviews were conducted both face to face and online. Although online interviews had the potential to make it difficult to establish rapport, it also offered the opportunity to reach participants during the COVID-19 period. Small sample size of our study could have an influence on the diversity of the experiences; still, the sample allowed us to obtain a good insight into return motivation.

References

Abadan-Unat, N. (2006). *Bitmeyen Göç: Konuk İşçilikten Ulus-ötesi Yurttaşlığa [Never ending migration: From guestworkers to transnational citizens]*. İstanbul Bilgi Üniversitesi Yayınları.

Apsite-Berina, E., Manea, M. E., & Berzins, M. (2020). The ambiguity of return migration: Prolonged crisis and uncertainty in the life strategies of young Romanian and Latvian returnees. *International Migration, 58*(1), 61–75.

Berry, J. W. (1997). Immigration, acculturation, and adaptation. *Applied Psychology: An International Review, 46*, 5–68. https://doi.org/10.1111/j.1464-0597.1997

Bolognani, M. (2007). The myth of return: dismissal, survival or revival? A Bradford example of transnationalism as a political instrument. *Journal of Ethnic and Migration Studies, 33*(1), 59–76.

Braun, V., & Clarke, V. (2006). Using thematic analysis in psychology. *Qualitative Research in Psychology, 3*(2), 77–101.

Bundesamt für Migration und Flüchtlinge (BAMF). (2016). *Migrationsbericht 2015*. Nuremberg: BAMF.

Christou, A., & King, R. (2006). Migrants encounter migrants in the city: The Changing context of 'home' for second-generation Greek American return migrants. *International Journal of Urban and Regional Research, 30*(4), 816–835.

Dona, G., & Ackermann, L. (2006). Refugees in camps. In D. L. Sam & J. W. Berry (Eds.), *The Cambridge handbook of acculturation psychology* (pp. 218–232). Cambridge University Press.

Dustmann, C., & Weiss, Y. (2007). Return migration: Theory and empirical evidence from the UK. *British Journal of Industrial Relations, 45*(2), 236–256.

He, Q., & Gerber, T. P. (2020). Origin-country culture, migration sequencing, and female employment: Variations among immigrant women in the United States. *International Migration Review, 54*(1), 233–261.

Hofmann, E. T., & Buckley, C. J. (2013). Global changes and gendered responses: The feminization of migration from Georgia. *International Migration Review, 47*(3), 508–538.

İçduygu, A. (2012). 50 years after the labour recruitment agreement with Germany: The consequences of emigration for Turkey. *Perceptions, 17*, 11–36. Retrieved from: http://sam.gov.tr/wp-content/uploads/2012/05/ahmet_icduygu.pdf

Kaya, A., & Kentel, F. (2008). *Belçika Türkleri: Türkiye ile Avrupa Birliği arasında bir engel mi? [Euro-Turks: A bridge, or a breach, between Turkey and the European Union?]*. İstanbul Bilgi Üniversitesi Yayınları.

Kılıç, Z., & Menjívar, C. (2013). Fluid adaptation of contested citizenship: Second-generation migrant Turks in Germany and the United States. *Social Identities, 19*, 204–220. https://doi.org/10.1080/13504630.2013.789217

Kim, Y. Y. (2001). *Becoming intercultural: An integrative theory of communication and cross-cultural adaptation*. Sage.

King, R. (2018). Theorising new European youth mobilities. *Population, Space and Place, 24*(1), e2117.

King, R., & Christou, A. (2011). Of counter-diaspora and reverse transnationalism: Return mobilities to and from the ancestral homeland. *Mobilities, 6*(4), 451–466.

King, R., Christou, A., & Ahrens, J. (2011). 'Diverse mobilities': Second generation Greek-Germans engage with homeland as children and as adults. *Mobilities, 6*(4), 483–501.

Konzett-Smoliner, S. (2016). Return migration as a 'family project': Exploring the relationship between family life and the readjustment experiences of highly skilled Austrians. *Journal of Ethnic and Migration Studies, 42*(7), 1094–1114.

Kunuroglu, F., Yagmur, K., Van de Vijver, F. J., & Kroon, S. (2015). Consequences of Turkish return migration from Western Europe. *International Journal of Intercultural Relations, 49*, 198–211.

Kunuroglu, F., Yagmur, K., Van De Vijver, F. J., & Kroon, S. (2018). Motives for Turkish return migration from Western Europe: Home, sense of belonging, discrimination and transnationalism. *Turkish Studies, 19*(3), 422–450.

Massey, D. S., Arango, J., Hugo, G., Kouaouci, A., Pellegrino, A., & Taylor, J. E. (1993). Theories of international migration: A review and appraisal. *Population and Development Review, 19*, 431–466.

Massey, D. S., Arango, J., Hugo, G., Kouaouci, A., & Pellegrino, A. (1999). *Worlds in motion: Understanding international migration at the end of the millennium: Understanding international migration at the end of the millennium*. Clarendon Press.

Nguyen, A.-M. D., & Benet-Martinez, V. (2012). Biculturalism and adjustment: A meta-analysis. *Journal of Cross-Cultural Psychology, 44*(1), 122–159.

Ní Laoire, C. (2008). Complicating host-newcomer dualisms: Irish return migrants as home-comers or newcomers. *Translocations: Migration and Social Change, 4*(1), 35–50.

Phalet, K., & Güngör, D. (2009). Cultural continuity and discontinuity in Turkish migrant families: Extending the model of family change. In S. Bekman & A. Aksu-Koç (Eds.), *Perspectives on human development, family, and culture* (pp. 241–262). Cambridge University Press.

Ralph, D. (2012). Managing sameness and difference: The politics of belonging among Irish-born return migrants from the United States. *Social & Cultural Geography, 13*(5), 445–460. https://doi.org/10.1080/14649365.2012.698747

Redfield, R., Linton, R., & Herskovits, M. H. (1936). Memorandum on the study of acculturation. *American Anthropologist, 38*, 149–152. https://doi.org/10.1525/aa.1936.38.1.02a00330

Reynolds, T. (2010). Transnational family relationships, social networks and return migration among British-Caribbean young people. *Ethnic and Racial Studies, 33*(5), 797–815.

Searle, W., & Ward, C. (1990). The prediction of psychological and sociocultural adjustment during cross-cultural transitions. *International Journal of Intercultural Relations, 14*(4), 449–464. https://doi.org/10.1016/0147-1767(90)90030-Z

Sussman, N. M. (2000). The dynamic nature of cultural identity throughout cultural transitions: Why home is not so sweet. *Personality and Social Psychology Review, 4*(4), 355–373.

Tezcan, T. (2022). Return migration intentions driven by parental concerns and the value of children. *Sociological Forum, 38*(1), 121–143.

Thomas, D. R. (2006). A general inductive approach for analyzing qualitative evaluation data. *American Journal of Evaluation, 27*(2), 237–246.

Todaro, M. P. (1969). A model of labor migration and urban unemployment in less developed countries. *The American Economic Review, 59*(1), 138–148.

Tsuda, T. (2009). Why does the diaspora return home? The causes of ethnic return migration. In T. Tsuda (Eds.), *Diasporic homecomings: Ethnic return migration in comparative perspective* (pp. 21–43). Stanford, CA: Stanford University Press.

TUSIAD (Turk Sanayicileri ve Isadamlari Dernegi). (2006). *Türkiye- Avrupa Birliği ilişkileri bağlamında göç tartışmaları*. İstanbul.

Virta, E., Sam, D. L., & Westin, C. (2004). Adolescents with Turkish background in Norway and Sweden: A comparative study of their psychological adaptation. *Scandinavian Journal of Psychology, 45*(1), 15–25.

Vlase, I. (2013). 'My husband is a patriot!': Gender and Romanian family return migration from Italy. *Journal of Ethnic and Migration Studies, 39*(5), 741–758.

Ward, C., & Geeraert, N. (2016). Advancing acculturation theory and research: The acculturation process in its ecological context. *Current Opinion in Psychology, 8*, 98–104.

Yehuda-Sternfeld, S. B., & Mirsky, J. (2014). Return migration of Americans: Personal narratives and psychological perspectives. *International Journal of Intercultural Relations, 42*, 53–64.

CHAPTER 8

Crisis, Circular Systems, and Return: A Case Study of Morocco

Frances D. Loustau-Williams and Abderrahim Zouggaghi

INTRODUCTION

With visibility of European continent, Morocco is a natural borderland that has relied on the benefits of mobility for decades. In the first two weeks of March 2020, a relatively fluid border system shutdown when the world deployed isolation in a way we have not seen in modern times. Economic and social systems that existed on account of the porous borders were suddenly immobilized. Border fluidity returned only to relive the same crisis in December 2021, during the Omicron variant outbreak, when Morocco once again closed its borders and canceled incoming and outgoing flights. What ensued after the border closures were short-run "immobility crises," where systems that relied on cross-border movement had to suddenly readjust. Such a significant shock to the movement system allows us to assess the reverberations over time, providing insights into its underlying structure of the migration system (Roehner et al., 2004).

F. D. Loustau-Williams (✉) • A. Zouggaghi
Al Akhawayn University, Ifran, Morocco
e-mail: f.williams@aui.ma

© The Author(s), under exclusive license to Springer Nature Switzerland AG 2024
J. Yeo (ed.), *Return Migration and Crises in Non-Western Countries*, Mobility & Politics,
https://doi.org/10.1007/978-3-031-53562-8_8

The following inquiry proceeds by asking the question, "How did the border closures impact circular systems of movement in Morocco?" To do this, we articulate three forms of circularity: return migration, seasonal return, and daily border crossings, considering the impact that circularity has on the migration system. The focus on immobility as opposed to mobility flips the typical migration narrative by presupposing cross-border movement to be the norm. This is in contrast to the often-discussed "migration crises," driven by the *sedentary bias* that implicitly assumes movement to be problematic (Castles, 2010).

The data presented in this chapter contribute to the arguments that traditional neoclassical migration paradigms, based on push-pull features, fail to adequately capture the relationship between short-term circular movements and long-term migration. The proceeding narratives, collected through qualitative and quantitative data, suggest that the "immobility crisis" tended to entrench more permanent movement patterns, but was highly disruptive to circular movements.

Exodus, Crisis, and Immobility

Morocco and the Exodus Narrative

Moroccans have been a particularly mobile population for decades. As one of the largest diasporas from the MENA region, approximately 5 million Moroccans live abroad in 2022 (Mohamed VI, 2020), amounting to about 10% of the Moroccan population (Natter, 2014). De Haas (2007) and Massey et al. (2011) refer to Morocco as a "labor frontier" country dominated by out-migration and internal rural to urban migration. The Moroccan Diaspora began to take shape in the colonial period in France. Bilateral agreements were made with European countries and Morocco to recruit temporary migrant labor. Ennaji (2014) describes Moroccan recruitment as a last resort after the recruitment of white labor failed (Ennaji, 2014). The first labor migrants were recruited in the agriculture and mining industries to account for the labor shortage driven by the war. Throughout both World Wars, North African regimes were mobilized to fight for the French, with many of them remaining during the period of reconstruction. The recruitment of Moroccan labor spread to Belgium and the Netherlands in the 1960s. The demographic makeup of these earlier waves of migrants was young, male, unskilled laborers. France,

Belgium, and the Netherlands are considered to be the traditional destination countries for Moroccan migrants.

These arrangements were initially intended to be circular, and some of them were. However, with the Oil crisis in 1973, the demand for labor dried up, work permits froze and migration controls tightened into the 1980s, leading to permanent settlement and the evolution of "irregular migration." From these original communities, informal networks formed, giving rise to to future chain migration via families and private employer connections (de Haas, 2007). Eventually, restrictions tightened so much that the only way to migrate was through family reunification programs. Many of the earlier migrants were already married, initially leaving their families in Morocco, only to later migrate them permanently (de Haas, 2007). Others subsequently got married and established their families in the destination country, creating more gender parity in the migrant population.

Despite the fact that many European migration restrictions became more strict, the emigration rate increased over time, with a particularly dramatic rise in the 1990s (Natter, 2014). In the 1980s, Spain joined the European Union and experienced economic convergence with the rest of the continent. As the economic gap between Morocco and Spain grew, Spain became a logical destination for the next wave of Moroccan migrants given the geographical proximity. Emigration rates skyrocketed on account of this new development. The Spanish agricultural sector currently depends heavily on Moroccan migrants. The Moroccan diaspora living in Europe currently has its own identity, that is partially transnational and partially an independent subcultural. Much of the literature on Moroccan migration explains the origins of this particular population (de Haas, 2007; Ennaji, 2014). We refer to this as "the exodus narrative," which is largely explained by macroeconomic structures and a focus on permanence.

More recently, North America, Germany, the Gulf countries have become common as migration destinations. Through the diversity lottery program, the United States gives 55,000 permanent residency cards to individuals from under-represented countries. Every Moroccan living in the United States interviewed for this chapter came to the States having won a lottery visa. Canada has also implemented programs to recruit skilled labor. According to the official Canadian Embassy website, 5000 Moroccan students go to Canada to study, on account of the shared *francophonie*. Increasingly, companies are recruiting skilled labor even in the anglophone parts of Canada. The Gulf countries have become a more common destination, recruiting Moroccans as domestic laborers, chauffeurs, and security personnel. Overall, the data indicates that movement patterns of Moroccans are diversifying.

Closure of the Moroccan Border: The "Immobility Crisis"

In the early days of the pandemic, Morocco got a head-start on implementing its lockdown meaning that the Covid risk was low. As such, it was suddenly and temporarily deemed more dangerous to be in Europe than in Morocco. Subsequently, the border systems momentarily flipped. Europeans were being kept out of Morocco's "safe space," rather than vice versa. Moroccans living abroad were blocked from coming home and often resorted to "illegally" crossing the border back to their home country, sometimes risking their lives by swimming across the border in the opposite direction of how it is usually reported (Hatim, 2020), essentially creating a momentary reverse migration crisis. National identity ties became strained as many Moroccans Residing Abroad (MRAs) described feeling abandoned by their governments.

The crisis-driven migration literature typically focuses on the movement that occurs in response to a crisis event such as a war or a natural disaster. Where "asymmetric shocks" occur, population redistribution allows the wider system to absorb the blow (Fidrmuc, 2004), leading to flows of displaced persons and refugees. In the case of COVID-19, this movement outlet was cut off, creating a second shock. This second shock to the system was rather the inability to move, hence, "the immobility crisis," making this scenario unique in relation to the typically assumed relationship between crisis and movement.

We examine these issues by reflecting upon what the after-effects of the shock to the system reveal about the migration system and in particular circularity. In physics, Dirac impulses are short pulses applied to a system with the purpose of analyzing the response to the shocks that reveal the internal workings of the system. Roehner (2004) revealed divisions in social cohesion by examining several crisis events. Applying this thinking to the current situation, the aim is to treat the shutter of the global system of movement as the primary shock that reveals the inner workings of the migration system. In this sense, rather than being the object of study, the crisis event has a methodological function whose purpose is to reveal the role that circularity has in the larger system.

Data and Methods

News Media Analysis

Contextual details were collected through news media accounts of the border closure items in order to piece together perspectives on both sides of the border and a specific timeline of the border closure. Overall, 87 news articles were collected in the periods around both border closures from March 2020 to February 2022. Articles were collected and coded using MAXQDA for events, dates, and political and economic narratives, taking into account the origin and reputation of the publication (Table 8.1).

Haut Commissariat au Plan Survey Data

Several surveys were performed by the Moroccan government on return migrant from the early 2000s (see Table 8.2). The census that is conducted every ten years also includes a question about migration. The survey populations are not consistent, nor were the questions asked in each survey, making them hard to use for comparative purposes. They do, however, provide snapshots of the characteristics of return migration. Informally, they provide the basis of a qualitative longitudinal analysis that can help piece together a broader picture.

Table 8.1 News articles used to build a timeline of events and perspectives

News source	# of articles	Publications
Moroccan	43	Moroccan World News, Bladi.net, FM5, MAP News, TelQuel, Hespress
Arab world (Non-Moroccan)	13	Al Jazeerah, Arab News, Arab Weekly, Middle East Eye, Middle East Monitor, Inside Arabia, North Africa Post
US/UK	14	CNN, BBC, Associated Press, Reuters, Brookings, Henrico County News
European	10	EuroNews, Agence-France Presse, Atalayar, Euronews, Schengen Visa News feed, The Irish Times, LaMoncloa
African (Non-Moroccan)	3	Africa News, Africa Report, Voice of Africa
Other	3	Eurasian Review, Jerusalem Post

Table 8.2 Surveys conducted by the Moroccan "Haut Commissariat au Plan"

Survey year	Publication	Scope
1982	Recensement Général de la Population et de l'Habitat	National
1994	Recensement Général de la Population et de l'Habitat	National
2003-2004	La Migration de Retour des Marocains Résidant à l'Etranger	Casablanca, Souss-Massa-Draa
2004	Recensement Général de la Population et de l'Habitat	National
2014	Recensement Général de la Population et de l'Habitat	National
2018-2019	Enquête nationale sur la migration internationale	National

Table 8.3 Interviews conducted

Interview location	Population	Number of interviews
Nador	Moroccan residents of Nador	9
Philadelphia, Spain, and Morocco	MRAs and family of MRAs	10

Interviews

To follow up, interviews were conducted to gather a range of perspectives within the migration system. The first group consisted of Moroccans living near the Melilla-Ceuta border that relied on smuggling prior to the border closure. The second set were among the Moroccan diaspora or relatives of diaspora living abroad or in Morocco. The interviews took place in January 2023 and in August 2023. They were short, taking approximately 15 minutes. Interviewees were selected by convenience and snowball sampling and thus are not representative. Almost all interviews were conducted in either Moroccan darija or Tarrifit (the local language of Nador) by a native speaker. They were then translated and transcribed into English and wiped of any sensitive information. The analysis consisted of coding for emergent themes using Grounded Theory (Table 8.3).

CIRCULARITY AND SYSTEMS OF RETURN

"Traditional Return (1 Departure, 1 Return)": HCP Survey Results

Return migration first became recognized in Morocco in the 1990s when the early labor migrants to Europe came of retirement age and decided to return to Morocco. A new migrant flow emerged, prompting the Moroccan Haut Commissariat au Plan (HCP) to begin collecting survey data on returnees. Prior to that, data can only be imperfectly gleaned from Census data. Thus far, narratives of return have yet to congeal into a clear consensus on when, why, and how Moroccans choose to return, and how this is changing over time.

According to these surveys, return migration is and has always been quite low. The most recent survey estimated roughly 200,000 return migrants. The 2018–2019 survey (Fainine, 2020) suggests that many of the earliest migrants moving to France did in fact return, albeit not the majority. This tendency sharply declined in the 1970s and 1980s as migration restrictions tightened. There are some indications that this tendency may be on the rise as of the last few decades. The most recent survey distributed the current returnees by the period of their return. The trend appears as a gradual increase with a spike in the 2010–2014 period, presumably on account of the financial crisis (see Table 8.4).

The HCP surveys suggest that return tendencies are changing. The 2018–2019 report states that the increase in return tendencies may correlate with the shift in migration destinations. Among the more recent destination countries (Spain, Italy, North American and Gulf countries), return appears to have increased. Returnees coming from the later European destination countries (Spain and Italy) accounted for 32.6% of those surveyed. Returnees coming from Arab countries accounted for 25.3% and those coming from North America accounted for 18.8%. The more traditional European destination countries (France, Belgium, and Holland which account for 80% of the Moroccan diaspora) accounted for only 10.6% of the those surveyed. This is in stark contrast with earlier surveys that indicated that the vast majority of returnees were coming from France. The data does not say why this relationship may exist.

Table 8.4 Return migrants by year of indicated return

Year of return	% of current returnees
2000–2004	15
2005–2009	20.3
2010–2014	35.1
2015–2018	28.7

Source: « Enquête nationale sur la migration internationale », Haut Commissariat au Plan, 2018–2019

The composition of return migrants may also be changing. While initial surveys indicated that returnees were retirees, the average age of returnees has lowered. In 2003, the average age was 64 years old and 87.7% were 50 or older. Only 5.5% were less than 40 (*Démographie: La Réinsertion Des Migrants de Retour Au Maroc: Analyse Des Résultats de l'enquête Sur La Migration de Retour Des Marocains Résidant à l'étranger de 2003-2004: Exemple Des Régions Du Grand Casablanca et de Souss-Massa-Draa | Téléchargements | Site Institutionnel Du Haut-Commissariat Au Plan Du Royaume Du Maroc*, 2011). In contrast, few of the returnees questioned in 2018–2019 were retirees. The largest age group for return in the period of 2000–2018 was ages 30–49 (40.6%). Again, without more contextual data to back up the surveys, it is not clear what the shift indicates.

The survey data collected by the Moroccan government cites "Marriage and family reunification" as the most common reasons for return (27.3%). A scant majority (56.9%) of the return migrants indicated that they wanted to stay in Morocco, while a little more than one-fifth (22.4%) stated they wanted to go leave the country again. The most commonly cited reason explaining why they wanted to stay (71.8%) was, once again, so they could stay with family. This creates an historical echo throughout all of the migration periods cited above. Family reunification was also a major reason for departure to traditional European countries in the 1970s. The theme emerged again in the 2003 survey as an explanation for the dismal rate of return, arguing that a head of household will rarely decide to return when their children have become well-established citizens of the destination country (Mohamed Mghari, 2011). Among those that did return, the 2003 survey demonstrates that they came back as a family. These findings are consistent with the New Economics of Labor Migration literature that posits the household as the primary unit of analysis rather than the individual (Stark & Bloom, 1985). They are also consistent with statements from the interviews, such as one participant that said, "going back to Morocco would not be easy, my kids were born and raised here. Even if I wanted to go back, they would not want to live in Lbled (Morocco). Their mentality is American, and they would not mix in well" (Participant 11, Interview, Jan 16, 2023).

Long-Term Return and the Immobility Crisis

With respect to the border closures during the COVID-19 pandemic, there was a range of experience among our interviewees. For established migrants with no immediate intentions of return, the border closure was inconsequential. One participant indicated that daily video discussions with family members made the border closure almost meaningless. "Every time I would get home, I would find my mother on a video call." For others, there was a desire to "go home" and be with family. Some were simply scared of losing family members and not being able to go home to either care for them or attend their funeral. Others feared dying themselves, not wanting to die in a foreign country. One participant stated, "You would think to yourself, if things were to remain this way it is better to go back home to your home country, somewhere in the countryside, you would be comfortable in your house." One participant described how the border closures increased the imagined distance between countries, "...the pandemic reminded them that Morocco is not as near as they think it is" (Participant 18, Interview, September 11, 2023).

For some the crisis hardened decisions that were already made. One interviewee had the opportunity to get his green card through the diversity lottery system. He initially opted against following through with it because he already had a decent job in Morocco. With the green card allotment set to expire if he did not move, he felt he needed to take the opportunity. He left a master's program and entered the United States a month before the Covid-induced shutdown. By this time, going back was not an option. Since he walked away from his contract in the public sector, he no longer had the option to return to the life he lived in Morocco prior to leaving. Notions of regret were evident in his voice. With his parents no longer alive, he was unsure what the future might bring. His hope was to go to graduate school. (Participant 12, interview, January 13, 2023)

For most of the long-term migrants, the border closure did not appear to change long-term intentions. Nonetheless, competing objectives seemed to make up transnational identities. When it comes to culture, values and religion, the Moroccan diaspora often identifies strongly with Morocco. "There is something in people that makes them want to return to their country where they were born and raised" (Participant 15, interview, September 6, 2023). Clifford Geertz refers to this as "primordial attachment," defined as presocial and instinctive (Geertz, 1973).

Seasonal Return – (1+ Departure, 1+ Return per Year)

The type of seasonal migration, typically discussed in the literature consists of migrants who work on a contractual basis. Several EU projects were launched to effectively facilitate these recruitment practices. This kind of circular migration is meant to serve as "triple win scenarios," where employment and labor needs are met without creating the integration/assimilation problem that many destination countries want to avoid. Several scholars contest the optimism of this approach, Wickramasekara arguing that these scenarios amount to migrant exploitation, social fragmentation or "a dead end" (Wickramasekara, 2011; Adunts, 2021; Ari, 2023).

Another seasonal movement that exists in far greater numbers but receives considerably less scholarly attention is that of the Moroccan diaspora coming "home" during the summer months. These movements are led often by Moroccans and descendants of Moroccans, many with European passports who may just as easily be classified as tourists. The summer influx is driven by an intrinsic attachment to one's "'usul" (origins) that is hardwired into Moroccan acculturation. The patterns amount to seasonal population explosions, turning the streets and family gatherings into linguistic smorgasbords and injecting life into local economies.

The sheer number of people coming across the border presents a logistical challenge. Since 2001, the Mohamed V Foundation for Solidarity runs "Operation Marhaba" (Welcome Operation) between mid-June and mid-August. Operation Marhaba offers services throughout Morocco and even in European countries to aid with social services, medical care, transportation, and information services. It involves many agencies and a partnership with Spain. According to the webpage designated for Operation Marhaba within the Mohammed V Foundation, in 2022, between June 15 and August 15, 3,080,984 Moroccans Residing Abroad came to Morocco. Just under half a million came through the Tanger-Med port alone in that period. The website reported that an average of 40,000 people came across the border on a daily basis (*Marhaba Operation*, 2023). This amounts to roughly increasing the total population during the summer months by 7%. Put another way, more than half of the entire Moroccan diaspora "returns" in the summer.

These population movements are an economic lifeline for many Moroccan towns. While most of these returnees take a vacation in typical high-density summer tourist areas, there are rural villages that remain almost uninhabited in winter but come to life in the summer. The economic impact tends to repair balance of payment deficits. The influx of European Moroccans has even led to classic migrant-native tensions that are commonly found in instances of mass population movements. Among those living in Morocco, pejorative associations exist of these "mazagri" (a colloquial term for immigrants) that are accustomed to lifestyle freedoms and practices in Europe, considered unacceptable in the more conservative Morocco (De Bree et al., 2010).

"Seasonal Return During the Immobility Crisis"

By summer 2020, the borders remained closed aside from sporadic repatriation movement. Operation Marhaba was formally cancelled. News media reported seasonal workers becoming stranded in Spain on account of the border closures. A years worth of tourist-based income was lost.

But the next year on June 15, 2021, Operation Marhaba opened with much fanfare as it does every year. On the same day, Morocco opened its sea and air borders after being closed for over a year. The vaccine campaign was underway and there was much anticipation for families to reunite and for an economic rebound after the dreadful economic consequences of the prolonged lockdown. Unfortunately, these hopes were dimmed by the midsummer Delta surge.

By the end of the summer however, about half of the normal cross-border traffic occurred and formal public responses for pleas for reimbursement were made. The Delta surge lasting approximately three months was the largest of all Covid surges, peaking in late July. The borders did not close, but people cancelled their travel plans en masse. The much needed and anticipated boost to the economy did not materialize.

Daily Return: The Nador-Melilla Border

Melilla and Ceuta are two Spanish enclaves on the Northern coast of Morocco. They are small cities, each inhabiting less than 100,000 people, surrounded by a double concrete wall with barbed wire rendering them more like European fortresses. They have been under Spanish control since the sixteenth century and were considered part of a precolonial ownership and thus were skipped over during the wave of decolonization to the dismay of Morocco who not so quietly wants them back. Currently, these are the only land borders between Europe and Africa, subsequently attracting attention from all corners of the migration debates.

Up until a few months before the start of the pandemic, Moroccan residents of Nador and Fnideq had the right to cross the border and stay for no longer than a day in the Spanish enclave of Melilla. This permission was limited to the enclaves and did not extend to the rest of Europe and gave rise to an elaborate smuggling operation. The selling of the products afterward evaded import taxes, thus turning the area into an ad-hoc tariff-free processing zone, with government authorities covertly participating in the system.

The border economy involved a variety of actors, from individual smugglers, the authorities, and those with significant resources who controlled the process. Before the border closures, most people worked as smugglers, known as "Ahemmal," and smuggled goods such as used clothes, food items, bags, alcohol, etc. across the border. The system was driven by the demand for cheaper goods, as well as the profit potential for those involved in smuggling. One participant described the system as employing "everyone": women, men, the elderly, and even disabled people were involved in the smuggling business. It was not always safe or fair. Several interviewees described problems that generally occurred with the Moroccan authorities and other smugglers. By and large, Melilla and Nador relied on one another economically and both were negatively impacted by the closures. As border guards accepted bribes to look the other way, contraband built the local economy of both Melilla and Nador.

"Daily Border-Crossings and the Immobility Crisis"

Starting in 2018, Morocco began exerting more control over these informal systems and enforcing restrictions on the border. This presented a twist on the typical narrative of Fortress Europe, where border regimes are intended to keep Africans out of Europe. In this case, Morocco restricted the movement of its own citizens to the dismay of the Spanish authorities who were well aware of its economic dependence on Moroccan visitors. A suspected reason reflected in the Spanish media for withdrawing border-crossing permission for residents of Nador was for the purposes of hurting the economies of the enclaves as a form of political pressure. The border formally closed to Moroccan citizens several months prior to the pandemic, leading some to forget the original politics of the border closure. In addition to the pandemic closures, political conflicts with Spain emerged prolonging and further confusing the motivations behind the closure. Currently, the border is open to Europeans and Schengen visitors, but not to the residents of Nador.

Throughout all of the interviews, the reality was apparent that the engine of the Nador economy was the border with Melilla, and its closure affected the entire local economy. Until a few years ago, the border economy between the cities of Melilla and Nador was thriving, driven by a vast informal network. The slowing down of the border economy was attributed to the tighter grip by the customs agents and even some infighting between them. Since the border closed, one participant explained that theft and mugging became a common occurrence in the area due to the high levels of unemployment and poverty caused by the economic crisis. Now, he says, people struggle to make ends meet, stating that daily wages are roughly half of what they were while the border was open.

One participant mentioned that many people are risking their lives by taking zodiac boats to escape to Spain, paying 10,000 Dh to 15,000 Dh for a trip that may not guarantee their safety or success. The participant himself lost 12,000 Dh on a zodiac boat that punctured. He was eventually caught. He described the low wages offered by companies and the lack of support from the government as having made life in Nador unbearable, leading many people to seek a better life in Spain and Melilla. Despite these challenges, one participant expressed hope that the borders will be re-opened in the future and that they would consider returning to work in the border economy if the opportunity arose. This is another instance of the immobility paradox, where constraining movement leads to an increase in another type of movement.

Conclusion

The pandemic brought into focus a primordial significance of mobility with which most people, on a sentimental level, probably identify after living through lockdowns. While everyone was affected by the immobility crisis, the shock to circular movement systems seemed to be more significant than to long-term movement. Interviews suggested that the crisis hardened decisions to stay in their destination countries. For those who did not have the option to leave, some interviewees referenced an increase in irregular migration. This reflects historical trends where the restriction of circularity leads to permanent and illegal migration, specifically in Europe in the 1970s and 1980s.

An examination of circularity confirms the transnationalism literature that people are constantly negotiating a cross-border existence rather than simply leaving and (possibly) returning. In Morocco, the influx of temporary returnees that occurs every summer attracts zero discussion in the migration literature but has significant impact on the economy and the transnational experience. The observed significance of circularity requires us to move away from the dichotomies that define so much of the field of

Migration Studies: push-pull, sending-receiving, migrant-nonmigrant, and think in terms of emergent transnational social fields (Bilecen and Lubbers, 2021). The "immobility crisis" highlights the importance of these circular systems. Bachmann-Medick and Kugele (2018, p. 10) state that "mobility ultimately challenges democracy as it incessantly points towards the paradox of democracy and to its inclusive-exclusive structure." In this case, we argue that *immobility* challenges democracy as it undermines one's fundamental ability to adapt to changing circumstances.

References

Adunts, D. (2021). Paternal Circular Migration and Development of Socio-Emotional Skills of Children Left Behind. *CERGE-EI Working Paper Series*, 696.

Ari, Y. O. (2023). Social and economic aspects of internal circular migration flows. *Theoretical & Applied Economics*, 30(4).

Bachmann-Medick, D., & Kugele, J. (Eds.). (2018). *Migration: Changing concepts, critical approaches*. De Gruyter.

Bilecen, B., & Lubbers, M. J. (2021). The networked character of migration and transnationalism. *Global Networks*, 21(4), 837–852.

Castles, S. (2010). Understanding global migration: A social transformation perspective. *Journal of Ethnic and Migration Studies*, 36(10), 1565–1586. https://doi.org/10.1080/1369183X.2010.489381

De Bree, J., Davids, T., & De Haas, H. (2010). Post-return experiences and transnational belonging of return migrants: A Dutch-Moroccan case study. *Global Networks*, 10(4), 489–509. https://doi.org/10.1111/j.1471-0374.2010.00299.x

de Haas, H. (2007). Morocco's migration experience: A transitional perspective. *International Migration*, 45(4), 39–70. https://doi.org/10.1111/j.1468-2435.2007.00419.x

Démographie: La réinsertion des migrants de retour au Maroc: *Analyse des résultats de l'enquête sur la migration de retour des Marocains Résidant à l'étranger de 2003-2004: Exemple des régions du Grand Casablanca et de Souss-Massa-Draa | Téléchargements | Site institutionnel du Haut-Commissariat au Plan du Royaume du Maroc*. (2011). Accessed from https://www.hcp.ma/downloads/Demographie-La-reinsertion-des-migrants-de-retour-au-Maroc-analyse-des-resultats-de-l-enquete-sur-la-migration-de-retour_t22426.html

Ennaji, M. (2014). Moroccan migration history: Origins and causes. In M. Ennaji (Ed.), *Muslim Moroccan migrants in Europe: Transnational migration in its multiplicity* (pp. 17–34). Palgrave Macmillan. https://doi.org/10.1057/9781137476494_2

Fainine, L. (2020). *Enquête nationale sur la migration internationale*. Site institutionnel du Haut-Commissariat au Plan du Royaume du Maroc. Accessed from https://www.hcp.ma/Enquete-nationale-sur-la-migration-internationale_a3237.html

Fidrmuc, J. (2004). Migration and regional adjustment to asymmetric shocks in transition economies. *Journal of Comparative Economics, 32*(2), 230–247. https://doi.org/10.1016/j.jce.2004.02.011

Geertz, C. (1973). The interpretation of cultures (Vol. 5019). Basic books.

Hatim, Y. (2020, April 7). Young Moroccans fleeing COVID-19 swim from Ceuta to Morocco. *Morocco World News*. Accessed from https://www.moroccoworldnews.com/2020/04/298913/young-moroccans-fleeing-COVID-19-swim-from-ceuta-to-morocco

Marhaba operation. (2023). Mohamed V foundation for solidarity. Accessed from https://www.fm5.ma/en/operations/marhaba-operation

Massey, D. S., Connor, P., & Durand, J. (2011). Emigration from two labor frontier nations: a comparison of Moroccans in Spain and Mexicans in the United States. *Papers: revista de sociologia*, 781–803.

Mghari, M. (2011). Profils démographique et socio-économique des migrants de retour. In *La réinsertion des migrants de retour au Maroc*.

Mohamed VI. (2020). *CCME - HM the king delivers a speech to the nation on 69th anniversary of the revolution of the king and the people (full text)*. Conseil de la Communaute Marocaine. Accessed from https://www.ccme.org.ma/en/what-s-new/54597

Natter, K. (2014). Fifty years of Maghreb emigration. *Working Paper, 95*.

Roehner, B. M., Sornette, D., & Andersen, J. V. (2004). Response functions to critical shocks in social sciences: An empirical and numerical study. *International Journal of Modern Physics C, 15*(06), 809–834. https://doi.org/10.1142/S0129183104006236

Stark, O., & Bloom, D. (1985). The new economics of labor migration. *American Economic Review, 75*(2), 173–178.

Wickramasekara, P. (2011). Circular migration: A triple win or a dead end. *SSRN Electronic Journal*. https://doi.org/10.2139/ssrn.1834762

CHAPTER 9

Building a New Home: Modes of Incorporation for 1.5-Generation Return Migrants in Mexico

Mónica Liliana Jacobo-Suárez

INTRODUCTION

Mexican migration to the United States (US henceforth) has a long history: with immigrant flows dating back to the 1880s, this migration corridor is unique in the world due to its continuity, volume, and neighborhood (Durand & Massey, 2003). It should be noted, however, that Mexican migration to the US presents a two-way pattern since its inception. For each flow of Mexican immigration coming to the US there has been a corresponding flow of Mexicans going back to their country of origin. Why, then, should we care about return migration to Mexico nowadays? Because the composition and volume of return migration experienced significant changes in the present century. Mexico's return migration since late twentieth century has been less circular and comparatively more involuntary

M. L. Jacobo-Suárez (✉)
CONAHCYT-El Colegio de México, Mexico City, Mexico
e-mail: mjacobo@colmex.mx

© The Author(s), under exclusive license to Springer Nature Switzerland AG 2024
J. Yeo (ed.), *Return Migration and Crises in Non-Western Countries*, Mobility & Politics,
https://doi.org/10.1007/978-3-031-53562-8_9

than the previous centuries (Jacobo & Cárdenas, 2022). First, we observed a net zero migration between 2005 and 2010 (Passel et al., 2012) to then witnessed a negative migration balance during the period 2009–2014 (González-Barrera, 2015). Both facts raised questions about whether we are beholding the collapse of the Mexican-US migration system (Durand & Arias, 2014) or just observing an increase in returning flows to Mexico triggered by the world economic crisis of 2009, deportation programs, and anti-immigrant legislation in the US (Canales & Meza, 2018). Mexican return migration as a phenomenon is relevant to comprehend returning migrant flows in other regions, particularly in Central America.

These demographic changes occurred under the two administrations of Barack Obama (2009–2013, 2013–2017), who gained the title of "deporter in chief" due to a record-high number of deportations carried out—mostly to Mexico and Central America. Some studies point to the US mass deportation policy as the cause of a humanitarian crisis (Golash-Bosa, 2015). Yet, this chapter argues that other factors, such as Mexico's unpreparedness to receive and adequately reintegrate their return migrants, also contribute to this crisis. The return flows experienced in the first decades of the twenty-first century surprised the Mexican government, accustomed to seeing its citizens leave but not to seeing them return in massive numbers, with few resources and weakened support networks. While return flows to Mexico reached its peak in 2009, it took five years for the Mexican government to design its first reintegration strategy aimed to support returnees, *Somos Mexicanos*. Yet, this program has shown many shortcomings: (1) it was designed to serve only those Mexicans who return forcedly leaving those who did not come back through deportation without support; (2) the program has been widely underfunded; and (3) its impact has not been assessed (Jacobo & Cárdenas, 2020). While support programs provided by Mexico's government have been limited, returnees experience labor, educational, bureaucratic, cultural, and even linguistic challenges upon their return to their home country, particularly for those migrants who have spent a considerable part of their lives in the US. This is the case of 1.5-generation Mexican immigrants, a concept widely used by Rubén Rumbaut (2004), and which refers to those immigrants who were brought by their parents to the US at an early age. Since these immigrants arrived in the destination country as infants or adolescents, their formative process occurs in the local schools, where they acquire values, habits, English proficiency, and a sense of belonging deeply related to the American culture.

This chapter examines the integration and reintegration trajectories of Mexican 1.5-generation immigrants that return, forcedly or under volition, to Mexico during their adulthood or late adolescence. In Mexico, they are considered return migrants with full rights. Nonetheless, Mexico usually constitutes an unfamiliar land for them: bureaucracy, educational institutions, identity documentation required for accessing services, and even speaking and understanding Spanish daily become difficult tasks. But returnees are not the only ones facing challenges. Mexico has gone from being a migrant sending country—mostly to the US—to a country of transit, destination, and return. While Mexico's federal government has reacted to the important number of Mexicans deported during the two Obama administrations, programs prioritize reception services (i.e., food, phones calls, and transportation to communities of origin) over reintegration support (labor training, transitioning education and language programs, etc.) (Jacobo & Cárdenas, 2020), which leaves the burden of reintegration mostly on returnees' shoulders and their families.

Thus, this chapter focuses on analyzing the reintegration experiences of 1.5-generation returnees in Mexico. It examines 45 Mexican returnees with two specific profiles: 25 of our participants were collegegoers (they had completed a degree or were studying one in a Mexican institution) at the time of the interview and 20 worked as customer service agents. The chapter investigates their educational and labor incorporation experiences in Mexico to uncover diverse adaptation strategies and agency manifestations developed by young returnees to adjust to their new environment. In the various cases examined, the nature of return (whether planned, with family, through deportation) as well as their ability to activate support networks in Mexico played important roles facilitating adaptation processes for 1.5-generation returnees. Most collegegoers returned to Mexico with family members who helped them navigate bureaucracy and culture and support them financially so they could continue studying. On the contrary, most of the returnees who worked in call centers experienced deportation, which usually involved family separation and a need to enter the labor market immediately to provide for themselves economically. The two scenarios are framed within the absence of long-term reintegration policies that promote educational continuity and delay entry into the labor market.

Mexico-US Migration: More than a Century of Coming and Going

The Mexico-US migration is a unique phenomenon within the history of international migration. Both countries have a neighborhood defined by 1954 miles of common border. Second, Mexican migration to the US is characterized by a long sustainability; more than 130 years of population flows from south to north and from north to south in a cyclical movement. Third, Mexican migration to the US is characterized by their massiveness; although population flows have varied along time due to political and economic changes, the volume of Mexican immigrants living in the US remains considerable (Durand, 2016). In fact, the US is the main destination for Mexican migrants in the world, accounting for 98 percent of the total Mexican immigrants in the world (CONAPO-BBVA, 2021). Even during the SARS-COVID 19 health emergency, the Mexican-US border remained as the major global migration corridor worldwide during 2020, registering 3.9 percent of global migration and 10.9 million migrants (CONAPO-BBVA, 2021).

It should be noted, however, that Mexican migration to the US migration has a two-way pattern since its inception: for each flow of Mexicans immigrating to the US, there is a corresponding flow of Mexicans returning to their origin country (Giorguli & Bautista, 2022). Until now, wage differences between the US and Mexico economies have worked as push and pull factors for more than a century. This bidirectional pattern is in turn characterized by a cyclical nature: in times of economic growth, Mexican emigration to the US becomes relevant; in times of economic austerity, Mexicans return to their origin country increasingly (Terán, 2022). Considering this cyclical pattern, Durand (2016) characterizes the history of Mexico-US as composed of six main stages. First, during the "enganche" (1880–1920) Mexican migration consisted primarily of men in productive ages emigrating to work on infrastructure. Then, it came the Bracero[1] Program (1942–1964) through which 4.6 million temporary work permits were granted to workers of Mexican origin. Although the Bracero program was unilaterally terminated by the US in 1964, circular migration between Mexico and the US was already consolidated so

---

[1] Bracero is the word used to refer to people who worked with their arms and were employed in agricultural tasks and in the maintenance of railroad tracks, see https://memoricamexico.gob.mx/es/memorica/programa_bracero

immigrant workers continued arriving regardless the termination of the program. The next stage, "the era of the undocumented" (1964 and 1986), was characterized by continuous flows of Mexican immigrants seeking to be employed in agriculture and industry. In fact, Mexican migrants began to spend longer stays in the US, thus promoting the establishment of a Mexican community in that country, which was estimated to be at 2.3 million at the time. The fifth stage of the Mexican-US migration is known as the "immigration reform", which started in 1986 and extended until the end of the twentieth century. During this period, the US government framed the issue of undocumented migration as a threat to national security and proposes the Immigration and Reform and Control Act (IRCA) as its solution. The sixth and most recent stage identified by Durand is known as the new migration pattern, characterized by massive deportations during both Barak Obama's administrations and the high politicization of immigration issues in the public agenda.

While return migration has been present since Mexican flows to the US started, there are important changes in the return population during the twenty-first century. First, a relevant feature of the new returnee profile is their prolonged stay in the US. About 75 percent of the Mexican immigrants have lived and worked in the US for more than 15 years. In these cases, deportation turns out to be particularly dramatic (Giorguli & Bautista, 2022). Second, return migration in Mexico is shaped by a growing heterogeneity (Jacobo & Cárdenas 2020; Giorguli & Bautista, 2022). Participation of retirees, women, and children of migrants born in Mexico (e.g., 1.5-generation immigrants) and in the US has gradually increased. In fact, US-born children of Mexican immigrants constitute a growing population group in Mexico: in 2005, there were 277,815 US-born minors who moved to Mexico[2] during the previous quinquennial; this number more than doubled in 2010, reaching 610,176 minors, then decreased to 601,346 children in 2015 (Aguilar, 2020). Third, uprooting and weakened support networks characterized the experiences of many returnees. As Durand (2022) rightly points out, long-stay migrants who are deported suffer a triple uprooting: for having been forced by circumstances to leave their homeland; for being uprooted from their destination where they tried to put down roots; and finally, because they are forced to

---

[2] Although US-born children are not return migrants in a strict sense, some scholars considered them as part of the return flow because they belong to a family unit that returns to Mexico.

reintegrate into a homeland that is already far away, where they lack strong social networks and where they have few resources to facilitate survival. In fact, young returnees belonging to the 1.5 generation fall within this profile as they spent most part of their lives in the US and coming back to Mexico is closer to a start-from-scratch (Silver, 2018) experience than one of "coming home".

Since 2014 Mexico's federal government implemented the program, We Are Mexican (*Somos Mexicanos*), which provides a wide range of reception services for returnees, i.e., short-term actions like food, water, free phone calls, and transportation from repatriation points to communities of origin. In the medium term, *Somos Mexicanos* includes some medical assistance and information on the educational options available, such as transferring education credits obtained in the US. The various actions included in this program are coordinated by the National Institute of Migration and implemented by various federal agencies. Yet, the coordination mechanisms are not clearly defined as there is not one single agency who is responsible for the results of the program or for managing the financial resources and implemented actions (Balança, 2016). Also, most actions designed by Mexico's government have a very limited timeframe as returnees must apply to these programs during the first six months upon arrival to benefit from them; however, we know reintegration is a complex process that may take several years.

1.5-Generation Return Migrants: Transitioning Between Two Worlds

Previous studies that examine reintegration among 1.5 generation migrants show that incorporation into the country of origin is a complicated and defiant process. Returning to Mexico may implicate family separation, particularly if a deportation occurred, in which case reunification with parents, children, or siblings becomes uncertain. In this regard, Silver (2018) points out the long-lasting effects and transnational consequences of US deportation, as they continue affecting the experiences of forced and voluntary returnees beyond its own borders. Also, young returnees may experience social stigma and even discrimination when they are positioned as criminals, social outsiders, or dangerous citizens in their communities of origin by the non-migrant population (Olvera & Muela, 2016). Furthermore, studies indicate that bureaucratic and administrative processes often block returnees' access to basic services and rights and ultimately hinders reintegration (Pinillos & Ortiz, 2021). On the bright side, even though returnees and deportees may contend with social exclusion, bureaucracy, and long-term adaptation processes, in Mexico they enjoy the freedom that comes with formal citizenship (Jacobo & Despagne, 2022).

Once in Mexico, the 1.5-generation youth experience various incorporation processes, among the most important, education and labor. The literature on returning children and youth in Mexico concentrates on two areas, those studies concerning their incorporation into the educational system (mainly in basic education) and research examining their integration into the labor market, which highlights integration into the call center industry. Within the literature that addresses the educational incorporation of returning children and youth, we find a predominance of studies that analyze the challenges experienced in basic education (elementary and middle school) over those that investigate upper higher education experiences. Research on basic education indicate that school insertion processes experienced by Mexican returnees are far from being inclusive. Students are often invisible for teachers and school authorities; teachers lack pedagogical tools to support students' curricular and cultural transition (Zúñiga & Giorguli, 2019); there are no language transitioning programs to help returnee students develop their oral and written Spanish skills (Jacobo, 2022), and extensive bureaucratic requirements often hinder formal registration, revalidation, and educational continuity (Petrone, 2020; Silver 2018).

The few studies that examine returnees' incorporation into higher education highlight the opportunity that Mexican universities offer to get a degree at an affordable cost. Once in Mexico, life course milestones, such as applying to college (Cortéz & Hamann, 2014; Jacobo & Despagne, 2022; Petrone, 2020) and embarking on new careers, are possible or, at least, more feasible to achieve than in the US if you lack legal status. Some studies show young returnees who move "voluntarily" to Mexico to pursue a professional career (Cortéz & Hamann, 2014; Cortéz et al., 2015); when 1.5-generation migrants encounter glass ceilings and limits to develop professionally or are unable to move up the social ladder in the American society, they decide to move to the country where they are citizens of. While moving to Mexico may illustrate their agency, it also points out to a constrained choice (Silver, 2018): 1.5-generation immigrants return to Mexico when they felt paralyzed by their limited opportunities for school or work, when they are immobilized by chronic anxiety, or when are compelled to leave the US due to a family member deportation.

Like their process of adjustment in the US, adaptation to Mexico depends on the local context of reception, that is, if they reintegrate to a rural or urban community, if they need to remigrate internally in search of job or school opportunities, and even if they are welcomed by relatives and community members. The previous experience in America provided returnees with English skills, highly valued in the Mexican labor market, in which they get incorporated as English teachers, as waiters in restaurants, as tourist guides, or as customer service agents in call centers. Regarding the call center industry, studies show they do a heavy recruitment of near-native English speakers such as deported 1.5-generation migrants in Mexico and Central America. On the one hand, call centers offer deportees with the means of immediate economic stability upon which to begin rebuilding after the trauma of expulsion (Anderson, 2015). For some of these deportees, working in a call center represents the best option in local job markets where they are frequently rejected as criminals and/or drug addicts. As they are employed as bilingual operators, their salaries are relatively high for Mexico's economic context, around 12,000 pesos, or about 600,000 dollars per month. Also, call centers offer a sheltered environment where 1.5-generation returnees realize that they were not alone as "Americanized" Mexicans back in Mexico. Thus, call centers allow American cultural expressions that in other spaces would be stigmatized. In other words, call centers offer a context of reception that nurtures migrants' feelings of belonging and security. On the other hand, call centers' jobs are repetitive and intense with little opportunity of advancement, benefits, and social security. In other words, this industry offers returnees limited opportunities to grow. In addition, by promoting an Americanized environment, returnees continue to feel as outsiders because they do not mingle with the Mexican society broadly (Da Cruz, 2021; Ogan & Ozakca, 2010). By working and socializing in English, their acquisition of Spanish is also hampered. In fact, speaking English, their mannerisms and dress code mark significant differences between returnees and other Mexicans, which provoke a social sanction from other Mexicans without migratory history (Jacobo & Despagne, 2022). Therefore, returnees often find themselves excluded from national membership, at least in the short term, despite their formal citizenship to Mexico. In this scenario, the existence of programs to assist and promote long-term reintegration processes is crucial although it is an issue still absent in Mexican government agenda.

In accordance with the literature, this chapter analyzes the labor and educational incorporation patterns of 45 young return migrants: 25 who chose to pursue a professional career by completing college education and 20 who joined the call center industry to integrate into the labor market. It examines the individual, family, and institutional conditions that encourage young returnees to continue studying, drop out of school, or join the labor market without completing their higher education. In other words, we ask what make young returnees to decide to study a university degree in Mexico while others choose to work in a call center? By asking about the factors that influence their decision, I emphasize the agency that these young people have for making decisions intentionally in the context of return. This recognition does not exclude, however, the existence of opportunity structures and specific challenges inherent to the diverse reception contexts in Mexico.

Data, Methods, and Participants

This research derives from a broader research project named Educational Trajectories and Labor Incorporation Prospects for Young Returnees, which received CONACYT funding (292078). The fieldwork was carried out during March, April, and May 2019 and consisted of utilizing focus groups, interviews, and a short survey with 90 young return migrants in five Mexican states. We decided to focus on 1.5-generation returnees as they encounter more obstacles during reintegration due to their strong emotional and cultural attachments to the US, the country where they spent their formative years. As we already pointed out in Sect.2, demographic changes show returnees who have spent long stays in the US, 15 years on average, which may weaken social networks and family ties in México. Returnees belonging to the 1.5 generation come back to Mexico in the late adolescence or early adulthood; therefore, school and labor incorporation are central themes to their reintegration and justify the importance of analyzing these two specific profiles. First, we examine the trajectories of 25 collegegoers, who return during their late adolescence and were able to incorporate and continue to higher education in a Mexican institution in Puebla, Veracruz, or Mexico City at the time of the interview. Second, we study 20 call center agents, one of the most popular jobs in Mexico available for 1.5 generation returnees, who at the time of the interview were hired by transnational companies in Guadalajara, Tijuana, and Mexico City. The sample was purposeful, i.e., we specifically reach universities and call centers and ask if they identify 1.5-generation returnees within their employees and students. Once we found our first participants, we apply a snowball technique to reach more returnees. The analytical approach used is retrospective, i.e., we reconstructed participants' migratory trajectories as well as educational and labor histories from the moment they first migrated to the US until the moment we interviewed them as college students or call center agents living in Mexico. We mostly relied on our survey to reconstruct life trajectories.

The purpose of using focus groups as a data collection technique was to promote self-disclosure among returnees with similar experiences and life histories and thus learn how participants really think and feel (Krueger & Casey, 2000) about some sensitive topics—such as returning to Mexico, experiencing exclusion and discrimination in both the US and Mexico, deportation, and the emotional shock of returning to Mexico. We asked participants about five central themes: life in the US; return and reintegration experiences; educational trajectory and use of languages in both countries; labor insertion in Mexico; and future expectations. Interviews were used to obtain deeper information with some of the participants. Both focus groups and interviews were audio-recorded with the permission of the participants, later transcribed verbatim and finally coded. In a first round, we used predetermined codes coming from the literature on reintegration and return migration. All names used are pseudonyms.

It should be noted that the goal of qualitative techniques is not to produce generalizable statements but rather to show the inherent complexity of social phenomena and their possible causal processes (Mahoney & Goertz, 2003). Therefore, the analysis, discussion, and conclusions of this research must be read within the context of the participants: Mexican returnees belonging to the 1.5 generation, who moved from the US to Mexico during the first two decades of the twenty-first century.

Table 9.1 illustrates some characteristics among participant returnees. We observe a variety of reasons to return to Mexico that go from a total lack of agency (when participants follow a deported parent or were themselves deported) to those situations that illustrate a constrained choice (e.g., by illness or death of a family member) or a conscious agency exercise (voluntary and planned return, either in family or by themselves). Deportation as a cause of return marks an important difference between returnees working in call centers and those pursuing higher education:

Table 9.1 Profile of participants

Cause of return	Collegegoers % (n = 25)	Call center agents % (n = 20)
Father/mother deported	8.34	0
Returnee deported	25	81.25
Inability to adapt to the US	4.17	0
Illness/death of a relative in Mx	12.51	0
Voluntary family return	29.17	0
Voluntary return	20.83	18.78

about 33 percent of collegegoers interviewed returned forcedly (following a deported parent or due to own deportation) in contrast with 81 percent of call center agents who were deported. Context of exit matters as immigrants who are forced to leave do not have time to active support networks in the country of origin, which in turn affects the resources available for their immediate reintegration.

On the other side of the spectrum, we find those immigrants who planned their return or came back to Mexico on their own volition, either by themselves or accompanied by family. About 42 percent of those returnees who now pursue or have completed a university degree come back voluntarily in comparison to 18 percent of the call center agents that did so. When asked about the year our participants returned to Mexico, 45 percent did so between 2008 and 2012, a period with the highest deportation numbers under President Barak Obama.

THE PURSUIT FOR HIGHER EDUCATION: COLLEGEGOERS

Studies on the 1.5 generation exhibit illegality as a defining feature of the late adolescence and adulthood among immigrant youth in the US. Undocumented status depresses aspirations (Abrego, 2011), causes frustration with the present and uncertainty about the future, and ultimately blocks educational aspirations and social mobility as higher education and labor opportunities are constrained for 1.5-generation immigrants (Gonzales, 2016). Yet, studies on the 1.5 generation carried out in the US underestimate the possibility that Mexican immigrant youth achieve a career path outside the US, in Mexico, for instance, where they have full rights as citizens. Coming back to the origin country allows young returnees to exercise formal citizenship and, with that, have access to opportunities that were not available to them as undocumented immigrants, such as scholarships, affordable tertiary education, a career path out of blue-collar jobs, an identification card, and the right to vote (Jacobo & Despagne, 2022).

Among the 25 young return migrants who have had access to higher education options, we observe that it has not been an obstacle-free path; on the contrary, the process to be a collegegoer in Mexico is rather full of challenges of a diverse nature. A salient obstacle for most of the returnees interviewed was the excessively bureaucratic nature of education processes in Mexico. Highly complex revalidation processes along with erroneous information about enrollment requirements are common experiences for returnees, as Rosa shared with us: "Between coming and going, the years passed, and after that time, the TOEFL exam that I had taken, it was no longer valid for enrollment". Rosa was finishing her degree on International Business at the *Universidad Veracruzana* when we met her. Even though she did research on the requirements to get into college, information was confusing and administrative processes complex. It took her two years to gather all documents (with apostilles and official translations) and do the admission tests to finally get accepted. In the meantime, her family provided her financially while she worked part-time as an English teacher. Bureaucratic barriers can also take the form of repeating school grades already completed in the US, a practice some Mexican schools ask when they do not recognize foreign education certificates. This was Viví's case, who moved with their parents from New York to Puebla: "I had to repeat some high school grades here, although I had already finished it [in the US], to have the [Mexican] certificate and enroll in the University". Viví has just started a bachelor's in business administration at the *Benemérita Universidad Autónoma de Puebla.*

In addition to administrative and bureaucratic issues, having a good command of Spanish plays a central role for all returnees during their educational re-insertion process in Mexico. Mastery of the language of instruction is even more important to carry out college studies due to the complexity of cognitive processes and what is demanded of a student at this level, for example, writing a thesis. Apart from two cases, all returnees who followed a university or professional path in Mexico experienced obstacles due to not having a full command of academic Spanish when they started college. As, who become a Programmer, narrates: "I couldn't follow the teacher (in the dictation). So, I would write some things, and, in the end, I couldn't understand what I had written. So far, there are things I don't know what they mean". At the classroom level, most returnees interviewed experienced some level of rejection by their peers or teachers due to their poor command of Spanish, as Giovani, who is also a Programmer, expressed: "When you start to speak and everyone tells you that you speak very weird, well, you feel quite uncomfortable trying to talk". For the most part, collegegoers did not receive school support to transition from English to Spanish, something that contrasts with their educational experience in the US where most of them had English as a Second Language class.

In addition to command of Spanish, knowledge of English influences educational choices of 1.5-generation returnees. In one case, a returnee considered enrolling in a private university where a percentage of their courses would be taught in English because he didn't consider himself to be proficient enough in Spanish. However, paying for private school, although more affordable than going to college in the US, might not be available to all returnees. English also influences returnees who may choose to study a career where this language is an advantage. For instance, we found various returnees who were enrolled in International Business, International Relations, Linguistics, and Tourism, where they already cover the graduation requirement of having a high command of English and could take some courses in that language.

We found a common trait among returnees that became collegegoers: the existence of a strong support network that worked as the main facilitator to overcome administrative obstacles, developing Spanish language skills, and navigating cultural and pedagogical codes inherent to the Mexican educational system. For those who experienced a family return, support was provided by nuclear and extended family, as the following testimonies illustrate:

> *My mother went around a lot, they (school authorities) asked her for a lot of documents, until she managed to enroll us in school. (Marian, Programmer, Mexico City)*
> *My uncles taught me Spanish at home so that I could understand the classes (in Mexico). (Fernanda, International Relations, Puebla)*
> *They (my uncles) sat me down and told me: you are going to have English, the teacher is always right. Don't argue with them. (Yadira, International Business, Veracruz)*

In the last quote, Yadira's uncles taught her a subtle trait of Mexican school culture: do not contradict the teacher. Such advice is particularly relevant to survive English classes in Mexico as returnees who attended

American schools get back with a high command of this language, which can be a potential source of conflict if they attempt to correct their Mexican English teachers. Hence, families support returnees to get through a wide variety of administrative requirements, substitute teachers in teaching returnees Spanish skills needed to survive school in Mexico, and provide knowledge about schools' cultural norms and accepted conducts. In other words, family and support networks work as facilitators for long-term adaptation in the post-return context.

Becoming a Customer Service Agent in an English-Speaking Call Center

The call center industry is not a uniform sector in Mexico. Some call centers pay more but offer less security, featuring short campaigns and short contracts; others give employees the opportunity to augment their salary with many bonuses; other call center jobs are lower paid but come with a wide array of social security benefits (permanent contract, medical care, vouchers, housing credits, and so on; Da Cruz, 2018). As a result, English-speaking Mexican call centers have become places where middle-class Mexicans mingle with 1.5-generation deportees who are native speakers of English thanks to their immigrant experience in the US. Differences between both groups are salient as many deportees also display visible tattoos, a trait associated with stigmatization and criminal behavior in Mexican white-collar jobs.

What makes young Mexican returnees to seek a job within the call center industry? Call centers offer specific advantages over other labor sectors and over going to college. First, the hiring process is almost immediate and does not require many documents, nor does it require translation of previous education diplomas completed in the US. Carlos, who worked at a call center in Guadalajara, confirmed this: "Yes, with ATNT they didn't ask me for any papers, just like… in the interview they told me 'Ah you come over, you're hired'". Alan, who also works in a call center in Guadalajara, elaborated on the hiring requirements: "Yes, they accept documents from there (US). The GED or high school, or even high school truncates". In second place, having an excellent command of English is often a necessary and sufficient condition to be hired in the industry. In this sense, Max, now a programmer in Mexico City, shared with us his previous experience as a call center agent: "I think it's one of the easiest jobs you can get [as returnee]. You don't need papers; you just have to show that you know how to speak English and you're almost hired".

Third, salaries offered by call centers are generally higher than those paid in other industries which also demand greater physical effort, e.g., agriculture, manufacturing, construction. Carlos shared: "I am earning 4,800 (Mexican pesos) a fortnight and then they give us a bonus, you can earn up to 12,000 as a bonus and, yes, I am doing fairly well". Pedro, who returned to Mexico just a year prior our interview, mentioned: "When I started [working] at call centers I came home and I told my aunt, 'Hey I'm going to be making this money' and she was like 'what?' you're rich!". These testimonies illustrate some important conditions of the Mexican labor market. On one side, wages offered by this industry are highly competitive in Mexico, where salaries and cost of living are much cheaper than in the US. On the other side, transnational corporations make a significant profit by hiring English-speaking returnees in Mexico and not in the US where the cost of their work would be much higher. Thus, the deportation system and a very constrained structure of opportunities faced by undocumented youth play in favor of transnational companies for whom the bilingualism and biculturalism of these return migrants are valuable commodities.

To these advantages we must add that working in a call center allows for a greater ability and skills transfer, like putting in practice their high command of the English language, knowledge of American culture, and familiarity with the culture of customer service. These elements make a significant difference within the call center, because unlike someone who has studied English professionally in Mexico, return migrants (even if they have not completed higher education) have knowledge of the North American culture, its holidays and festivities, and the prevailing codes and values learned during their formative years in American schools. Such knowledge has a direct impact on the culture of customer service, the cornerstone of call centers, and in which returnees are good at.

Despite these advantages, returnees working at call centers did try alternative career options. At least half of those interviewed had tried to revalidate their studies to start higher education in Mexico. Yet, extremely complex revalidation systems, incorrect information provided by education authorities, lack of support networks to help navigating bureaucracy, not having a good command of the Spanish language, and the need to provide for themselves were reasons to cut short their college-dreams in Mexico. Testimonies pointed to, again, a structure of constrained choices where college education oftentimes is not feasible in Mexico if deportees lack family or support networks in Mexico, as we can see below:

> *I'm not studying... I don't think I'll last 4 or 5 years studying because I'm alone (in Mexico), so I want to study something easy. (Javier, Tijuana)*
>
> *Well, yes, I have wanted to study to become an English teacher, because I already know English... but you also have to work to be able to support yourself. (Octavio, Guadalajara)*
>
> *One of the biggest drawbacks is the lack of correct information. I studied high school [again] to enter college in Mexico. And when I finished, they told me that I needed to complete middle school. (Linos, Guadalajara)*
>
> *They asked me for 7,000 pesos to revalidate my previous education, and then other 30,000 for the paramedic training. There was no way to pay that with salaries of 700, 800 pesos a day. (Daniel, Cd. Mx.)*

Discussion: Modes of Incorporation and the Role of Public Policy

When reconstructing the migratory histories and educational trajectories of the young people interviewed, several findings are observed. First, young returnees use their own resources—mostly family resources—to reintegrate into the Mexican educational system, since the federal government lacks specific programs to facilitate education and work incorporation. In our interviews, no young returnee reported government or school support to guide them in the enrollment process, revalidation of studies, much less access to welcoming programs for students with migrant trajectories, or support for language transition. A second finding points out to the relevance of returning to Mexico accompanied by family, which in turns facilitates school enrolment and educational continuity up to college. For the young university students interviewed, the presence of the nuclear and/or extended family was decisive to navigate the Mexican educational bureaucracy and thus guaranteeing school access. From their relatives, returnees learn important cultural codes to survive the Mexican schools and even improve their command of Spanish. No less important, family support networks also provided necessary economic resources to finance returnees' educational continuity and delay entry into the labor market.

Even though getting a professional career could be more affordable in Mexico than going to college in the US, it may not be a feasible option for all returnees. Experiencing a deportation process during adolescence or youth is a risk factor for abandoning studies in Mexico, due to the need of young people to provide themselves financially, the absence of scholarships to support their educational continuity, and the possible effects that having their lives abruptly interrupted have on their mental health (Silver, 2018). Among returnees employed in call centers, the "need" to provide for themselves was the main reason for not continuing their higher education in Mexico, in addition to the excessive bureaucracy that prevented most of them from revalidating studies completed in the US, a requirement necessary to continue your education in Mexico. Given the lack of support networks that guides their educational insertion and provide them economically, and the absence of long-term reintegration government programs, these young people have been pushed into precarious labor markets. Call centers offer a competitive salary, few or no documentation requirements, and the creation of friendship networks among returning youth (Gutiérrez, 2017; Da Cruz, 2018). However, the social dynamics within them perpetuate returnees' social isolation (Ogan & Ozakca, 2010), while working conditions offer few opportunities for social and economic mobility (Hualde, 2017). This discussion must be contextualized to the Mexican labor market in which working conditions are precarious; whether you are a migrant or have never left the country, there are low wages, little access to social security, and housing benefits (Hualde, 2017).

What, then, could be done from a policy perspective to facilitate the educational incorporation of young returnees? We must first acknowledge the great diversity of experiences, which in turn suggest that returnees have different resources for reintegration once in Mexico: while some youth return accompanied by their nuclear family and/or are received by extended families who help them get through multiple learning processes needed for their adaptation, there are others whose return was unplanned, sudden, and even forced, which constrains their ability to activate valuable resources and support networks upon return. Hence, policy-oriented actions can facilitate returnees' cultural, linguistic, social, institutional, educational, and labor transition in Mexico. Based on the testimonies discussed, we propose specific recommendations:

1. Creating scholarships at the upper secondary and higher level for young returnees. It is a priority that these scholarships are flexible in terms of age limits and the time elapsed since they come back to Mexico, since not all returnees can continue their higher education immediately upon return.

2. Training school and administrative staff to report on the registration and revalidation processes clearly and correctly, as we observed bureaucratic requirements are common obstacles most of our participants experienced.
3. Establishing welcoming programs that support the linguistic and curricular transition of return students at all educational levels and thus facilitate their permanence and continuity through the Mexican education system.
4. Designing short career options with high economic returns to allow social mobility of returning youth. It is desirable that these options consider the command of English as an added value. The testimonials presented here also illustrate experiences in which bilingualism and biculturalism have been used as symbolic capital associated with economic and professional benefits, as in the case of the call centers. Yet, it is pertinent to create labor opportunities beyond this industry for this untapped labor force.
5. Invest in bilateral partnerships, US-Mexico, to better prepare teachers and schools to implement programs that can promote the bilingualism and biculturality of these group while in the US and when they come back to Mexican schools.

References

Abrego, L. (2011). Legal consciousness of undocumented Latinos: Fear and stigma as barriers to claims-making for first and 1.5 generation immigrants. *Law and Society Review, 45*(2), 337–370.

Aguilar, R. (2020, August 12). ¿Dónde quepo? ¿De dónde soy ahora? Análisis de las barreras que enfrentan los migrantes de retorno en el Estado de México. In *Conference Presented at the Permanent Seminar Migration, Return and Infancy*, UNAM-IIA.

Anderson, J. (2015). "Tagged as a criminal": Narratives of deportation and return migration in a Mexico City call center. *Latino Studies, 13*(1), 8–27.

Balança, I. L. (2016). Los desafíos de la coordinación intergubernamental: la atención a migrantes mexicanos deportados en el estado de Baja California. (Masters thesis). El Colegio de la Frontera Norte, México.

Canales, A., & Meza, S. (2018). Tendencias y patrones de la Migración de Retorno. *Migración y Desarrollo, 16*(30), 123–155.

Consejo Nacional de Población, Fundación BBVA y BBVA Research. (2021). *Anuario de Migración y Remesas México 2021*. Conapo-Fundación BBVA-BBVA Research. México, pp. 200. Retrieved from https://www.bbvaresearch.com/

publicaciones/anuario-de-migracion-y-remesas-mexico-2021/#:~:text=El%20 Anuario%20de%20Migraci%C3%B3n%20y,el%20mundo%2C%20haciendo%20 %C3%A9nfasis%20en

Cortéz, N., & Hamann, E. T. (2014). College dreams à la Mexicana ... Agency and strategy among American-Mexican transnational students. *Latino Studies, 12*(2), 237–258.

Cortéz, N., García, A., & Altamirano, A. (2015). Estudiantes Migrantes de retorno en México: Estrategias emprendidas para acceder a una educación universitaria. *Revista Mexicana de Investigación Educativa, 20*(67), 1187–1208.

Da Cruz, M. (2018). Offshore migrant workers: Return migrants in Mexico's English-speaking call centers. *Journal of the Social Sciences, 4*(1), 39–57.

Da Cruz, M. (2021). El retorno como experiencia para romper el techo de cristal. Trayectorias migratorias y profesional de los jóvenes mexicanos de la generación 1.5 en los call centers bilingues de la Ciudad de México. In A. Hualde, M. Paris, & O. Woo (Eds.), *Experiencias de retorno en migrantes mexicanos en contextos urbanos*. El Colegio de la Frontera Norte.

Durand, J. (2016). *Historia Mínima de la Migración México-Estados Unidos*. El Colegio de México.

Durand, J. (2022, September 11). Perfil del Migrante Retornado. *La Jornada*. Retrieved from https://www.jornada.com.mx/2022/09/11/opinion/012a2pol

Durand, J., & Arias, P. (2014). Escenarios locales del colapso migratorio. Indicios desde los Altos -de Jalisco. *Papeles de Población, 20*(81), 165–192.

Durand, J., & y Massey, D. (2003). Clandestinos. Migración México-Estados Unidos en los albores del siglo XX. Universidad Autónoma de Zacatecas/ Miguel Ángel Porrúa.

Giorguli, S., & Bautista, A. (2022). Introducción: nuevos patrones de retorno y los retos institucionales para su integración. In S. Giorguli & A. Bautista (Eds.), *Derechos Fragmentados Acceso a Derechos Sociales y Migración de Retorno a México*. El Colegio de México.

Golash-Bosa, T. (2015). *Deported: Immigrant policing, disposable labor and global capitalism*. New York University Press.

Gonzales, R. (2016). *Lives in Limbo. Undocumented and coming of age in America*. University of California Press.

González-Barrera, A. (2015). *More Mexicans leaving than coming to the U.S.* Pew Research Center. Retrieved January 15, 2021, from https://www.pewresearch.org/hispanic/2015/11/19/more-mexicans-leaving-than-coming-to-the-u-s/

Gutiérrez, M., Jr. (2017). Fragmented identities: Contention of space and identity among Salvadoran deportees. In B. Roberts, C. Menjivar, & N. Rodríguez (Eds.), *Deportation and return in a border-restricted by Borders: Experiences in Mexico, El Salvador, Guatemala and Honduras* (pp. 111–129). Springer.

Hualde, A. (2017). *Más trabajo que empleo. Trayectorias laborales y precariedad en los call centers de México.* El Colegio de la Frontera Norte.

Jacobo, M. (2022). La niñez y juventud migrante de retorno en México: Hallazgos, avances y pendientes (2015-2022). *Norteamérica, 17*(2), 1–35.

Jacobo, M., & Cárdenas, N. (2020). Back on your own: migración de retorno y la respuesta del gobierno federal en México. *Migraciones Internacionales, 11*(11), 1–24.

Jacobo, M., & Cárdenas, N. (2022). Return migration to México. In A. Feldman, X. Bada, J. Durand, & S. Schutze (Eds.), *The Routledge history of modern Latin American migration* (pp. 369–382). Routledge.

Jacobo, M., & Despagne, C. (2022). Jóvenes migrantes de retorno: construyendo nociones alternativas de ciudadanía en México. *Estudios Sociológicos, 40*(119), 455–486.

Krueger, R., & Casey, M. (2000). *Focus group. A practical guide for applied research.* Sage.

Mahoney, J., & Goertz, G. (2003). A Tale of Two Cultures: Contrasting Quantitative and Qualitative Research. *Political Analysis, 14*(3), 227–249.

Ogan, C., & Ozakca, M. (2010). A bridge across the bosphorus returned migrants, their internet and media use and social capital. *Social Science Computer Review, 28,* 118–134.

Olvera, J., & Muela, C. (2016). Sin familia en México: redes sociales alternativas para la migración de retorno de jóvenes mexicanos deportados con experiencia carcelaria en México. *Mexican Studies, 32*(2), 302–320.

Passel, J., Cohn, D., & González-Barrera, A. (2012). *Net migration from Mexico falls to zero—And perhaps less.* Pew Research Center. Retrieved January 15, 2021 from https://www.pewresearch.org/hispanic/2012/04/23/net-migration-from-mexico-falls-to-zero-and-perhaps-less/

Petrone, E. (2020). A DREAMer's transnational pursuit for higher education and the impenetrable wall of neoliberalis. *Latino Studies, 18,* 558–580.

Pinillos, G., & Ortiz, L. (2021). Recovering citizenship after-deportation in Mexico-US border. *Frontera Norte, 33*(8), 1–25.

Rumbaut, R. (2004). Ages, Life Stages, and Generational Cohorts: Decomposing the Immigrant First and Second Generations in the United States. *International Migration Review, 38*(3), 1160–1205.

Silver, A. M. (2018). Displaced at "home": 1.5-generation immigrants navigating membership after returning to Mexico. *Ethnicities, 18*(2), 208–224.

Terán, D. (2022). *Análisis de la Situación de la Migración de Retorno de México a Estados Unidos.* Fondo de Población de las Naciones Unidas. Retrieved from https://mexico.unfpa.org/es/publications/an%C3%A1lisis-de-la-situaci%C3%B3n-de-la-migraci%C3%B3n-de-retorno-m%C3%A9xico-desde-estados-unidos

Zúñiga, V., & Giorguli, S. (2019). *Niños y niñas en la migración de Estados Unidos a México: la generación 1.5.* El Colegio de México.

CHAPTER 10

Venezuelan Migration in Peru: Exploring the Causes for Venezuelans' Return Migration

Maritza Concha and Rasha Mannaa

INTRODUCTION

In recent years, the surge of Venezuelan migration has had a profound impact on various countries in the Latin American region (Freier & Parent, 2019). Peru has been significantly affected by this migratory phenomenon, witnessing an influx of Venezuelan immigrants seeking refuge, economic opportunities, and stability. The complexities surrounding the return of Venezuelan migrants to their home country have emerged as a compelling area of study.

The multifaceted nature of the return migration phenomenon necessitates a comprehensive examination of the factors contributing to its occurrence. One crucial aspect explored in this chapter is the impact of migratory policies led by various Peruvian administrations. These policies have played

M. Concha (✉) • R. Mannaa
University of Central Florida, Orlando, FL, USA
e-mail: maritza.concha@ucf.edu; rasha@ucf.edu

© The Author(s), under exclusive license to Springer Nature Switzerland AG 2024
J. Yeo (ed.), *Return Migration and Crises in Non-Western Countries*, Mobility & Politics,
https://doi.org/10.1007/978-3-031-53562-8_10

a key role in shaping the experiences and decisions of Venezuelan migrants regarding their potential return to their homeland. Furthermore, this chapter also investigates the xenophobic attitudes that have pervaded certain sectors of Peruvian society, fueling discrimination and animosity towards Venezuelan migrants. Understanding the prevalence and manifestations of xenophobia is crucial for comprehending the challenges faced by returning migrants and the potential barriers they encounter upon their arrival in Venezuela.

While the Peruvian context is at the forefront of this analysis, it is essential to explore the efforts led by President Nicolás Maduro to facilitate the safe return of Venezuelan migrants. By examining the initiatives and policies implemented by the Venezuelan government, we can gain valuable insights into their approach to attract their citizens back to their home country. Comparisons will be drawn between these efforts and similar undertakings by other authoritarian regimes in the Latin American region, providing a broader perspective on the dynamics of return migration.

This chapter not only contributes to the academic discourse on migration but also provides practical insights for policymakers, humanitarian organizations, and governments grappling with the challenges posed by return migration in the region.

Understanding Return Migration

Return migration has always existed. Particular attention was devoted to this topic back in the 1980s when Western European nations started promoting the repatriation of migrants (Kerwin et al., 2018). Nevertheless, there is limited consensus among scholars on how to frame return migration. Some definitions include repatriation while others see it as expulsion, aided return, and voluntary return (Michiel Baas & International Institute For Asian Studies, 2015). Pérez-López (2001) defines return migrants as people who spent a substantial amount of time living abroad as immigrants in a nation other than their own before returning to their home country to establish themselves.

The Migration Data Portal identifies two forms of return migration: Voluntary return, "the assisted or independent return to the country of origin, transit or another country based on the voluntary decision of the returnee" (MDP, 2022, Definition section, p. 3) and forced return, "a migratory movement which, although the drivers can be diverse, involves force, compulsion, or coercion" (MDP, 2022, Definition section, p. 4).

Return migration literature has focused on four main topics, namely the size and direction of migration flows; the characteristics of migrants as defined by demographic, economic, social, and cultural variables; the reasons for migration; and the means by which migrants adapt to and integrate into the host society can differ between and within migrant groups (Richmond, 1983).

A study from Batistella (2018) recognizes several patterns in the return processes. First, is the *Return of achievement*. This reflects the conclusion of the migration project or plan, where the immigrant returns willingly after having accomplished the goal for which they traveled overseas. *Return upon completion* involves migrants returning after the contract is over, but not voluntarily since they would prefer to stay in the host country for an additional amount of time or travel abroad once again. *Setback return* happens when the migrant returns to their home country before the migration process is complete which may be caused by a variety of reasons such as dissatisfaction with working circumstances, familial considerations, personal experiences of abuse, or even trafficking. Lastly, *Crisis return* or forced return, is one in which migrants are brought back on by events like political unrest or natural calamity. A forced departure is due to security concerns or political decisions made by the migrant's country of origin or destination. The repatriation of undocumented immigrants is another possibility in this scenario.

RETURN MIGRATION TO AUTHORITARIAN COUNTRIES IN THE LATIN AMERICAN AND CARIBBEAN REGION

In the 1980s, scholars in several Latin American nations began to study the phenomenon of return migration as a result of the increasingly frequent return of those who had been exiled during the military dictatorships in conjunction with the restoration of democracy. To motivate skilled workers to return to their home country, several developing nations, like Cuba, Mexico, and Argentina, implemented return-incentive programs. Incentives used in these programs typically include housing assistance, exemptions from customs restrictions and duties, employment and tax benefits, coaching, travel expenses covered, business loans, and initiatives to support the education of migrants' children (Pérez-López, 2001). The main reason for returning to their home countries is based on *Return of achievement*, which is based on a voluntarily return after achieving a goal

(Barcenas Alfonso et al., 2022). Other common reasons for returning include reuniting with family members and for education purposes.

When individuals contemplate returning to their home country, they often find themselves facing a decision that bears similarities to the one they made when they initially departed. It involves a series of considerations and evaluations of various factors. Just as individuals carefully weigh their options and assess the potential benefits and drawbacks before embarking on a journey to a new land, they go through a similar thought process when contemplating a return to their place of origin. However, it can be challenging to understand why immigrants from authoritarian regimes would want to return to their country of origin.

Brief History of Venezuelan Authoritarian Regime

In order to understand the Venezuela exodus, we must first review the implementation of an authoritarian government in Venezuela and its consequences. The authoritarian government in Venezuela started to take shape under President Hugo Chávez two decades ago, and has hardened ever since under his successor, Nicolás Maduro. The forced convening of a constituent assembly in 1999, through a consultative referendum to impose the "will of the people" over the Constitution, was the first step in undermining democratic principles and values. It is important to highlight that the Constitution itself, does not recognize this mechanism to be legitimate for a constitutional reform. As a result, the newly elected Constituent Assembly, which the president of the republic fully controls, interfered with and took control of all previously elected bodies of government. The Constitution was approved without any type of agreement, an electoral system for the Assembly was enacted, and conditions were set for the establishment of an authoritarian, centralized government that has since abolished and replaced any checks and balances and the rule of law (Brewer-Carías, 2010).

Following the Venezuelan experience of 1999, a new method was developed in which those who took the initiative to call the referendum, rather than political actors, determined the general bylaws for the election of a Constituent Assembly, which was also not established in the 1961 Constitution as a method for constitutional review. In this instance, the formation and growth of a framework for the emergence of an authoritarian government using democratic instruments, rather than a democratic government, was the final outcome (Brewer-Carías, 2010). President

Hugo Chávez unilaterally constituted the assembly in a way that prevented the creation of a plural political entity, a popular consultation or consultative referendum was gathered to overturn the constitution.

Opposition has been present through all the democratic regressing processes in Venezuela. Some literature finds the survival of the authoritarian regime in Venezuela, impressive at the most. Political opposition has come from party leaders, the media, civil society, military units, and international players since Maduro assumed office as Chávez's chosen successor upon the latter's death from cancer in March 2013. He was not elected in a primary; rather, Chávez personally chose him to be the next head of what he called "Bolivarian revolution." (Corrales, 2020).

A series of political, institutional, military, and economic problems that Maduro has faced since 2015 are likely to have toppled any democratic administration. Maduro has turned the inherited semi-authoritarian system into a complete dictatorship by his autocratic responses. Internationally, Maduro has changed his great-power backers and created new, primarily illegal exports. According to Corrales (2020), he has employed two authoritarian toolkits domestically. The traditional one includes brutal repression, rigged elections, violations of the separation of powers, exclusions of opposition leaders, and attacks on them, as well as grants of impunity to purchase the support of the financial elite. The more inventive one combines functions in a variety of ways including delegating economic responsibilities to the military, giving paramilitary and criminal roles to organized civilians, transforming a fraudulently elected constituent assembly into a multifunctional political machine, and delegating sovereignty to a group of non-state actors, among others.

Along with transitioning from a restricted democracy to an authoritarian government, during the late 2010s, Venezuela has encountered a persistent series of crises that no other contemporary Latin American country could begin to compare to (Bull & Rosales, 2020). These crises have substantial social, cultural, and even human rights dimensions in addition to its political system and economic foundations. From 2013 and 2019, the nation's Gross Domestic Product (GDP) decreased by 62%. Child and infant mortality increased sharply, as did death from a wide range of illnesses. Public services were completely destroyed and due to the country's current situation, more than 4 million individuals have migrated from the nation in recent years (Bull & Rosales, 2020).

The COVID-19 pandemic further exacerbated the challenges faced by Venezuelans, both within the country and abroad. The pandemic led to widespread job losses, economic contraction, and a strained healthcare system. Many Venezuelans abroad faced difficulties in accessing healthcare, financial support, and employment opportunities due to the pandemic-related restrictions. The United Nations High Commissioner for Refugees (UNHCR, 2023) reports that the pandemic had intensified the vulnerability of Venezuelan migrants and refugees.

Finally, according to the International Labour Organization (2021), natural disasters have also played a role in increasing migration from Venezuela. The country has been hit by severe floods, landslides, and other environmental crises, particularly in recent years. These disasters have resulted in loss of lives, displacement, and further strain on already fragile infrastructure.

To sum up this section, Venezuela has been characterized by one of the highest rates of systemic inequality in the region (Di John, 2005). The country's socio-economic disparities were pronounced, with a significant wealth gap between the privileged few and the majority of the population. This inequality manifested in various aspects of life, including access to basic services, education, healthcare, and employment opportunities. The stark contrast between the affluent minority and the impoverished majority underscored the deep-rooted structural issues that plagued Venezuelan society, contributing to the challenging conditions that many Venezuelans faced on a daily basis.

COMMUNITY PROFILE OF VENEZUELANS IN PERU

Venezuelans left their home country due to the implementation of socialist policies in an authoritarian regime (Weyland, 2013; Corrales, 2020; Handlin, 2018). For the last 5 years, there have been almost 5 million Venezuelans migrating to different parts of the world. In the Latin American region, Peru received the second highest number of Venezuelan immigrants, after Colombia, with more than 1,043,460 Venezuelans (IOM, – DTM round 5, 2019). The majority of Venezuelans reside in the larger cities, such as Lima, La Libertad, and Arequipa.

In a recent study to display a community profile of Venezuelans in Peru, it was found that there is almost an equal distribution between males, representing 52.3% and females, accounting for 47.7%. In addition, at least 40% of Venezuelans reported to be between 18 and 29 years of age. Due to the challenges found to leave their home country, at least 80% of study participants indicated it had taken them at least a month to arrive in Peru

(INEI, 2018). In a similar study conducted by the Pontificia Universidad Catolica del Peru (Durán Lora, 2020) regarding the socio-economic situation of Venezuelans in Lima, Peru's capital, it was found that more than half of surveyed participants indicated to have legal authorization to work. Regardless of this, the vast majority of study participants stated to work as street vendors, taxi drivers, restaurant servers and housekeepers due to lack of employment opportunities (Durán Lora, 2020). They show signs of mental illness, which include depression and anxiety (Durán Lora, 2020). The combination of all these factors may have contributed to discontent and cultural isolation, which can affect their path to acculturation in the Peruvian culture; and eventually, may be a cause of return migration.

Peru's Migration Policies Towards Venezuelans

Migration policies in Peru can be summarized into 2 phases prior to President Castillo (Said & Jara, 2020). Phase 1 is part of Pedro Pablo Kuczynski presidency from 2016 to 2018. During his administration, President Kuczynski opted for the protection of Venezuelans and encouraged their stay in Peru. This "open door policy" allowed millions of Venezuelans to migrate to Peru, with minimum restrictions. During this time, Venezuelans were able to apply for the Temporary Residence Permit, which facilitated their stay and allowed them to work for at least one year, with the opportunity to re-apply up to 4 times (González Levaggi & Freier, 2022).

However, this policy changed during the administration of President Martin Vizcarra, which corresponds to phase 2 (from 2018 to 2020). Because of political pressure by opponents and the media, President Vizcarra required Venezuelans to obtain a humanitarian visa prior their arrival in Peru. Hence, this new policy restricted Venezuelans from working legally. Although almost half a million Venezuelans applied for this visa, the vast majority of these applications were not processed due to incomplete documentation of required paperwork (González Levaggi & Freier, 2022). Further initiatives for additional restrictions were aggregated by an increase in delinquent acts committed by some Venezuelan immigrants. This continued to worsen with the negative image of migrants portrayed by the media, which contributed to increased discrimination against Venezuelans by Peruvians (Freier & Pérez, 2021).

During the presidential campaign in 2021, candidate Pedro Castillo used discriminatory rhetoric against Venezuelan migration to gain more political support from Peruvian citizens. In a press release, candidate Castillo stated that as soon as he takes the presidency, foreign delinquents would have only 72 hours to leave Peru. He also mentioned that youth born outside Peru who were not enrolled in the school system or employed, must enroll into military service (La Silla Vacia, 2021). When Castillo won the Peruvian Presidency (from 2021 to 2022), his proposed migration policies were not as aggressive as he initially advertised. Instead, he announced a new initiative of return migration. This initiative was created in collaboration with the Venezuelan embassy to ease the return of Venezuelans who have committed crimes. At this moment, there have been more than 5000 expulsions of foreigners residing in Peru, in which at least 98% are from Venezuela (El Comercio, 2022).

Xenophobic Attitudes Against Venezuelans and Their Consequences

Xenophobia has been defined by different scholars as fear of the unknown or the new when it relates to foreigners' arrivals to a new society (Kim & Sundstrom, 2014; Achiume, 2021). Other feelings associated with xenophobic attitudes can be envy or resentment, which leads foreigners to feel unwelcomed by host country residents (Sundstrom, 2013; Kim & Sundstrom, 2014). In some instances, xenophobic attitudes can be embedded into a nation's *modus operandi* which creates systemic challenges that can minimize immigrants' role of participating in cultural or traditional activities because they are not seen as children of the host county (Sundstrom, 2013). Therefore, it is not surprising that xenophobia has been closely associated with the concept of nationalism, a sentiment that stresses the superiority of a nation over others (Klein & Licata, 2001). Within this view, individuals from a country may believe that national identity can only be obtained by birth rather than association in civic or cultural institutions, which feeds to negative sentiments towards foreigners or immigrants (Esses et al., 2005).

Negative attitudes towards foreigners are also often associated with deteriorating the stability of the host country, as they are seen as contributors to political and economic instability, social unrest, increased violence, and crime (Cowan et al., 1997). It is not uncommon that foreigners are seen as violent criminals who lack formal education (Espenshade & Calhoun, 1993; Muller & Espenshade, 1985) and who have the tendency of taking over informal jobs, which comprise an important, and sometimes the only, source of income of many people in developing countries. Venezuelans in Peru are not the exception in this context as xenophobic and nationalist attitudes have augmented through time in a negative and unwelcome manner.

Peruvians' perception of Venezuelans has worsened throughout the years, especially during Vizcarra's administration. In a study led by IDEHPUCP & IOP (2020) an increase of Peruvians' perceptions related to fear and delinquency against Venezuela migration was noted. For perceptions related to delinquency acts, this percentage increased from 55% of survey participants in 2018 to 80% in 2019. Regarding perceptions of fear, the percentage of fear increased from 24% in 2018 to 52% in 2019. Hence, fear can increase when immigrant groups are perceived by locals as culturally different, which at the same time creates stereotypes and prejudice (UPC, 2021). More data related to stereotypes and attitudes against Venezuelans is shown in Table 10.1.

Additional findings in Table 10.1 provide a clear direction on xenophobic attitudes. There is a general agreement that Venezuelans should learn more about the cultural traditions of Peru. In addition, there is an increase in the level of mistrust for newcomers from Venezuela as well as the strong belief that Venezuelans are taking employment opportunities that belong to Peruvian nationals. In fact, at the end of 2019, at least 650,000 Peruvians were seeking employment (Gamero & Pérez, 2020). The

Table 10.1 Attitudes and stereotypes against Venezuelans

	2018	2019
Venezuelans living in Peru should learn about Peruvian culture, customs, and traditions	81.0	88.7
Many Venezuelans are involved in criminal activities in Peru	55.0	81.0
The arrival of so many Venezuelans will harm the economy of Peruvians, both men and women	72.0	76.6
Venezuelans are taking jobs away from many Peruvians	73.3	76.3
I do not trust the Venezuelans arriving in Peru	39.8	67.8
Most Venezuelans are untrustworthy or dishonest people	38.8	61.2
I'm afraid of the Venezuelan, both men and women, who are arriving in Peru	24.3	52.4
Total %	100.0	100.0
Number of cases	400	680

Source: IDEHPUCP & IOP (2020)

current economic situation of Peru exacerbated discontent towards Venezuelans due to additional competition in the formal and informal job markets. What remains unclear is whether Venezuelans feel that there is enough governmental support that would allow them to integrate into Peruvian culture.

Venezuelans' perception of xenophobic and discriminatory policies in Peru has also been examined by scholars. Freier and Pérez (2021) found that at least 60% of Venezuelans have experienced nationality-based xenophobia and at least 30% have suffered from discrimination, which often occurs in public space by using slurs to express negative perceptions against Venezuelans. These perceptions included being accused of thieves or murders, which sometimes has been extended to children at school age. In this study, it was also inferred that Peruvians' negative reactions towards Venezuelans were exacerbated by political rhetoric during campaigns and the way Venezuelans were portrayed by the media (Freier & Pérez, 2021). For instance, municipal authorities used hate speech against Venezuelans by describing them as criminals who must return to Venezuela (Berganza & Blouin, 2021). Peruvian media and political rhetoric opened doors for the normalization of xenophobic attitudes, which can lead to violence against this migrant group (Stefoni et al., 2021).

Return Migration to Venezuela

The combination of socio-economic factors, lack of health access and xenophobia as well discriminatory policies contributed to a recent return migration of Venezuelans to their home county. Venezuelan President Nicolas Maduro created a "Plan Vuelta a la Patria" or 'plan to return to home', to facilitate this process. In this plan, President Maduro provided assistance to Venezuelans who voluntarily want to return. This is an effort that requires ongoing diplomatic collaboration of Venezuelan embassies in the Latin American region. It consists of three phases, which are: (1) registration plan, (2) logistical operation for safety return, and (3) inclusion of social protection in the República Bolivariana de Venezuela. This plan targets Venezuelan migrants who live under poverty lines in their host country, complicating their return to Venezuela due to financial constraints (Consulado de Venezuela, n.d.).

In a study led by Mixed Migration Centre (2022) to assess why Venezuelans returned to their home country, it was noted that the main reasons for their return were related to the lack of access to primary services, barriers to make a living, lack of integration in their host country—which often led to discrimination, impediment to regularizing their migratory status as well as nostalgia. There is also uncertainty as to whether they will stay in Venezuela for a short or long period of time due to the economic, political, and social consequences of the Venezuelan authoritarian regime.

Conclusion

Return migration, which includes both forced and voluntary returns, is a complex multiphase phenomenon. Several factors, including available economic opportunities, prevailing political conditions, personal circumstances, and the need to reunite with family, have an impact on it. Policymakers, humanitarian organizations, and governments dealing with the effects of migration must have a thorough understanding of the reasons behind and difficulties encountered by return migrants.

The case of Venezuela, with its authoritarian regime and socio-economic crisis, exemplifies the complex dynamics of return migration. The country's descent into authoritarianism under President Hugo Chávez and his successor Nicolás Maduro has led to a severe deterioration of living conditions, human rights abuses, and economic collapse. These factors have driven millions of Venezuelans to seek refuge and opportunities in neighboring countries like Peru.

Peru, as one of the primary destinations for Venezuelan migrants, has experienced the impacts of this migratory phenomenon. The Peruvian government initially adopted an open-door policy, allowing Venezuelans to enter and work in the country. However, political pressure and negative media portrayal of migrants led to a shift in policy, with increased restrictions and discrimination against Venezuelans. President Pedro Castillo's election campaign further fueled anti-immigrant sentiments but ultimately resulted in a return migration initiative aimed at facilitating the repatriation of Venezuelans who have committed crimes.

For many individuals, returning to an authoritarian socialist regime can be seen as an incomprehensible event. There are still limitations in studying return migration for immigrants born in unstable countries due to lack of reliable data. In many countries such as Venezuela, having an accurate number of returnees is undermined by the lack of transparency in developing and authoritarian countries. Future studies should focus on documenting the inter-collaboration between Venezuelan embassies and local host governments, including non-governmental organizations to track the number of Venezuelans who return to their country regardless of their legal status.

Reintegrating into a nation experiencing socioeconomic and political crises, as well as potential stigmatization and discrimination, are just a few of the significant difficulties faced by Venezuelan return migrants. Governments and aid agencies must support and assist migrant workers who are returning home by attending to their needs and ensuring their safety and well-being.

By focusing on the particular context of Venezuelan return migration in Peru, this chapter adds to the academic discourse on migration. For organizations and policymakers tackling regional migration-related issues, it also offers useful insights. Stakeholders can create more informed and efficient strategies to deal with the opportunities and challenges brought on by this phenomenon by understanding the dynamics and complexity of return migration.

References

Achiume, E. T. (2021). Governing Xenophobia. *Vanderbilt Law Review, 51*(2), 333. Retrieved from https://scholarship.law.vanderbilt.edu/vjtl/vol51/iss2/1

Barcenas Alfonso, J., Martín Fernández, C., Peña Pino, I., & Robaina Figueroa, M. (2022). Los múltiples retornos: estudio psicosocial sobre la migración de retorno a Cuba. *Revista Novedades en Población, 18*(35), 1–21. Retrieved June 16, 2022, from http://scielo.sld.cu/scielo.php?script=sci_arttext&pid=S1817-40782022000100001&lng=es&tlng=es

Batistella, G. (2018). *Return migration: A conceptual and policy framework - The Center for Migration Studies of New York (CMS)*. The Center for Migration Studies of New York (CMS). Retrieved February 17, 2023, from cmsny.org/publications/2018smsc-smc-return-migration

Berganza, I., & Blouin, C. (2021). Lima as a welcoming city for Venezuelan migrants? Transformations, tensions and challenges in a new urban destination. In L. Faret & H. Sanders (Eds.), *Migrant protection and the city in the Americas* (pp. 261–284). Palgrave Macmillan.

Brewer-Carías, A. (2010). *Dismantling democracy in Venezuela: The Chávez authoritarian experiment*. Cambridge University Press. https://doi.org/10.1017/CBO9780511762062

Bull, B., & Rosales, A. (2020). The crisis in Venezuela: Drivers, transitions, and pathways. *European Review of Latin American and Caribbean Studies/Revista Europea de Estudios Latinoamericanos y Del Caribe, 109*, 1–20. Retrieved from https://www.jstor.org/stable/26936900

Consulado General de Venezuela en Cuba. (n.d.). *PLAN VUELTA A LA PATRIA | Consulado General de Venezuela en Cuba*. Retrieved February 1, 2023, from http://www.consuladovenezuela.co.cu/planvpatria.

Corrales, J. (2020). Authoritarian survival: Why Maduro hasn't fallen. *Journal of Democracy, 31*(3), 39–53. https://doi.org/10.1353/jod.2020.0044

Cowan G, Martinez L, & Mendiola S (1997). Predictors of attitudes toward illegal Latino immigrants. *Hispanic Journal of Behavioral Sciences, 19*, 403–415. https://doi.org/10.1177/07399863970194001

Di John, J. (2005). Economic liberalization, political instability, and state capacity in Venezuela. *International Political Science Review, 26*(1), 107–124.

Durán Lora, B. I. (2020). *Duelo migratorio de venezolanos en Lima Metropolitana* (Undergraduate thesis, Universidad Peruana de Ciencias Aplicadas, Facultad de Psicología, Programa Académico de Psicología). Retrieved from https://repositorioacademico.upc.edu.pe/bitstream/handle/10757/650453/Durán_LB.pdf?sequence=1&isAllowed=y

El Comercio. (2022, August 12). *Pedro Castillo anuncia comienzo del programa "Retorno a su país" para extranjeros ilegales y con antecedentes rmmn | LIMA*. El Comercio Perú. Retrieved from https://elcomercio.pe/lima/sucesos/pedro-castillo-anuncia-comienzo-del-programa-retorno-a-su-pais-para-extranjeros-ilegales-y-con-antecedentes-rmmn-noticia/

Espenshade, T. J., & Calhoun, C. A. (1993). An analysis of public opinion toward undocumented immigration. *Population Research and Policy Review, 12*, 189–224. https://doi.org/10.1007/BF01074385

Esses, V. M., Dovidio, J. F., Semenya, A. H., & Jackson, L. M. (2005). Attitudes toward immigrants and immigration: The role of national and international identity. In D. Abrams, M. A. Hogg, & J. M. Marques (Eds.), *The social psychology of inclusion and exclusion* (pp. 317–337). Psychology Press.

Freier, L. F., & Parent, N. (2019). The regional response to the Venezuelan exodus. *Current History, 118*(805), 56–61. Retrieved from https://www.jstor.org/stable/48614415

Freier, L. F., & Pérez, L. M. (2021). Nationality-based criminalisation of south-south migration: The experience of Venezuelan forced migrants in Peru. *European Journal on Criminal Policy and Research, 27*(1), 113–133. https://doi.org/10.1007/s10610-020-09475-y

Gamero, J., & Pérez, J. (2020). *Perú: Impacto de la COVID - 19 en el empleo y los ingresos laborales*. Organización Internacional del Trabajo. https://www.ilo.org/wcmsp5/groups/public/%2D%2D-americas/%2D%2D-ro-lima/documents/publication/wcms_756474.pdf

González Levaggi, A., & Freier, L. F. (2022). Immigrants' Contribution to Development in the Global South: Comparing Policy Responses to Venezuelan Immigration in Peru and Argentina. *International Development Policy | Revue internationale de politique de développement, 14*. https://doi.org/10.4000/poldev.4963

Handlin, S. (2018). The Logic of Polarizing Populism: State Crises and Polarization in South America. *American Behavioral Scientist, 62*(1), 75–91. https://doi.org/10.1177/0002764218756922

IDEHPUCP. (2020). *Cambios en las Actitudes hacia los Inmigrantes Venezolanos en Lima-Callao 2018-2019*. Retrieved from https://repositorio.pucp.edu.pe/index/bitstream/handle/123456789/169459/IOP_1119_01_R2.pdf?sequnce=1&isAllowed=y

Instituto Nacional de Estadística e Informática (INEI). (2018). Encuesta Nacional de Hogares: Módulo de Medición del Nivel de Vida. Retrieved from https://www.inei.gob.pe/media/MenuRecursivo/publicaciones_digitales/Est/Lib1544/00TOMO_01.pdf

International Labour Organization. (2021). *Migration from Venezuela: Opportunities for Latin America and the Caribbean*. Retrieved from https://www.ilo.org/wcmsp5/groups/public/%2D%2D-americas/%2D%2D-ro-lima/documents/publication/wcms_775183.pdf

International Organization for Migration – DTM round 5 (IOM). (2019). *Flow monitoring of the Venezuelan population in Peru*. Retrieved from https://www.r4v.info/sites/default/files/2021-06/DTM_R5_digital_en.pdf

Kerwin, D., Appleby, K., Battistella, G., Carciotto, S., Rabben, L., Nicholson, M., Skoda, A., Demurtas, P., Vitiello, M, Accorinti, M., Carola, P., & Carafone, L. (2018). *2018 international migration policy report: Perspectives on the content and implementation of the global compact for safe, orderly, and regular migration*. Retrieved from https://www.researchgate.net/publication/327871068_2018_International_Migration_Policy_Report_Perspectives_on_the_Content_and_Implementation_of_the_Global_Compact_for_Safe_Orderly_and_Regular_Migration

Kim, D. H., & Sundstrom, R. R. (2014). Xenophobia and Racism. *Critical Philosophy of Race 2*(1), 20–45. https://www.muse.jhu.edu/article/538481.

Klein, O., & Licata, L. (2001). Explaining differences between social groups: The impact of group identification on attribution. *Swiss Journal of Psychology / Schweizerische Zeitschrift für Psychologie / Revue Suisse de Psychologie, 60*(4), 244–252. https://doi.org/10.1024/1421-0185.60.4.244

La Silla Vacia. (2021, August 2). *Pedro Castillo reitera discurso xenófobo en Perú*. Retrieved from https://www.lasillavacia.com/historias/historias-silla-llena/pedro-castillo-reitera-discurso-xen%C3%B3fobo-en-per%C3%BA/

Michiel Baas, & International Institute for Asian Studies. (2015). *Transnational migration and Asia: The question of return*. Amsterdam University Press. Retrieved from https://legacy.prio.org/utility/DownloadFile.ashx?id=526&type=publicationfile

Migration Data Portal. (2022, July 28). *Return migration*. Migration Data Portal. Definition Section. Retrieved from https://www.migrationdataportal.org/themes/return-migration#definition

Mixed Migration Centre. (2022). Mixed Migration Review 2022. Retrieved from https://mixedmigration.org/mixed-migration-review-2022/#:~:text=The%20Mixed%20Migration%20Review%202022%2C%20the%20Mixed%20Migration%20Centre%27s%20flagship,approaches%20to%20current%20migration%20policies.
Muller, T., & Espenshade, T. J. (1985). *The fourth wave: California's newest immigrants*. Urban Institute Press.
Pérez-López, J. F. (2001). Pazos' Economic Problems of Cuba During The Transition: Return Migration of Skilled Persons and Professionals. *Annual Proceedings, The Association for the Study of the Cuban Economy*, 11.
Richmond, A. H. (1983). Explaining return migration. *International Migration Review*, 17(1 suppl), 269–275. https://doi.org/10.1177/019791838301701s39
Said, V. A., & Jara, S. C. (2020). Reacting to Change within Change: Adaptive Leadership and the Peruvian Response to Venezuelan Immigration. *International Migration*, 60(1), 57–76. https://doi.org/10.1111/imig.12761
Stefoni, C., Bravo, A., & Liberona, N. (2021, December 1). Migrar en tiempos de pandemia: entre el cierre de fronteras y el crecimiento de la xenofobia y el racismo Revista Común. *Revista Común*. Retrieved from https://revistacomun.com/blog/migrar-en-tiempos-de-pandemia-entre-el-cierre-de-fronteras-y-el-crecimiento-de-la-xenofobia-y-el-racismo/
Sundstrom, R. (2013). Sheltering Xenophobia. *Philosophy*, 49. Retrieved from https://repository.usfca.edu/phil/49
The United Nations High Commissioner for Refugees (UNHCR). (2023). Retrieved from https://reporting.unhcr.org/operational/situations/venezuela-situation
Universidad Peruana de Ciencias Aplicadas (UPC). (2021). Trayectorias migrantes: la juventud venezolana en el Perú. Retrieved from https://idehpucp.pucp.edu.pe/lista_publicaciones/trayectorias-migrantes-la-juventud-venezolana-en-el-peru/
Weyland, K. (2013). The Threat from the Populist Left. *Journal of Democracy*, 24(3), 18–32. Retrieved from https://journalofdemocracy.org/wp-content/uploads/2013/07/Weyland-24-3-1.pdf

CHAPTER 11

Return Migration and Return Intention in Times of Crisis: Dominican Return During the COVID-19 Pandemic

Carlos Manuel Abaunza

INTRODUCTION

Over the last few decades, migration dynamics and human mobility processes have changed dramatically. Two independent processes have reshaped the way in which migration phenomena is lived by social actors, namely the democratization of international travel and changes in naturalization laws which have facilitated the acquisition of dual or multiple citizenships. In the past, experts on migration studies used to frame return migration as the last stage of the migration process, whether it happened voluntarily, as a planned process, or involuntarily, as an *impromptu* event; in any case, it used to be seen as a one-way ticket back home (Bovenkerk, 1974; European Council, 2002; King, 1986). Current empirical data suggests that this simplistic view of return can no longer explain today's

C. M. Abaunza (✉)
Nazarbayev University, Astana, Kazakhstan
e-mail: carlos.abaunza@nu.edu.kz

© The Author(s), under exclusive license to Springer Nature Switzerland AG 2024
J. Yeo (ed.), *Return Migration and Crises in Non-Western Countries*, Mobility & Politics,
https://doi.org/10.1007/978-3-031-53562-8_11

migratory dynamics, which is why there is a push to reconceptualize return migration incorporating new analytical frameworks and conducting new empirical research (Abaunza, 2020; Cassarino, 2004, 2008; Lozano Ascencio & Martínez Pizarro, 2015; Stark, 2019).

The exploratory research that informs this chapter had a particular interest on examining which factors had a greater impact on return migration and return intention processes during the COVID-19 pandemic. A series of state policies and state actions were introduced in Spain as a response to the global health crisis; however, very little is known as to how these measures impacted migrant communities, particularly with respect to their ability or necessity to go back to their countries of origin. An unprecedented combination of macro socioeconomic changes took place in a very short period which affected virtually all spheres of human activity, including restrictions to human mobility, international traveling, loss of livelihoods, and wellness. Initial observations suggest that state policies had very little impact on Dominican return migration and return intention; other factors such as socioeconomic asymmetries, sociocultural differences, strategies of family re/production, and family expectations appear to be more consequential in these processes.

Brief Migratory Profile of Dominican Republic

Dominican Republic (DR) is a country of emigration as it is of immigration (Abaunza, 2017). According to the Institute of Dominicans Living Abroad, over 2.8 million Dominican nationals are currently living overseas (INDEX, 2022); this equates to around 26% of the total population. At the same time, there is a large number of Haitian migrants and Dominican-born Haitian-descent individuals who comprise somewhere between 5 and 8% of the population according to official sources (Abaunza et al., 2017; ONE, 2022) and almost 20% according to unofficial ones. More recently, Venezuelan migrants have increased their presence in the country amounting to 115 thousand people toward the end of 2022 (Licheri et al., 2022), making DR the hosting country with the largest number of displaced Venezuelans in the Insular Caribbean. With respect to return migration, apart from the number of deportees, who are systematically registered, little to no official information is available. The Dominican government puts little effort into quantifying the scope of permanent and seasonal returnees, and this tendency did not change during the pandemic.

Dominican Migration to Spain

Dominicans began migrating to Spain thanks to the formation of a transnational religious network that operated between Vicente Noble and Tamayo in Dominican Republic and Madrid, Spain (Martínez-Buján, 2007). In the 1970s and 1980s, a religious order comprised of Spanish nuns arrived in the region to work with poor rural communities in the country. These nuns first established literacy and religious education programs, but later acted as intermediaries between Dominican households in need of income, and Spanish households in need of domestic help (Abaunza, 2020). Around the death of Dictator Francisco Franco, Spain experienced a powerful economic growth stimulated by its industrial modernization and the diversification of its economic activity; these macro socioeconomic changes required Spanish women to enter the formal labor force, which created the need for migrant workers to relay their counterparts as domestic services providers and caregivers (Gallardo Rivas, 1995; Sørensen, 1998).

The Spanish demand for foreign workers, especially but not exclusively for the domestic and care sectors, was meet by an influx of Latin American women, initially coming from Dominican Republic, Bolivia, and Ecuador. Some authors have explained the reason why these nationalities were preferred over others with more geographical proximity, as it is the case of Moroccan women, due the sociocultural affinity between Latin America and Spain (Izquierdo & Cornelius, 2012; Pedone & Gil Araujo, 2008). Factors such as sharing the same language and religion—Spanish and Catholicism—given a common colonial past, undoubtedly played an important role in the recruitment of these women (Abaunza, 2020). Interestingly, before the influx of these foreign workers, Spain was almost exclusively a country of emigration—except for some British pensioners—which is why the country was not ready to deal with what would eventually become over 5 million immigrants (Cachón Rodríguez, 2009).

The inability of the Spanish government to deal with a large influx of immigrants resulted in a series of processes of migrant regularization which not only contributed to granting permanent residency to irregular migrants present in the country but more importantly allowed and fomented processes of family reunification developing in a stronger pull effect (see Table 11.1). Thus, the migrant population grew exponentially in the 2000s, positioning Spain as a country of immigration for the first time in its history (Aja, 2012). The Dominican population in Spain

Table 11.1 Dominican population resident in Spain

	2002	2007	2012	2017	2018	2019	2020	2021	2022
Women	31,895	61,694	90,361	100,132	103,570	107,015	110,654	111,842	113,865
Men	13,992	36,557	57,632	64,177	66,931	69,925	73,118	74,723	77,381
Total	45,887	98,251	147,993	164,309	170,501	176,940	183,772	186,565	191,246

Source: Own elaboration based on the Spanish National Institute of Statistics (INE, 2022)

Note: This data set begins in 2002 as provided by the INE and it follows a sequence of every five years until 2017; then, the last five years are included in order to see the trend just before and during the pandemic followed a pattern where women migrated first and then were followed by men; later, through processes of family reunification, their children and parents also came along. Separate processes of market labor specialization resulted in women working in the domestic services and care sectors while men joined the construction, landscaping, and maintenance industries (Cachón Rodríguez, 2009).

Dominican Return in Times of COVID: A Type of Shock Mobility

The Shock Mobility Theory as proposed by Xiang et al. (2022) explains how natural disasters and human-induced crises can lead to a sudden movement of people—which later may or may not evolved into unexpected migration patterns such as "protracted forced migration" processes (Xiang & Sørensen, 2020, para. I). The theory argues that such "shocks" can be so disruptive to people's lives and livelihoods that they effectively force people to seek out new opportunities elsewhere or, at least, move temporarily to avoid the negative consequences of the source of disruption. The global pandemic is a perfect example of these types of disruption *en masse*, this theory can help explain some of the patterns of return migration and return intention of Dominican nationals during COVID-19 global crisis. Part of what makes this theory highly appealing to analyze return processes during the pandemic is imbedded in the idea that different factors hold different power when the decisions to return are taken during a period of "normalcy" or during a period of emergency; in the latter, not only are the pressures different but the strategies that have to be formulated in order to implement an exit plan—or a plan to stay—have to be articulated under heavy stress due to the unexpected circumstances resulting from a rapidly changing environment.

The quick—if not unpremeditated—measures taken by governments as a response to the unexpected outbreak of the new coronavirus and its rapid propagation around the world, led to an unprecedented disruption of economic activity from virtually every country in world (Durant, 2022; Mencutek, 2022). Interestingly, for many different factors—some of which are still under scrutiny—the virus hit particularly hard certain countries more than others, and within those countries certain sectors and industries. It so happens that Spain was one of the hardest hit countries in Europe (Chislett, 2021). In Spain, the health emergency was confronted with strict lockdown measures which effectively closed certain sectors and industries that, again, coincide with the jobs of low-skilled populations (Oliver, 2021), thus affecting much of the Dominican community in the country.

As it is often the case, the pandemic hit harder those segments of society that are the most vulnerable to begin with, such as migrant communities—among other minority groups (Arango et al., 2020). The sudden and unexpected loss of income resulting from massive business closures, international border closings, confinement measures, restricted urban and rural mobility, and remote working practices, created the context for the destruction of livelihoods for thousands of families both autochthonous and foreign. These macrostructural conditions exacerbated the inequality gap which allowed for certain established asymmetries to affect some families and individuals positively while affecting many others negatively. Given the strict official measures taken by the local and national governments, it must have been incredibly difficult for individuals and/or families to articulate a survival strategy while, at the same time, having to comply one way or another to the ever more pressing restrictions and constant policy changes. This is the context with which Dominicans in Spain had to decide to go back—or to stay put—with little, if any, time to reflect. In the first months of the pandemic, these circumstances sparked waves of shock returns.

METHODS

Using a transnational perspective and shock mobilities theory and based on empirical data collected through qualitative research in 2021 and 2022, and official statistical data sets from the National Office of Statistics of the Dominican Republic, this exploratory research analyzes the factors that have a greater impact on return migration and return intention as well as the kinds of return migration that materialize in times of crisis. Seventeen semi-structured interviews were conducted, nine in Spain and eight in Dominican Republic, the former followed a classical face-to-face process using all the health protocols mandate by the Community of Madrid, while the latter were carried out remotely. The instrument used was the same for both sides of the Atlantic and was comprised of three general areas, namely (1) how is the pandemic affecting you; (2) how did you arrive to the intention of staying or returning; and (3) what factors were the most pressing in the actual implementation of this decision. During the interview, there was an exploration of different issues at greater length as they appeared in the conversation. A snowball approach was used where some Dominican migrants led to other informants both locally and transnationally. The ages of the informants ranged from 24 to 67 and ten of the informants were women while seven were men. Given the limited scope of this independent exploratory research, we reached saturation with this many informants which is why we only included seventeen interviews.

Key Findings

Our data suggests that the global pandemic affected Dominican migrants in Spain in different ways; some findings seem to demonstrate that even though the virus did not discriminate who to infect, there were socioeconomic asymmetries that did (López-Ruiz & Cabrera Cabrera, 2021; Oliver, 2021). The loss of livelihoods that resulted from a drastic reduction in the economic activity of sectors such as the care, the construction, and the hospitality industries, particularly affected low-skilled migrant workers (Chander et al., 2021), including thousands of Dominican nationals. In Spain, a large percentage of the Dominican labor force works in these sectors which has proven to be one of the diaspora's greatest weaknesses—as it never reached an appropriate level of diversification. Historically, in the 1970s, 1980s, and 1990s Dominican migrants were hired mainly to work as domestic help, construction workers, maids, dishwashers and cooks in private homes, hotels, and restaurants (Herranz Gómez, 1997; Tejeda et al., 2018). This speaks of a process of labor specialization that developed over time which, unfortunately, resulted in low levels of diversification. The lack of a collective strategy to acquire the mid-level and high-level skills to work in other sectors eventually created the conditions for labor stagnation, which has negatively impacted the more recent influxes of Dominican migrants in Spain.

Drawing from the seventeen interviews that were conducted within the context of this study, two main outcomes were identified with respect to the processes of return migration and return intention during the pandemic: first, there was a twofold mechanism of simultaneously motivating processes of return as well as preventing them from happening; second, migrant communities were disproportionately impacted with respect to the local population. Our analysis also determined four main factors that seem to be the most important drivers of return migration and return intention during the pandemic, which could help explain, at least in part, how the crisis simultaneously enable and prevented return processes, these factors are: (1) having access to the health care system; (2) being able to receive social benefits and legal protections; (3) assuming family roles and renegotiating family expectations; and (4) being able to move back and forth from Spain based on the migratory status.

Another unexpected finding is how the migratory status of the informants did not seem to have played a stable role in the processes of return but rather an ambiguous one, especially in the decision-making stages. Dominicans whose migratory status in Spain was uncertain did not experience any kind of discrimination, harassment, or exclusion, when compared to Dominicans who were residents or Spanish citizens. This is to say that whatever type of discriminatory practices that Dominicans faced during the pandemic did not occur because of their migratory status but rather from the fact that they were foreigners in Spain. Again, in theory the Spanish government mandated that all migrants, regardless of their migratory status and country of origin, would have the same treatment as any other Spanish citizen during the pandemic. Therefore, in this context people's migratory status was not a decisive factor when considering whether to stay in the country or go. On the other hand, those who had the legal credentials to leave the country and come back without any problems did report having a sense of freedom in knowing that they could escape the crisis in Spain and come back once things went back to normal.

Access to the Health Care System

Having access to the health care system during a global pandemic is crucial for a myriad of obvious reasons, one of which is related to the fact that many migrant workers did not have the luxury to stay home and work remotely, condition which made them more vulnerable to getting infected and becoming ill. The official campaigns that the Spanish government put in place forced—and even harassed—people into getting constantly tested for the virus, and eventually vaccinated and boosted, as part of a "civic duty", which evidently required having access to the testing centers and vaccination points. Even though the Spanish government announced that all Spanish nationals as well as regular and irregular migrant communities would have full access to these services, many migrants, especially those with an irregular status feared making use of these programs for fear of violence, apprehension and/or deportation (Mahía, 2021). Perna and Moreno Fuentes (2021) illustrate that even "the president of the

Community of Madrid, Isabel Díaz Ayuso, stated [publicly] that "migrants' lifestyles" is one of the causes of new outbreaks in the districts of the south of Madrid" (p. 118).

Fear became an important factor, as a generalized resentment grew among the local population against migrant communities. One of the informants recalls how her friend, also Dominican, went to a vaccination center and was turned away:

> *She went, right, and the people there said to her that she did not have a previous appointment, so they would not see her. But we all know that this center also sees people without previous appointments. The irony is that she actually works in a hospital as cleaning lady, but not every hospital has access to the new vaccines (…) It has to do with the color of her skin, no more.*

Local authorities have accepted responsibility in blocking certain migrants from accessing health services during the pandemic, despite the central government's orders to see everyone regardless of their migratory status, due to administrative hassles (Ocaña et al., 2022). Be it as it may, there was a generalized sentiment in the Spanish population that foreigners were competing for the same state-owned resources and were taking advantage of these services amidst the pandemic. Altogether, this became a crucial point for people with preexisting conditions.

There were many incidents that were reported where the shortages of vaccines, hospital beds, and intensive care units provoked the local population to discriminate and even deny treatment to foreigners regardless of their migratory status as irregular or regular migrants or even naturalized Spanish citizens (Mahía, 2021). As this news propagated and reached the main media outlets and social media platforms, certain migrants became increasingly more hesitant to resort to COVID testing points, vaccination centers, and/or hospitals, which sparked even more fear among migrant communities. Two informants, who at the time of the interview were in the DR, affirmed that the main reason why they returned was because of their preexisting condition(s) and their fear of not being admitted into a hospital. One of them shared:

> *I am diabetic and hypertense and if something happens to me, you know like receiving bad news or if I fall, I need immediate medical attention; and knowing that there [in Spain] being admitted became like a lottery, I said I'd better*

return. And I am a Spaniard [meaning a Spanish citizen]. Here, hospitals are not as well equipped as they are there, but at least they see you.

The notion that migrants are abusing the medical system follows the same 'migrants-are-stealing-our-jobs' logic that often autochthonous populations adopt; however, in this case, the health system was visibly overwhelmed. As Spain tried to cope with the pandemic which created the conditions for real shortages of masks, tests, and then vaccines and booster shots, where the local population—especially the elderly and the sick—resented migrants for "taking those resources away".

Indeed, some migrants "benefited" from early vaccination programs, but it was only because these migrants were essential workers that kept the country running. Some worked in the transportation industry bringing food and essential goods to supermarkets and stores, while others were cleaning hospitals, clinics, or vaccination points, cooking in restaurants, or delivering food home, for example. As most of these people needed to take public transportation to go to work and their jobs demanded a constant exposure to other individuals, it was clear that their risk of contagion was higher and had to be mitigated by receiving vaccines and booster shots before those who could stay home. Local authorities were not looking to favor any migrant population above their own citizenry; rather they were following public health measures. Unfortunately, the main reason behind the prioritization of some migrant workers over other segments of the general public was largely missed by the public opinion.

Social Benefits and Legal Protections

Even though the Spanish government allocated resources for anti-discrimination campaigns, migrant communities in the country were discriminated against and violently harassed. Migrants reported to have witnessed retaliatory practices against them, which resulted in a distrust with respect to the institutions that provided social benefits and legal protections for the population at large. These specific tensions were happening in parallel to the collapse of the Spanish health care system. In the backdrop, the Spanish government was dealing with a political crisis where little to no decisions could be achieved via consensus. This crisis was overcome by governing through executive orders allowed by calling for the state of alarm, emergency, or exception (see Table 11.2). This high level of uncertainty and risk was the context that effectively triggered a shock

Table 11.2 Policies and regulations in response to the pandemic during the first year of the pandemic

March 12, 2020	RD Law 7/2020	Urgent measures against the economic impact of COVID-19
March 13, 2020	RD 463/2020	First State of Alarm Declaration. The government becomes the competent authority to deal with defense, interior affairs, transport, and health. Restrictive measures taken to limit human mobility and confinement
March 24, 2020	Act CM	Distribution of 300 million euro from the Extraordinary Social Fund
March 27, 2020	RD 476/2020	Harsher restrictive measures on mobility and confinement
March 30, 2020	Act CM	Distribution of 300 million euro for financing health care costs
April 24, 2020	RD 492/2020	Measures for deconfinement
June 16, 2020	RD 20/2020	Creation of the COVID-19 Fund, endowed with €16,000 M
July 20, 2020	Agreement among Member States	Advance Procurement Agreement (APA) with vaccine manufacturers for the procurement of vaccines for the purpose of combating the COVID-19 pandemic within the European Union
October 25, 2020	RD Law 926/2020	Second State of Alarm Declaration
December 12, 2020	National Technical Committee	Inoculation strategy for COVID-19
March 29, 2021	Law 2/2021	Urgent prevention, containment, and coordination measures to address the health crisis caused by COVID-19

Source: Own elaboration based on Pérez Medina (2021)

response by many migrant families sparking shock returns and return decisions.

Due to the alarming number of deaths and the incapacity of the central and local governments to provide essential services and even dispose of the deceased, lockdown measures rapidly intensified which resulted in the destruction of thousands of livelihoods of both autochthonous as well as migrant families (Fernández Jurado et al., 2021). As a response to the economic crisis linked to the sanitary emergency, the Spanish government quickly instituted in June of 2020 the minimum vital income social assistance scheme, calling for an endowment of some €500 to €1000 per month depending on the family composition and employment situation (Pérez Medina, 2021). Likewise, other legal measures were implemented that effectively halted evictions for lack of payment and froze monthly bank payments that would strip away resources from families that were in very vulnerable conditions. Some believe that these measures were insufficient; assessing the response as "too little and too late" (Médicos sin Fronteras, 2020), while others dispute the real impact of such policies in people's lives. According to a Human Rights Watch report:

> *The Minimum Vital Income scheme, which, as of June 2022, allowed applicants to claim between €491 and €1081 per month based on household size, while admirable in its objectives, proved extremely difficult to access due to stringent eligibility criteria and documentation requirements. Investigative journalists have discovered that exclusions baked into the system, some of which are evidently arbitrary, as well as a system overwhelmed by demand, may have contributed to very high rates of refused applications. Studies of official social security data show that three quarters of applications for IMV were rejected. Moreover, the levels of support are inadequate to meet basic needs.* (Raj, 2022, para. VI)

As stated in this report, a great number of families were never able to benefit from this government initiatives from what seemed to be arbitrary reasons on the part of the Spanish authorities. Be it as it may, the reality on the ground suggested that thousands of households were left alone to their luck during these times of crisis, making them resort to multiple charity organizations and NGO food banks for their weekly sustenance and survival (Cáritas Española, 2020).

All in all, even though the Spanish government allocated a lot of resources for helping families cope with the economic effects of the pandemic, many of these families did not get nearly the help they needed (López-Ruiz & Cabrera Cabrera, 2021). This scenario most certainly created the conditions for many shock returns, especially in households where reverse remittances could not help individuals or families face the negative socioeconomic impact of the pandemic. Some of the most pressing issues during the hardest months of the pandemic were lack of access to the health care system, food insecurity, illegal evictions, and inhuman living conditions (Corrado & Palumbo, 2022). In fact, judging from the numbers of Dominican residents who entered the island in 2020, 2021, and 2022, it is obvious that during the last two years of the pandemic, the number of entries almost doubled the amount registered for 2020 (see Table 11.3). Even though, these absolute numbers only allow for a limited interpretation and extrapolation of ideas, one can assume that the reasons behind this sharp increase might be linked to the hardships that Dominicans were experiencing abroad.

One of the informants shared the circumstances that she experienced in Madrid during the global economic crisis that started in 2008, recalling how difficult and "inhumane" it was to be in a one-bedroom apartment with 8 other people, plus her own family. She remembered that she had sworn that she would never put herself in that situation ever again. In fact, in the beginning of the pandemic when she saw how many of her extended family members and friends were losing their jobs, she decided to leave Madrid to go back to Santo Domingo, where she at least has a place to live comfortably:

> *Look, when I saw all the measures to keep us inside, and everything became prohibited I decided to go back. I couldn't bare it anymore, you felt trapped. Besides, one of my cousins already wanted to move in with me, with us, because they couldn't continue making rent payments… and I knew that this would be like during the crisis, so I said to her that I couldn't have them because I was*

Table 11.3 Number of international entries of Dominican residents to the national territory

Month	2020 Monthly	2020 Total	2021 Monthly	2021 Total	2022 Monthly	2022 Total
January	83,079	83,079	75,218	75,218	94,276	94,276
February	76,951	160,030	71,796	147,014	91,822	186,098
March	43,484	203,514	104,660	251,674	98,552	284,650
April	115	203,629	101,259	352,933	112,814	397,464
May	321	203,950	117,578	470,511	107,953	505,417
June	664	204,614	129,488	599,999	130,654	636,071
July	81,058	285,672	151,797	751,796	143,986	780,057
August	60,216	345,888	118,513	870,309	119,674	899,731
September	57,065	402,953	88,038	958,347	88,414	988,145
October	67,375	470,328	93,637	1,051,984	91,424	1,079,569
November	73,261	543,589	94,774	1,146,758	94,674	1,174,243
December	162,532	706,121	192,334	1,339,092	183,802	1,358,045

Source: own elaboration based on the data provided by the Dominican Office of National Statistics

going back. Plus, if I had to die because of the damn virus, I prefer to die in my country.

It is obvious that her level of frustration with respect to the strict confinement measures reached a limit. However, her decision to go back was also motivated by the fact that she held dual citizenship, in which case she could always come back to Madrid if she wanted to. In the end, she confessed that she considers herself to be lucky as some of her friends also wanted to return but could not.

Family Roles and Family Expectations

As observed during the field research conducted for this study, family roles and expectations usually translated into strategies of family re/production, and effectively play a crucial role in different processes of return migration and return intention, in some cases to enable these processes and in other cases to prevent them from happening. Within the first six months of the pandemic, three out of the nine informants whose interviews were conducted in Spain, became the only source of income for their own nuclear—and in two cases even their extended—family. According to them, assuming the role of the sole breadwinner in the family is a heavy burden, one that imposes a set of expectations that result in the modification of their own life plans to support others. It seems that in the case of the Dominican diaspora in Spain, these roles also play an important transnational function, as migrants are usually expected to send money in the form of remittances to cater to the needs of their loved ones back at "home". This is particularly true during times of crisis or economic hardships.

The three informants—two women and one man—indicated how they wanted to go back to DR to "ride the pandemic but sadly had to stay". Based on family expectations, they felt solely responsible for the survival of their family members who "did not even have enough money to pay for rent". These stories are particularly striking because the three had their own houses in the DR and enough savings to live comfortably once they did not have to pay for rent in Spain; however, instead of going back "home", had to stay in Spain fulfilling the role of the breadwinner. Two other informants—also in Spain—expressed that they also wanted to go back to the island but decided to stay to help take care of their grandchildren as their daughters needed to go to work but no longer had the means to pay for daycare. These five cases are examples of no returns associated with family expectations. The other four informants that were in Spain during the time of the interview did not want to go back to the DR; three of them were working and one was unemployed.

Thus, family roles and expectations seem to be a very important factor in the decision-making processes related to return migration and return intention for individuals as well as for family groups. Interestingly, these constraints seem to carry such a considerable social weight that they can disrupt personal plans and migration projects completely. More research is needed to understand how the re/negotiations of roles and the assumptions of new expectations take place. The limited data collected here suggests that when a family is forced to establish an economy of survival, the pressures on those who can provide become absolute.

Individual and Family Migratory Status

Finally, return migration and return intention seem to be greatly affected by the migratory status held at the time of the action or the decision-making process. Being regular or irregular in any country has far more reaching consequences than just being considered a "legal" or "illegal" migrant. In fact, it is instrumental in accessing social services, requesting legal protections, and, more importantly, knowing that one can always come back to the country of destination at will. Being a naturalized citizen holds a different set of rights and obligations before the law than someone who is undocumented. Based on the interviews conducted to informants in Spain and DR, the two most important points they all—without exception—attach to this are: first, being able to maintain a transnational life, that is having the credentials to travel back and forth, and second, being able to bring family members to the country of destination through family reunification processes. According to the interviews, Dominicans associate their migratory status with the ability to see their relatives on both sides of the Atlantic, rather than with the ability to rip any social benefits from the "host" society.

As the numbers of foreign-born nationals increase in the global north, many developed nations have passed legislation over the last few decades to make it harder for third country nationals to acquire their citizenship and easier to lose the right to become naturalized citizen (Parrenas, 2020). In the Spanish case, citizenship laws continue to favor nationals coming from its ex-colonies, but still display stringent laws that could potentially disrupt people's plans of acquiring its citizenship. For instance, most Latin

American migrants can obtain the Spanish citizenship only after five years of living "legally" in the country; however, if in the process of or after obtaining the residency the migrant leaves the country for a period of twelve months or more, the person loses the privileges acquired through time, and gets their residency taken away (Pasettin & Cumella de Montserrat, 2020). In this light, three out of the five informants who were in Spain and responded that they did not want to leave the country during the pandemic, two were in the process of acquiring the citizenship for themselves and one was obtaining a residence permit for a family member. As stated before, becoming a legal resident and eventually a naturalized citizen is high in the list of family re/production strategies and, in fact, takes precedence over other considerations.

Conclusions

In conclusion, the COVID-19 pandemic did not affect all migrants the same way, while some individuals and families had the material conditions to "ride" the virus in situ or "ride it" back home, others did not. Having to choose between going back to the country of origin or having to stay in the country of destination is undoubtedly a difficult decision, but it is even more problematic when those decisions must be taken in a rapidly changing environment, full of uncertainty, chaos, and risk. These two very different scenarios reveal how certain asymmetries played a crucial role in the ways in which migrants responded to the sanitary and economic crises. In short, while the virus itself did not discriminate who to infect, the socioeconomic conditions in which people lived during the pandemic did. In fact, these conditions became key class determinants and predictors of success or failure in the face of contagion, sickness, or hospitalization. Thus, we arrived at the conclusion that those socioeconomic conditions played a greater role in return migration and return intention processes than state policies or state actions during the pandemic.

This study found that the structural changes brought by the pandemic fomented both processes of shock return and no return; this finding effectively contests the notion that people resort to the country of origin when there is an absolute loss of income in the country of destination and other conditions also deteriorate as a result of this major change. In the case of the Dominican diaspora in Spain, processes of return migration and return intention seem to be closely related to two crucial factors, namely the type strategies of family re/production re-negotiated during the pandemic and the type of migratory status exhibited by the person(s) at the time of the crisis. Other important factors were also present in the decision-making processes but did not alone shift the balance one way or another. These factors are having access to the health care system, being able to benefit from social assistance programs, and fearing violence associated to discrimination and xenophobia.

Family expectations played a crucial role in return migration and return intention; more specifically, they translated into the actual materialization of returns and no returns. Whether consciously or unconsciously, these expectations are part of larger strategies of family re/production, where some members sacrifice for the sake of others. These strategies are usually put in place through tacit negotiations which are constantly revised depending on the changing conditions sparked by the crisis. The pandemic undoubtedly brought serious changes that most likely did not exonerate people from their obligations but rather contributed to establishing those expectations as more formal and pressing demands. According to the data gathered for this study, these obligations are as material as they are symbolic, and develop over time into real emotional burdens, often leading to economic precarity and psychological distress.

Family expectations are not only economic in nature. In some particular cases, they are associated with providing care for other family members, usually the young, and/or sponsoring newcomers in their process of obtaining their residency and work permits at destination. These expectations can effectively anchor a person(s) to the country of destination despite their desire to leave. This was the case for some informants who would not have stayed in Spain during the pandemic if not for the fact that they needed to help take care of their grandchildren or remain in the country while other family members were obtaining their legal residency papers. It is important to note that even though there are drastic differences between these kinds of expectations and those that are strictly economic, the latter are not necessarily more restrictive than the former. In fact, the levels of sacrifice that both situations present are daunting, especially when one considers the fact that the living conditions in Spain during the pandemic were truly problematic to say the least. Nevertheless, these informants willingly fulfilled their part of their bargain, despite the socioeconomic constraints they were facing in Spain and that most likely would not have faced in Dominican Republic.

The type of migratory status individuals and families held at the time of the pandemic proved to be consequential in many ways for different processes of return migration and return intention. Even though the Dominican government does not educate its emigrants in knowing how to best rip the benefits of their migration projects, the population has an idea of the sacrifices and the many hurdles that are present in migration processes. It is in this light that, all informants consulted understood and cherished the importance of having the credentials to go back and forth between Spain and DR. In fact, only those who had acquired the Spanish citizenship expressed their desire to go back to their country of origin knowing that, if need be, they could always move back to Spain. The rest of the informants who, at the time of the interview did not have their Spanish citizenship, knew that moving back to DR could put at risk their Spanish residency, and none was willing to take the chance. Thus, in some cases this precaution was more important than having better living standards during the pandemic. Being incredibly mindful of their migratory status could be particularly important for families whose newer generations are Spanish-born citizens and will most probably never live in DR regardless of the circumstances they might face in Spain. After all, the pandemic came to remind us of all that nation-states are still containers whose hard borders can materialize at any given moment.

References

Abaunza, C. (2017). Dominican emigration: Numbers and tendencies. In N. Riveros (Ed.), *State of the art of migrations related to Dominican Republic*. OBMICA.

Abaunza, C. (2020). *Dominican return migration. Towards a typology of transnational return*. Complutense University of Madrid.

Abaunza, C., Riveros, N., & Wooding, B. (2017). *Perfil Migratorio de la República Dominicana*. Organización Internacional para las Migraciones.

Aja, E. (2012). *Inmigración y Democracia*. Alianza.

Arango, J., Garcés, B., Mahía, R., & Moya, D. (2020). Inmigración en tiempos de COVID-19. *Anuario CIDOB de la Inmigración, 4*(17).

Bovenkerk, F. (1974). *The sociology of return migration: A bibliographic essay*. Martinus Nijhoff.

Cachón Rodríguez, L. (2009). *La "España inmigrante": marco discriminatorio, mercado de trabajo y políticas de integración*. Anthropos.

Cáritas Española. (2020). *El primer impacto en las familias acompañadas por Cáritas. Observatorio de la Realidad Social: la crisis de la COVID-19*. Cáritas.

Cassarino, J. P. (2004). Therorising return migration: The conceptual approach to return migrants revisited. *International Journal on Multicultural Societies*, 6(2), 253–279.

Cassarino, J. P. (2008). The conditions of modern return migrants. *International Journal on Multicultural Societies*, 10(2), 95–105.

Chander, R., Murugesan, M., Ritish, D., Damodharan, D., Arunachalam, V., Parthasarathy, R., Raj, A., Sharma, M. K., Manjunatha, N., Bada Math, S., & Kumar, C. N. (2021). Addressing the mental health concerns of migrant workers during the COVID-19 pandemic: An experiential account. *International Journal of Social Psychiatry*, 67(7), 826–829. https://doi.org/10.1177/0020764020937736

Chislett, W. (2021). Challenges and opportunities for Spain in times of COVID-19. *Working paper 01/2021 April*.

Corrado, A., & Palumbo, L. (2022). Essential farmworkers and the pandemic crisis: Migrant labour conditions, and legal and political responses in Italy and Spain. In A. Triandafyllidou (Ed.), *Migration and pandemics. Spaces of solidarity and spaces of exception. IMISCOE research series*. Springer. https://doi.org/10.1007/978-3-030-81210-2_10

Durant, I. (2022). *Impact of the on trade and development*. UNCTAD.

European Council. (2002). *Proposal for a return action Programme, 14673/02*. European Communities.

Fernández Jurado, M. Y., Ramos Llamos, A. J., & García Santos, N. (2021). La economía española ante la COVID-19: efectos, retos y soluciones. In A. Blanco, A. Chueca, J. A. López-Ruiz, & S. Mora (Eds.), *Informe España 2021*. Kadmos.

Gallardo Rivas, G. (1995). *Buscando la vida: dominicanas en el servicio doméstico en Madrid*. IEPALA/CIPAE.

Herranz Gómez, Y. (1997). Mujeres dominicanas en el servicio doméstico de Pozuelo-Aravaca. *Cuadernos de Relaciones Laborales*, 10, 75–101.

INDEX – Instituto de Dominicanos y Dominicanas en el Exterior. (2022). *Informe del registro sociodemográfico de los dominicanos residentes en el exterior 2022*. Ministerio de Relaciones Exteriores.

INE – Instituto Nacional de Estadística. (2022). *Población dominicana residente por fecha. Series detalladas desde 2002*. INE.

Izquierdo, A., & Cornelius, W. A. (2012). *Políticas de control migratorio: Estudio comparado de España y EE.UU*. Bellaterra.

King, R. (1986). *Return migration and regional economic problems*. Croom Helm.

Licheri, D., Spitale, S., Silvera, C., Romero, M. L., & Boccia, B. (2022). *Estudio de Impacto Económico de la Migración Venezolana en República Dominicana: Realidad VS Potencial*.

López-Ruiz, J. A., & Cabrera Cabrera, P. J. (2021). Desigualdad y pobreza en tiempos de la COVID-19. In A. Blanco, A. Chueca, J. A. López-Ruiz, & S. Mora (Eds.), *Informe España 2021*. Kadmos.

Lozano Ascencio, F., & Martínez Pizarro, J. (Eds.). (2015). *Retorno en los procesos migratorios de América Latina. Conceptos, debates, evidencias.* ALAP.

Mahía, R. (2021). Los efectos del COVID-19 sobre la inmigración en España: economía, trabajo y condiciones de vida. In J. Arango, B. Garcés, R. Mahía, & D. Moya (Eds.), *Inmigración en tiempos de COVID-19. Anuario CIDOB de la Inmigración* (Vol. 4, pp. 68–81). https://doi.org/10.24241/AnuarioCIDOBInmi.2020

Martínez-Buján, R. (2007). *Bienestar y cuidados: el oficio del cariño. Mujeres inmigrantes y mayores nativos (Tesis Doctoral).* Universidad da Coruña, La Coruña, España.

Médicos sin Fronteras. (2020). *Poco, tarde y mal. El inaceptable desamparo de los mayores en las residencias durante la COVID-19 en España.* Retrieved from http://static.msf.es/web/archivos/cov-19/AAFF-MSF-Informe-COVID19-Residencias-BAJA.pdf?_ga=2.62768942.384267787.%201597826316-745549122.1597826316

Mencutek, Z. S. (2022). Voluntary and forced return migration under a pandemic crisis. In *Migration and pandemics* (IMISCOE research series). https://doi.org/10.1007/978-3-030-81210-2_10

Ocaña, C., Bandrés, E., Chuliá, E., Fernández, M. J., Malo, M. Á., Rodriguez, J. C., & Torres, R. (2022). *Impacto social de la pandemia en España. Una evaluación preliminar.* FUNCAS.

Oliver, M. Á. (2021). Desigualdad social y políticas públicas: impacto del COVID-19 en España. *Revista Em Pauta, 19*(48), 92–106. https://doi.org/10.12957/rep.2021.60298

ONE – Oficina Nacional de Estadística. (2022). *Encuesta Nacional Demográfica y Socioeconómica 2017.* Ministerio de Economía, Planificación y Desarrollo.

Parrenas, R. (2020). The mobility pathways of migrant domestic workers. *Journal of Ethnic and Migration Studies, 47,* 3. https://doi.org/10.1080/1369183X.2020.1744837

Pasettin, F., & Cumella de Montserrat, C. (2020). Las políticas de integración en España según el índice MIPEX. *CIDOB Notes Internacionals, 238*(244), 1–14. Retrieved from https://www.cidob.org/en/publications/publication_series/notes_internacionals/n1_220/the_world_in_2020_ten_issues_that_will_shape_the_global_agenda

Pedone, C., & Gil Araujo, S. (2008). Maternidades transnacionales entre América Latina y el Estado español. El impacto de las políticas migratorias en las estrategias de reagrupación familiar. In *Nuevos retos del transnacionalismo en el estudio de las migraciones* (pp. 149–176). OPI-Ministerio de Trabajo e Inmigración.

Pérez Medina, J. M. (2021). El sistema autonómico y la crisis sanitaria causada por la COVID-19. In A. Blanco, A. Chueca, J. A. López-Ruiz, & S. Mora (Eds.), *Informe España 2021.* Kadmos.

Perna, R., & Moreno Fuentes, F. J. (2021). Inmigración y atención sanitaria en un contexto de pandemia: vulnerabilidades y (escasas) respuestas en Europa y en España. In J. Arango, B. Garcés, R. Mahía, & D. Moya (Eds.), *Inmigración en tiempos de COVID-19. Anuario CIDOB de la Inmigración* (Vol. 4, pp. 68–81). https://doi.org/10.24241/AnuarioCIDOBInmi.2020

Raj, W. (2022). *"We can't live like this". Spain's failure to protect rights amid rising pandemic-linked poverty.* Human Rights Watch.

Sørensen, N. (1998). Narrating identity across Dominican worlds. In M. P. Smith & L. E. Guarnizo (Eds.), *Transnationalism from below* (pp. 241–269). Transaction Publishers.

Stark, O. (2019). Behavior in reverse: Reasons for return migration. *Behavioural Public Policy, 3*(1), 104–126. https://doi.org/10.1017/bpp.2018.27

Tejeda, E., Wooding, B., & Abaunza, C. (2018). Impacto de la crisis económica internacional en la población dominicana en España. *Fondo para la Investigación Económica y Social, 1,* 1–59.

Xiang, B., & Sørensen, N. N. (2020). *Shock mobility: Long-term impacts of the COVID-19 pandemic and lock-down.* Danish Institute for International Studies. Retrieved from http://www.jstor.org/stable/resrep26348

Xiang, B., Allen, W. L., Khosravi, S., Kringelbach, H. N., Ortiga, Y. Y., Liao, K. A., Cuéllar, J. E., Momen, L., Deshingkar, P., & Naik, M. (2022). Shock mobilities during moments of acute uncertainty. *Geopolitics, 28,* 1632. https://doi.org/10.1080/14650045.2022.2091314

PART III

Conclusion

CHAPTER 12

Return Migration and Crises in Non-Western Countries: Contributions and Lessons Learned

Jungwon Yeo

Introduction

This edited volume aims to enhance our current understanding of migration and crises, with a particular focus on the issues arising at the intersection of return migration and crises within the context of non-Western nations. Crises influence various factors that affect people's migratory decisions and movements, leading to a series of challenges and opportunities in both migrant-sending and receiving countries (Mencutek, 2022). As we can all attest, for instance, the COVID-19 pandemic became an enormous shock to all countries, resulting in panic-driven return migration around the world (as discussed in Chaps. 2, 4, and 8). Additionally, response measures to the disease, such as immediate border closures and lockdowns, halted daily economic activities, leading to waves of returns by

J. Yeo (✉)
School of Public Administration, University of Central Florida, Orlando, FL, USA
e-mail: Jungwon.Yeo@ucf.edu

© The Author(s), under exclusive license to Springer Nature Switzerland AG 2024
J. Yeo (ed.), *Return Migration and Crises in Non-Western Countries*, Mobility & Politics,
https://doi.org/10.1007/978-3-031-53562-8_12

migrants who lost their jobs in their host countries (as described in Chaps. 4, 8, and 11). The reception of an unexpectedly large number of returnees may have created a more noticeable burden for non-Western countries (Zaiceva & Zimmermann, 2016). Many of these nations and societies were not sufficiently prepared in terms of awareness, understanding, and strategies to address the needs of returning individuals who had distinctly different requirements and requests. The crisis may have also prompted migrants from non-Western countries to prioritize factors they had never considered before as reasons for their return. Despite its growing importance and impact, the intersection of crises and return migration in non-Western countries remains a relatively underexplored area in both theory and practice (Bastia, 2011).

To contribute to enhancing the currently limited knowledge of issues arising at the intersection of return migration, crises, and non-Western countries, this book presents a diverse array of cases, engaging in theoretical dialogues and practical discussions within this topic area. The chapters explore the role of crises on various types of return migration in non-Western countries and discuss the policy and political significance of return migration in either the countries of origin or the countries of destination. In the process, the chapters also examine both theoretical and practical implications for various approaches and strategies to address issues arising from the intersection of return migration and crises in non-Western countries.

CONTRIBUTIONS

Expanded Horizons of Return Migration

This volume expands upon the definition and dimension of return migration, highlighting the limitations inherent in the traditional understanding of this phenomenon. Traditionally, return migration has been explained through a lens that focuses on the duration of migrants' stay abroad, with an emphasis on their long-term experiences in their destination countries, and it often views return as the permanent and ultimate stage of migration. Many existing studies primarily focus on a specific demographic—international male labor migrants, typically of aged and low-skilled.

However, these descriptors may not be sufficient for a comprehensive understanding of return migration in contemporary society, especially in times of crises. In response to this, this edited volume broadens the perspectives on duration, stages, and the subjects of migration when defining and examining return migration. This volume sheds light on the fluid, short-term, or transient nature of return migration (as discussed in Chaps. 6, 8, and 10), in addition to the longer-term migration experiences (as discussed in Chaps. 2 and 11). Moreover, this book addresses issues related to various categories of returnees, including female domestic workers (Chap. 2), high-skilled migrants (Chap. 5), family migrants (Chap. 7), 1.5 generations/young migrants (Chap. 9), war refugees (Chap. 6), political asylum seekers (Chap. 10), and internal/international migrant workers (Chaps. 3, 4 and 11). All of these groups contribute to the multifaceted landscape of return migration in today's world (as evidenced in chapter citations).

Furthermore, this volume extends the dimension of return migration by considering internal remigration or relocation as part of the dynamics of return migration (as presented in Chap. 2). This expansion can offer valuable insights into understanding the return journeys of temporary or seasonal domestic migrant laborers, for whom returning to different cities or locations may constitute an essential aspect of their ultimate journey back to their hometowns.

Expanded Types of Crises in Migration Studies

This edited volume expands upon the types of crises that set specific contexts for migration. Existing studies exploring migration and crises often focus on a single crisis, with most of them concentrating on economic or financial crises. Since the recent pandemic, studies highlight the pandemic as the focal event affecting migration. However, existing studies often miss that crises sometimes lead to other types of crises and become cascading events that significantly and severely affect people and society. For instance, the 2011 Tsunami in Tohoku, Japan led to unprecedented damage to nuclear power plants near the coast, causing the release of nuclear waste into the sea. Similarly, the wind gusts from Hurricane Dora on the west coast of the U.S.A affected the speed of wildfire spread in Manoa, Hawaii in 2023. Migrants return may be greatly affected by the types and scopes of crises they face.

Furthermore, migration trends can be affected by a series of different crises at the same time or over the years. For example, as Yap and Opiniano (2024) presented in Chap. 2, the return trends and policy response to the return during the Asian financial crisis in 1997 are different from those during the pandemic in 2020. However, the previous experience can support the current policy response to return. These varying scopes, types, and durations of crises may provide different insights into migrants' return decisions and processes, as well as the policy measures of their home countries.

Regarding the aforementioned issues, this book explores return migration during different scopes, types, and durations of crises. Chapter authors are allowed to define the scope and types of focal crises, including a single crisis as a focal event, cascading crises occurring simultaneously, as well as a series of events over a period of time. For example, while some chapters may focus on a primary focal event, such as COVID-19 (Chaps. 3, 8, and 9) or war (Chap. 6), authors explore return policies by reviewing the return trends and policy adaptations over a series of crises (Chaps. 2, 7, and 11) and/or exploring return during cascading crises (Chaps. 4, 5, 10, and 11).

Multidisciplinary Approach to Exploration/Examination

This volume incorporates diverse perspectives on the topic by featuring authors with various disciplinary backgrounds. The contributing authors possess expertise in a range of fields, including Anthropology, Emergency Management, Humanities, Journalism, Migration Studies, Nonprofit Management, Political Science, Psychology, Public Administration, Public Policy, and Sociology. In each chapter, the author(s) introduce different theoretical frameworks to explain the topic, as well as adopt various methods to empirically and theoretically investigate the issues emerging at the intersection of return migration and crisis in non-Western countries.

The diverse approaches in theories and methods contribute to triangulating the common findings and lessons learned throughout the volume. Furthermore, the diverse perspectives and varied disciplinary expertise suggest fresh implications and insights for both the theories and practices of migration and crisis management. All efforts of authors from different disciplines are undertaken with the overarching goal of enhancing our understanding of return migration and crises in non-Western nations, while also providing more comprehensive insights to the relevant fields.

Lessons Learned

This edited volume explores a wide range of topics related to return migration and crises in non-Western countries, covering regions including Asia, Europe, Africa, Latin America, and the Caribbean. Each chapter delves into and sheds light on various aspects of return migration. These themes encompass factors and motivators influencing immigrants' decisions to return during crises, the role of crises in shaping return migration dynamics in non-Western contexts, the repercussions of return migration on the relationships between migrants' countries of origin and their countries of destination, and the policy responses aimed at facilitating the reacculturation and reintegration of returnees. Therefore, each chapter maintains its distinct focus as it addresses its respective questions.

However, it is noteworthy that, despite the variations among the chapters, there is a general consensus on the increase in return migration in non-Western countries during times of crises and the importance of addressing this issue. Additionally, despite different focuses and geographical contexts, the chapters, overall, present common findings, particularly regarding the role of crises in return migration, and emerging factors influencing return decisions.

Centering on the overarching consensus and shared findings gleaned from eleven cases, the key lessons that have emerged from the edited volume are as follows:

Non-direct but Significant Role of Crisis

Multiple chapters consistently point out that a crisis or crises may not directly cause the return of migrants from non-Western countries. However, these crises do amplify contextual uncertainty and risks while reshuffling the influence of other existing factors on the decision or intention of returnees. For instance, in Chap. 3, Zheng and Zhang (2024) found no statistically significant impact of the COVID-19 pandemic on the intention of migrant workers to remigrate. Nevertheless, their findings highlight that pandemic did significantly affect the perception of unemployment risk among these migrant workers, which in turn had a significant impact on their remigration intentions.

Similarly, Vaidelytė et al. in Chap. 5 and Abaunza (2024) in Chap. 11 explain that the COVID-19 pandemic did not have universal impact on all migrants alike but it reshaped the socio-economic conditions, which could become crucial for the migrants' continued survival or success in their host countries.

In Chap. 6, Yeo and Pysmenna (2024) explain how the full-scale Russian invasion served as a catalyst, strengthening the patriotism of Ukrainian war refugees, and fueling their determination to return and participate in the reconstruction of their war-torn home country. They also explain that the war led to unprecedented and involuntary separation of families and communities, intensifying the longing of Ukrainian war refugees to reunite with their families and reestablish connections with the communities they left behind in Ukraine.

Non-economic Factors as Emerging Determinants

This edited volume emphasizes non-economic factors as the primary determinants of returns to non-Western countries amid crises. Traditional migration studies often emphasize economic determinants or geopolitical events as explanations for migration (Massey et al., 1999; King, 2018). While not undermining the impact of economic factors, the chapters in this volume consistently report that, in the face of crises, migrants are returning to less developed or less safe homes in non-Western countries, prioritizing emotional and psychological security, and social support stemming from personal, familial, ethnic, or communal ties and connections over economic factors.

Concha and Mannaa (2024) in Chap. 10 explored the multifaceted factors that drive the return of Venezuelan migrants from Peru. In particular, the authors reviewed the role of policies—discriminatory migration policies in Peru, and recent return support policies in Venezuela—as facilitators of Venezuelans' return. Additionally, they also pointed out that Peruvians' xenophobic, discriminatory, or discontented attitudes toward Venezuelans impede the stabilization of the migrants in Peruvian society and drive them to return home.

In Chap. 7, Künüroğlu and Yüzbaşı (2024) point out emotional motives, family ties, ethnic roots, and a sense of belonging as key determinants of Turkish migrants' return from developed Western countries and their continued stay in Turkey, particularly in the midst of public health and economic crises. Similarly, in Chap. 5, Vaidelytė, Butkevičienė, and Vaičiūnienė argue that the return of high-skilled professionals to Lithuania depends heavily on various non-economic factors, including education, professional achievements, career prospects, family relations, and concerns for human rights.

Furthermore, the volume highlights that familial and communal support are the primary factors that facilitate the successful reintegration and re-acculturation of returnees in their home countries. In Chap. 9, Jacobo-Suárez (2024) explains the importance of family and extended community support networks in the reintegration of young returnees into Mexican society, especially in the absence of relevant government programs. She explored the migratory histories and educational trajectories of two groups of young returnees and identified that young returnees who are well-integrated into the educational system and labor market has extended familial supports. In contrast, the other groups of young returnees lacking such support network are pushed into precarious labor markets that might cause social isolation of the returnees.

Transnational Approach

Return migration is inherently a transnational issue. The process and consequences of return migration simultaneously affect the home and host countries of returnees. Such effects can extend to reshape the existing relationship between the returnees' home and host countries. In this volume, chapter authors ponder, either implicitly or explicitly, about the relationships between the concerned nation-states in their discussion of international return migration.

In Chap. 4, Kahn (2024) points out that the massive Indian return migration following the COVID-19 pandemic, along with ongoing returns due to changes in the domestic labor market in Persian Gulf countries, may strain the diplomatic ties that were built through economic exchanges, labor, remittances, and cultural and religious interactions between India and countries in the Persian Gulf.

Loustau-Williams and Zougghaghi (2024) in Chap. 8, approach return migration amid crises from a translational perspective. They explain how the immobility crisis and restrictions on circular migration during the recent pandemic facilitated irregular migration in both destination countries and home countries. They suggest addressing migration circularity through transnational socio-economic orders.

Given the transnational nature of return migration, this volume seeks translational solutions to relevant issues and problems. Particularly for less developed non-Western home countries, partnerships with developed host countries would be critical to tackle relevant challenges due to return. In line with this, Chaps. 2, 6, 9, and 10 suggest building bilateral/transnational partnerships between countries (origin/destination) to address the issues and challenges that emerge at the intersection of return migration, crises, and non-Western countries.

Conclusions

In conclusion, this edited volume underscores the critical importance of diversifying and expanding the horizon of current migration studies to provide a clear and innovative perspective on the complex phenomenon of return migration in non-Western countries affected by crises. The book features cases from countries around the world, including Asia (Philippines, China, South Korea, and India), Europe (Lithuania, Turkey, and Ukraine), North Africa (Morocco), and South America and the Caribbean (Mexico, Peru, and the Dominican Republic). The authors present various distinctive aspects of theories, methods, and perspectives in research and practices of return migration during times of crisis.

Common findings across the chapters in this edited volume confirm some claims of existing studies. However, they also reveal information that differs significantly from the arguments and findings of studies focusing on immigration in Western countries or return migration during periods of normalcy. The findings of this volume are also distinct from the information and narratives shared through select media and policy debates.

This book makes a substantial contribution to the comprehension of return migration and crisis dynamics in non-Western countries, transcending institutional, geographic, economic, political, psychological, and social boundaries across various policy domains. By applying diverse theoretical and methodological approaches to study crisis-induced, crisis-affected, or crisis-situated return migration in non-Western contexts, this volume lays the groundwork for future research in this area. Moreover, it aligns with the United Nation's Sustainable Development Goals, offering numerous case studies that scrutinize multiple facets of return migration and crises in non-Western countries. These insights are invaluable for practitioners seeking credible solutions and accountable governance in managing return migration, an increasingly pressing global issue.

Therefore, this edited volume provides a unique opportunity to critically explore current thinking on return migration and investigate the relationship between migration and crises from varying policy and operational viewpoints. With its encompassing diverse theories, methods, contexts, and findings, it inspires researchers and studies to expand the horizon of crisis and migration research. Furthermore, the information and findings attend to practitioners, helping them develop creative solutions for both global and local policies and practices related to return migration management in non-Western countries. These solutions will support and accommodate both returnees and residents during challenging times.

REFERENCES

Abaunza, C. M. (2024). Return migration and return intention in times of crisis: Dominican return during the COVID-19 pandemic. In J. Yeo (Ed.), *Return migration and crises in non-Western countries (Chapter 11)*. Palgrave Macmillan.

Bastia, T. (2011). Should I stay or should I go? Return migration in times of crises. *Journal of International Development, 23*(4), 583–595.

Concha, M., & Mannaa, R. (2024). Venezuelan migration in Peru: Exploring the causes for Venezuelans' return migration. In J. Yeo (Ed.), *Return migration and crises in non-Western countries (Chapter 10)*. Palgrave Macmillan.

Jacobo-Suárez, M. L. (2024). Building a new home: Modes of incorporation for 1.5-generation return migrants in Mexico. In J. Yeo (Ed.), *Return migration and crises in non-Western countries (Chapter 9)*. Palgrave Macmillan.

Kahn, S. (2024). Soft power amidst a crisis: Return migration and India's soft power in the Persian Gulf. In J. Yeo (Ed.), *Return migration and crises in non-Western countries (Chapter 4)*. Palgrave Macmillan.

King, R. (2018). Theorising new European youth mobilities. *Population, Space and Place, 24*(1), e2117.

Künüroğlu, F., & Yüzbaşı, D. V. (2024). Family return migration from Europe to Turkey in the time of crises. In J. Yeo (Ed.), *Return migration and crises in non-Western countries (Chapter 7)*. Palgrave Macmillan.

Loustau-Williams, F., & Zouggaghi, A. (2024). Crisis, circular systems and return – A case study of Morocco. In J. Yeo (Ed.), *Return migration and crises in non-Western countries (Chapter 8)*. Palgrave Macmillan.

Massey, D. S., Arango, J., Hugo, G., Kouaouci, A., & Pellegrino, A. (1999). *Worlds in motion: Understanding international migration at the end of the millennium*. Clarendon Press.

Mencutek, Z. S. (2022). Voluntary and forced return migration under a pandemic crisis. In *Migration and pandemics: Spaces of solidarity and spaces of exception* (pp. 185–206). Springer.

Yap, C. A. D., & Opiniano, J. M. (2024). A generation of crisis-responsive reintegration in migration management: Reflections from the Philippines. In J. Yeo (Ed.), *Return migration and crises in non-Western countries (Chapter 2)*. Palgrave Macmillan.

Yeo, J., & Pysmenna, O. (2024). Lives on hold between the European Union and Ukraine: Ukrainian migrants' return before and after the war. In J. Yeo (Ed.), *Return migration and crises in non-Western countries (Chapter 6)*. Palgrave Macmillan.

Zaiceva, A., & Zimmermann, K. F. (2016). Returning home at times of trouble? Return migration of EU enlargement migrants during the crisis. In M. Kahanec & K. F. Zimmermann (Eds.), *Labor migration, EU enlargement, and the great recession* (pp. 397–418). Springer.

Zheng, A., & Zhang, H. (2024). Does environmental uncertainty affect the remigration intention of Chinese migrant workers in the pandemic. In J. Yeo (Ed.), *Return migration and crises in non-Western countries (Chapter 3)*. Palgrave Macmillan.

Index

NUMBERS AND SYMBOLS
1.5 generation
   immigrants, 161, 163, 167
   Mexican immigrants, 158
   migrants, 6, 162–167, 170, 219
   returnees, 159, 165, 166, 169
   return migrants, 10, 162, 223

A
Acculturation, 123, 124, 129, 137, 183
Africa, 7, 145, 151, 221
African countries, 6
Africans, 142, 145, 152
Agarwal, S., 77
Agency manifestations, 10
Aided return, 178
American cultural expressions, 164
American culture, 158
Animosity, 178
Antecedents, 9
Anthropology, 220

Anti-immigrant legislation, 158
Anti-immigrant sentiments, 187
Arequipa, 182
Argentina, 179
Asia/Asian, 7, 8, 221, 224
   countries, 6
   financial crisis, 219
Asylum seekers, 6
Authoritarian government, 180, 181
Authoritarian regime, 181
Authoritarian socialist regime, 187

B
Bahrain, 70
Bangladesh, 74
Behavioral psychological analysis, 46
Bhagat, R., 78
Bilateral relationship, 8
Bolivia, 195
Border closures and lockdowns, 4, 141, 142, 145, 148, 152
Borderland, 141

Border systems, 141, 144
Bracero program, 160
Brexit, 84, 99, 100, 122
Bureaucracy/bureaucratic, 163
 and administrative processes, 163
 barriers, 168
 requirements, 163

C
Call center agents, 165, 170
Call center industry, 164
Capacity-building programs, 114
Career prospects, 223
Caregivers, 195
Caribbean countries, 7, 10, 221, 224
Cascading crises, 5, 9, 220
Cases, 218
Case study, 141–154
Castillo, Pedro (President), 183
Catholicism, 195
Central America, 7, 158, 164
Chávez, Hugo (President), 180, 181
Child and infant mortality, 181
China/Chinese, 33, 45, 46, 48–50, 52, 224
 internal migration, 48
 migrant workers, 8, 45–63
Circular migration, 160, 223
Circular systems, 141–154, 157, 223
Circulatory movement, 6, 9, 142, 144, 153, 223
Citizens, 167
Collegegoers, 159, 165, 167, 169
Colombia, 182
Community connections, 114
CONACYT funding, 165
Concerns, 10
Conflictive migratory policies, 10
Contextual conditions, 4
Contextual factors, 123
Contextual perspectives, 127

Contextual uncertainty and risks, 221
Contributions of return migrants, 7
Country of origin, 200, 208
COVID-19 pandemic, 3, 5, 8, 10, 16, 17, 28, 33, 35–38, 45–63, 72, 73, 76–80, 84, 85, 87, 89, 90, 100, 121, 134, 135, 137, 144, 148, 151–153, 181, 193–210, 217, 220, 221, 223
Crisis/crises, 3–11, 15–38, 49, 77, 79, 121–137, 141–154, 193–210, 217–225
Crisis-hit, 32
Crisis-induced, 28
Crisis management, 220
Cross-border, 141, 142, 151, 153
Cuba, 179
Culture/cultural, 171
 challenges and opportunities, 3
 diplomacy, 70
 distance, 136
 exchanges, 69, 70
 factors, 70
 group, 71
 isolation, 183
 relations, 69, 72
 similarities, 75
Customer service agents, 159
Cycle, 105
Cyclical pattern, 160

D
Daily border-crossing, 9
Deep-rooted structural issues, 182
Democratic instruments, 180
Democratic regressing processes, 181
Demographic characteristics, 108
Deportation programs, 158, 159, 162, 166, 172
Deportees, 163, 164
Deporter in chief, 158

Destination, 160
Destination country, 158
Devastation, 104
Diaspora, 76, 81
Dictatorship, 181
Diplomatic relations, 70
Diplomatic ties, 8
Discontent, 183
Discrimination, 9, 136, 162, 178, 183
Discriminatory rhetoric, 183
Displaced citizens, 104
Displacement, 103
Domestic services providers, 195
Domestic workers, 111, 219
Dominican Republic (DR), 194, 195, 200, 207, 209, 224
 community, 198
 diaspora, 206, 208
 government, 194, 210
 labor force, 199
 migrants, 10, 199
 nationals, 197
 population, 195
 residents, 204
 return migration, 10, 194
 in Spain, 198
Duration of migration, 6

E
Eastern Europe, 7
Economic and institutional disparities, 9
Economic austerity, 160
Economic challenges and opportunities, 3
Economic crises, 121, 122, 134, 203, 208
Economic determinants, 222
Economic engagement, 109
Economic events, 122, 125, 135, 136
Economic factors, 87, 99, 100, 122
Economic failures, 5
Economic growth, 160
Economic hardships, 206
Economic interests, 70
Economic migrants, 78
Economic opportunities, 106, 110
Economic persepctives, 85, 86
Economic policies, 78
Economic prosperity, 114
Economic reasons, 75, 84–86
Economic resources, 172
Economic shocks, 78
Ecuador, 195
Education, 10, 222
Educational incorporation, 163, 173
Educational Trajectories and Labor Incorporation Prospects for Young Returnees, 165
Emergency Management, 220
Emerging circumstances, 105
Emerging issues, 7
Emigrants, 84, 86
Emigration, 83–90, 94, 99, 100, 105, 110, 113, 143, 194
Emotional attachment, 107
Emotional motives, 222
Emotional reasons, 123
Empirical data, 198
"Enganche," 160
English speakers, 164
Environmental uncertainty, 8, 45–63
"The era of the undocumented," 161
Essential workers, 202
Ethnic identities, 127
Ethnic origin, 124
Ethnic roots, 136, 222
Ethnic ties, 9, 123, 127, 136
Europe, 7, 9, 104, 121–137, 197, 221, 224

European countries, 83, 105, 113, 124, 125
European governments, 103
European Union, 9, 103–115
European Voluntary, 91
Expat, 77
Exploratory research, 194, 198
Expulsions, 178, 184
Extended community support, 223

F
Factors and motivators, 87, 221
Familial factors, 122, 123, 127, 129, 133, 134
Family, 6, 121–137, 223
 connections, 9
 expectations, 194, 207, 209
 migrants, 219
 relations, 223
 re/production strategies, 208
 resources, 172
 reunification, 148, 195
 roles and expectations, 206, 207
 separation, 159
 social, 114
 and support networks, 170, 172
 ties, 136, 222
Family Return Migration, 222
Fears, 10, 201
Female domestic workers, 6
Fieldwork, 165
Final stage of the migratory process, 6
Focus groups, 165, 166
Forced migration, 114, 167
Forced return, 10, 85, 178
Foreigners, 200, 201
Foreign policy, 76, 80, 81
Foreign workers, 195
Formal citizenship, 167
Formal responses, 7

G
GCC region, 71
Geographical contexts, 221
Geopolitical events, 222
Global economic crisis, 205
Global health crisis, 194
Global migration, 3
Global pandemic, 197, 199, 200
Governmental support, 10
Government interventions, 10, 108
Government programs, 173
Government reports, 9
Govil, D., 78
Guadalajara, 166
Guest-workers, 69, 71
Gulf Cooperation Council (GCC), 69–80
Gulf countries, 70, 73, 74

H
Hall, I., 80
Harihar, S., 78
Haut Commissariat au Plan Survey Data, 145
HCP surveys, 147
Health care system, 10, 200
Health emergency, 197
Health services, 201
Higher education, 163, 173
High skilled migrants, 6, 100, 219
High skilled professionals, 9, 83–101, 221, 222
History of migrant management policies, 8
Home countries, 122, 123, 128, 136, 137
Homeland security, 107, 162
Host countries, 109, 113, 114, 122–126, 128–130, 133–137
Host society, 109
Human displacement, 3

Humanitarian crises, 103, 158
Humanitarian visa, 183
Humanities, Journalism, 220
Human migration, 5, 105
Human migratory processes, 5
Human mobility, 193, 194
Human movement, causes and consequences of, 5
Human rights, 223

I
Illegal migration, 10
Immigrant workers, 161
Immigration, 24, 105, 194
  countries, 24
  process, 105
  reform, 161
Immigration and Reform and Control Act (IRCA), 161
The "Immobility" Crisis, 9, 141, 142, 144, 153, 154
Incorporation, 163, 165
Increasing social discrimination, 10
In-depth interviews, 9
India, 8, 69–81, 223, 224
  diaspora, 72
  subcontinent, 69, 70
Individual factors, 6, 9, 105, 107
Individual's perceptions of the life, 9
Inequality, 182
Inequality gap, 198
Institute of Dominicans Living Abroad, 194
Institutional factors, 6
Institutional failures, 5
Integrate, 179
Integration, 159
Intention of returnees, 221
Intentions to remigrate, 8
Internal/international migrant workers, 219

Internal re-migration, 219
International Labour Organization, 182
International migration, 160
International Organization for Migration (IOM), 6, 15, 27, 28, 32, 77, 85
Intersection of migration and crises, 4
Interviews, 88, 89, 91, 100, 126, 127, 134, 137, 146, 148, 152, 153, 165, 166, 199
Involuntary, 157, 193
Irregular migration, 143, 153
Irregular status, 200

J
Jiangsu Province, 55, 63

K
Knowledge, 171
Kuczynski, Pedro Pablo, 183
Kuwait, 70

L
Labor incorporation experiences, 10
Labor migrants, 142, 146
La Libertad, 182
Landscape of return migration, 219
Language, 171, 195
Language transitioning programs, 163
Latin America, 7, 195, 221
Latin American
  and Caribbean countries, 10
  migrants, 208
  nations, 179
  region, 177, 178, 182, 186
  women, 195
Legal resident, 208
Lessons, 220

Lima, 182
Lithuania, 8, 9, 83–101, 221, 224
Lithuanian Official Statistics, 85
Local context of reception, 164
Longer-term return, 9
Long-term adaptation processes, 163
Low-skilled migrant workers, 199
Low-skilled populations, 198

M
Maduro, Nicolás (President), 178, 180, 181, 186
Market labor specialization, 197
Mastery of the language, 168
MAXQDA, 145
Mega-crisis, 16
Mexican, 157–160, 172
 community, 161
 educational system, 172
 emigration, 160
 flows to the US, 161
 government, 158, 165
 immigrants, 160, 161
 immigration, 157
 labor market, 171, 173
 migrants, 161
 migration, 157, 160
 1.5 generation immigrants, 159
 returnees, 159, 163, 166
 returning, 160
 return migration, 158, 160
 society, 164, 223
 states, 165
Mexican-US migration system, 158, 160, 161
Mexico, 10, 157–159, 162–173, 179, 224
 federal government, 158, 159, 162
Mexico City, 165, 166, 170
Middle East, 7, 75–77
Middle Eastern countries, 6

Migrants, 61, 109, 201
 communities, 201, 202
 regularization, 195
 workers, 45–53, 55, 58, 60–63, 195
Migration, 15, 16, 18, 21, 22, 24, 25, 28, 30, 31, 33, 35–37, 46, 60, 69–78, 80, 81, 83–101, 121, 122, 124–126, 136, 141–143, 154, 193–210, 217
 crises, 142, 144
 decision-making, 60, 61
 intention, 48
 management, 15–38, 219
 patterns, 8
 policies, 183
 studies, 220
Migration Data Portal, 178
Migration in Countries in Crisis (MICIC), 32
Migratory decisions, 217
Migratory policies, 177
Migratory processes, 9
Migratory status, 200, 201, 207, 209, 210
Moroccan diaspora, 142, 143, 146, 147, 150
Moroccan Haut Commissariat au Plan (HCP), 147
Moroccan Border, 144
Moroccans, 142–144, 146, 147, 149, 150
Morocco, 9, 141–144, 146–153, 224
Muslim minority, 71
Muslims, 69, 79, 80

N
National Bureau of Statistics' Peasant Workers Monitoring Survey Report, 55
National Institute of Migration, 162
Nationalism, 184

National Office of Statistics of the Dominican Republic, 198
National Reintegration Center for OFWs (NRCO), 20, 27
Natural disasters, 182
Nature of return, 159
Negative attitudes, 184
Negative image, 183
Negative migration, 158
Negative reactions, 186
Net zero migration, 158
New initiative of return migration, 184
News Media Analysis, 145
Non-crisis, 37
Non-economic factors, 84, 136, 222
Non-migration, 25, 35, 38
Nonprofit Management, 220
Non-Western countries, 3–11, 217–225
Non-Western Europe, 8
Non-Western nations, 217
No returns, 206, 208
North Africa, 7, 224
North America, 7
Nupur Sharma incident, 71

O
Obama, Barak (President), 158, 159, 167
Oil crisis, 143
Oman, 70
Open door policy, 183
Outsiders, 164
Overseas Workers Welfare Administration (OWWA), 15, 16, 18, 21, 33, 37

P
Pakistan, 75, 76
Pandemic-related uncertainity, 8, 52–54, 56, 58, 60–62

Pandemic uncertainty, 58
Patriotism, 9, 107, 222
Patterns in return processes, 179
Perceptions, 185
 of unemployment risk, 8
Permanent and seasonal returnees, 194
Permanent migration, 10
Persian Gulf, 8, 69, 71–73, 223
Personal factors, 122, 125, 126, 131, 136
Peru, 10, 177, 182–184, 188, 222, 224
Peruvians, 185
 administrations, 10, 177
 government, 187
 nationals, 185
 society, 178
Pethiyagoda, K., 70
The Philippines, 8, 15–38, 224
Pivotal roles, 7
Planned process, 193
'Plan to return to home', 186
"Plan Vuelta a la Patria ", 186
Policy challenges, 7
Policy efforts, 8
Policy failures, 5
Policy interventions, 105, 108–109, 111, 113
Policy support, 111
Political asylum seekers, 219
Political challenges and opportunities, 3
Political decisions, 179
Political freedom, 114
Political Science, 220
Pontificia Universidad Catolica del Peru, 183
Post-pandemic era, 17, 38
Post-return context, 170
Post-war reconstruction, 104
Practices of migration, 220
Pre-COVID-19 pandemic, 33
Preexisting condition(s), 201

Pre-pandemic, 37
Primary focal event, 220
Professional achievements, 223
Protracted forced migration, 197
Psychological challenges, 7
Psychological factors, 107, 122, 124
Psychology, 220
Public Administration, 220
Public health and economic crises, 5, 9
Publicly available data sources, 110
Public Policy, 220
Public responses, 7
Public services, 181
Puebla, 165
Push/Pull factors, 6, 84, 85, 87–92, 94, 99, 100, 106, 123, 125, 127, 136, 160

Q
Qualitative analysis, 9
Qualitative content analysis, 110
Qualitative data analysis, 88, 91, 126, 136, 142, 145, 166
Qualitative research, 198
Qualitative study designs, 109

R
Re-acculturation, 124, 221
Readaptation strategies, 10
Rebuilding, 114
Reception services for returnees, 162
Reconceptualize return migration, 194
Re-emigration, 88, 91, 94, 100
Refugees, 6
Reintegration/reintegrate, 7, 9, 15–38, 125, 134, 136, 159, 162, 163, 165, 172, 173, 188, 221, 223
  crisis, 10
  policies, 8
  strategy, 158
Reintegration Program Department, 27
Religion/religious, 195
  exchanges, 69, 70
  factors, 70
  groups, 76, 79
  relations, 69
  similarities, 75
  tensions, 76
Relocation, 219
Remigrate/remigration, 6, 45, 51, 53–55, 58, 60–63, 105, 164, 221
Remigration intention, 47, 48, 50, 56, 58, 61–63
Remittances, 8, 70–74, 204, 206
Repatriation, 178, 179
Reshmi, R., 78
Return, 16, 85, 104, 106, 113, 122, 123, 141–154, 158, 179
  decisions, 203
  emigration, 84
  intention, 9, 10, 193–210
  migrants, 6, 84, 85, 87, 99, 100, 123, 124, 135, 136, 158, 159, 171, 178
  migration, 3–11, 32, 70, 78, 84–88, 92, 99, 100, 105, 107, 121–137, 145–147, 157, 177–179, 187, 193–210, 217–225
  migration trends, 7
  support, 10
  types of, 6
  of Venezuelan migrants, 177
Return and Reintegration Key Highlighted, 85
Returned citizens, 7

INDEX 235

Returnees, 6, 16, 20, 21, 25, 27, 30, 35, 37, 105, 121, 123, 125, 136, 147, 148, 150, 153, 159, 163–166, 168–171, 173
  home and host countries, 223
Return-incentive programs, 179
Returning migrants, 24, 38
Returning migrant workers, 21, 25, 33, 38
Returning overseas workers, 24, 37
Return of achievement, 179
Return upon completion, 179
Reunification, 162
Risk factor, 173
Roy, A., 78
Russian invasion of Ukraine, 3, 9, 103, 112, 113

S
Sanitary emergency, 203, 208
Saudi Arabia, 69, 70, 73, 74, 77, 79
Scalabrini Migration Center, 18, 20, 28
Seasonal migrant laborers, 6
Seasonal migration, 149
Seasonal return, 9
Second generation, 122
Security concerns, 179
Semi-authoritarian system, 181
Semi-structured interviews, 198
Sense of belonging, 136, 158, 222
Series of crises, 220
Series of interconnected events, 5
Setback return, 179
Sharma, Nupur, 79
Shock mobilities theory, 197, 198
Shock response, 203
Shock returns, 198, 203, 204, 208
Short survey, 165
Short-term circularity, 10
Short-term laborers, 6

Significant wealth gap, 182
Skilled labor, 143
Skill sets, 108
Snowball technique, 166, 199
Social
  assistance, 10
  challenges and opportunities, 3, 7
  and cultural connections to communities, 107
  exclusion, 163
  isolation, 173
  networks and family ties, 162, 165
  welfare, 10
Sociocultural affinity, 195
Sociocultural differences, 194
Socio-economic asymmetries, 194, 199
Socio-economic conditions, 208, 221
Socio-economic cultural conditions, 9
Socio-economic disparities, 182
Socio-economic situation, 183
Sociology, 220
Socio-political, 125
Soft power, 8, 69, 71, 72, 76, 79
Somos Mexicanos, 158, 162
South America, 7, 224
South Asia, 69, 70, 72, 73, 75, 76
South Korea, 224
Spain, 10, 195, 197, 199, 200, 202, 206, 209
Spanish, 195
  citizenship, 208, 210
  government, 195, 200, 202, 203
  health care system, 202
  residency, 210
Sri Lanka, 70
Standalone event, 5
State actions, 194, 208
State policies, 194, 208
Statistical analysis, 8
Statistics, 9

Stigma/stigmatization/stigmatized, 162, 164, 170
Strategies of family re/production, 194, 206, 208, 209
Strong support network, 169
Structural determinants, 105
Structural factors, 6, 9, 106, 111
Support networks, 158, 159, 173
Survey data, 8, 55
Systematic content analysis, 105
Systematic preparation, 114
Systemic inequality, 182

T
Temporary protection, 113
Temporary Residence Permit, 183
Theories, 220
Tijuana, 166
Times of India, 78
Training opportunities, 109
Transition, 163, 173
Translational solutions, 223
Transnational approach, 223–224
Transnational contexts, 106
Transnational linkages, 148
Transnational perspective, 198
Transnational religious network, 195
Triangulating, 220
Turkey, 9, 121–137, 222, 224
Turkish, 123–125, 128, 130, 132–134, 136, 137
  families, 9
  migrants, 121, 122, 124

U
UAE, 70, 72, 73, 79
Ukraine, 9, 103–115, 224
Ukrainian, 3, 103, 104, 106, 114
  decision on resettlement in host countries/return to Ukraine, 105
  government, 104, 114, 115
  migrants, 9, 111, 112, 114, 222
  migrant workers, 110, 111
  migration and return, 109
  refugees, 9, 103, 104, 113–115
  return, 105
  war refugees, 105, 222
Undocumented immigrants, 167, 179
Undocumented migration, 161
Unexpected circumstances, 197
Unexpected migration patterns, 197
United Nations High Commissioner for Refugees (UNHCR), 103, 104, 111, 182
United States (US), 32, 157, 159, 161, 166
  deportation, 162
  government, 161
  mass deportation policy, 158
Unprecedented disruption, 197
Urban migration intention, 50
US-born children of Mexican immigrants, 161

V
Venezuela/Venezuelan, 178, 180–183, 185–187
  embassies, 184, 186
  exodus, 180
  government, 10, 178
  immigrants, 177, 182, 183
  migrants, 178, 182, 187
  migration, 10, 177, 183, 185, 222
  return migrants, 188
  return migration, 188
  society, 182

Veracruz, 165
Vizcarra, Martin (President), 183
Volatility, 6
Voluntary return, 122, 162, 178, 179, 193

W
War, 5, 104, 109
War refugees, 219
We Are Mexican (*Somos Mexicanos*), 162
Western countries, 110, 224
Western Europe, 7
World economic crisis of, 158, 2009

X
Xenophobia, 178, 184, 186
Xenophobic attitudes, 10, 178, 184, 185

Y
Young Mexican returnees, 10, 170
Young people, 173
Young returnees, 10, 162, 165, 172, 223

Z
Zhejiang Province, 55, 63

Printed in the USA
CPSIA information can be obtained
at www.ICGtesting.com
LVHW011825041124
795688LV00004B/366